VOCABULARY POWER 1

PRACTICING ESSENTIAL WORDS

Jennifer Recio Lebedev

PEARSON

Longman

Vocabulary Power 1: Practicing Essential Words

Pearson Education, 10 Bank Street, White Plains, NY 10606

Staff credits: The people who made up the *Vocabulary Power 1* team, representing editorial, production, design, and manufacturing, are Rhea Banker, Christine Edmonds, Laura LeDréan, Francoise Leffler, Christopher Leonowicz, Amy McCormick, Linda Moser, Diana Nam, Edith Pullman, and Barbara Sabella.
Cover and text design: Barbara Sabella
Cover photos: (wave) © P. Wilson/zefa/Corbis; (car) © Schlegelmilch/Corbis; (windmills) © Firefly Productions/Corbis; (bulb) © Chris Rogers/Corbis; (train) © Tim Bird/Corbis; (volcano) © Jim Sugar/Corbis; (type) © Don Bishop/ Getty Images; (shuttle) © Stock Trek/Getty Images
Text composition: GGS Book Services
Text font: 11/12.5 New Aster Medium

Library of Congress Cataloging-in-Publication Data
Lebedev, Jennifer.
    Vocabulary power 1 : practicing essential words / Jennifer Lebedev. – 1st ed.
        p. cm.
    Includes index.
    ISBN 978-0-13-228356-4 (student book 1 : alk. paper) – ISBN 978-0-13-228357-1 (answer key 1 : alk. paper) – ISBN 978-0-13-222150-4 (student book 2 : alk. paper) – ISBN 978-0-13-222151-1 (answer key 2 : alk. paper) – ISBN 978-0-13-243178-1 (student book 3 : alk. paper) – ISBN 978-0-13-243179-8 (answer key 3 : alk. paper) 1. Vocabulary. I. Title. II. Title: Vocabulary power one.
    PE1449.L37 2007
    428.1–dc22

                                                              2007000501

LONGMAN ON THE **WEB**

Longman.com offers online resources for teachers and students. Access our Companion Websites, our online catalog, and our local offices around the world.

Visit us at **longman.com**.

Printed in the United States of America
1 2 3 4 5 6 7 8 9 10—VHG—11 10 09 08 07

CONTENTS

TO THE TEACHER vii

TO THE STUDENT ix

CHAPTER 1 2

Key Words: consider, feast, generous, guilt, load, mean, occasion, proof, settle, spirit

Readings: *The First Noodles, What Men and Women Eat*

CHAPTER 2 10

Key Words: allow, attempt, cause, cure, damage, disease, raise, record, risk, shore

Readings: *River Surfing, Powerful Women in the Air*

CHAPTER 3 18

Key Words: coast, compare, contain, develop, effect, experiment, public, sense, skill, system

Readings: *The Van Gogh Drawings, The Man Who Loved to Build Parks*

QUIZ 1 26
Key Words from Chapters 1–3

CHAPTER 4 28

Key Words: bold, certain, creature, degree, exist, pattern, rise, serve, shallow, stick

Readings: *Smart Enough to Use Tools, Little Known Facts about the Killer Whale*

CHAPTER 5 36

Key Words: doubt, gain, habit, handle, improve, lead, origin, reduce, result, reward

Readings: *Small Changes Make a Difference, What to Do When You're Stressed*

CHAPTER 6 44

Key Words: admit, beam, board, crime, destroy, disturb, faith, population, ripe, warn

Readings: *A Darkness in German Soccer, Safety for College Students*

QUIZ 2 52
Key Words from Chapters 4–6

CHAPTER 7 54

Key Words: blow, compose, duty, exact, inquire, miserable, pity, probable, proper, sympathetic

Readings: *Push Dad into Action?, Making Mom Understand*

CHAPTER 8 62

Key Words: ancient, blame, course, entire, gather, motion, practical, purpose, ruin, threat

Readings: *Green Buildings, The Truth Is in the Ice*

CHAPTER 9 70

Key Words: compete, dismiss, divide, field, include, industry, opinion, produce, train, treat

Readings: *Bollywood, Beijing Film Academy*

QUIZ 3 78

Key Words from Chapters 7–9

CHAPTER 10 80

Key Words: battle, charm, cheat, due, forbid, interfere, permit, protect, puzzle, rush

Readings: *Old Enough to Drive?, A New Kind of Ride on the Streets of New York*

CHAPTER 11 88

Key Words: artificial, base, obey, pause, race, succeed, supply, trap, wonder, worship

Readings: *Ant Farms: A Family Business, Doing Business Like a Child*

CHAPTER 12 96

Key Words: brave, cheer, crowd, modest, post, raw, replace, slave, slip, stir

Readings: *So You Want to Be a Rock Star?, From the Football Stadium to the Opera House*

QUIZ 4 104

Key Words from Chapters 10–12

CHAPTER 13 106

Key Words: eager, fortune, freedom, horizon, ideal, operate, reserve, standard, steady, wise

Readings: *Soon to Be a Millionaire, How Rich is Rich?*

CHAPTER 14 114

Key Words: ache, actual, blind, concern, courage, expect, mention, peace, pretend, separate

Readings: *New Book, New Author, New Beginnings; No Direction Home*

CHAPTER 15 122

Key Words: block, deaf, defend, dozen, grateful, inform, patience, relieve, respect, sharp

Readings: *What Your Doctor Never Told You, Medicine From Around the World*

QUIZ 5 130

Key Words from Chapters 13–15

CHAPTER 16 132

Key Words: bunch, condition, loan, official, postpone, praise, rough, shelter, sincere, wage

Readings: *A Time to Think and a Time to Help, Lessons About the World outside School*

CHAPTER 17 140

Key Words: balance, deal, guide, hesitate, honor, local, loyal, matter, position, support

Readings: *First Jobs, First Lessons, Keeping Workers Happy*

CHAPTER 18 148

Key Words: arrest, beat, beg, envy, evil, guard, point, poison, rot, sore

Reading: *What's Right or Wrong*

QUIZ 6 156

Key Words from Chapters 16–18

CHAPTER 19 158

Key Words: class, exchange, fresh, interrupt, liquid, mild, opportunity, permanent, quality, trick

Readings: *When Drinking Water Becomes a Lifestyle, Home Is Anywhere*

CHAPTER 20 166

Key Words: accept, appear, determine, examine, express, formal, frequent, hook, increase, limit

Readings: *Who Lives in Cyworld?, Can a Computer Understand Our Emotions?*

CHAPTER 21 174

Key Words: border, century, former, hire, immediate, native, necessary, split, spread, suit

Readings: *Ride Through History, A Tour Just for You*

QUIZ 7 182

Key Words from Chapters 19–21

CHAPTER 22 184

Key Words: apply, bargain, confess, disappoint, gradual, host, literature, private, regret, shame

Readings: *We Want to Study German, Choosing a College Across the Ocean*

CHAPTER 23 192

Key Words: companion, curious, desire, heal, manner, observe, prevent, pure, remind, suffer

Readings: *The Need to Watch Bad News, The Pet Dog: A Mirror of Its Owner*

CHAPTER 24 200

Key Words: adopt, advantage, committee, depend, possess, property, realize, responsible, solve, tax

Readings: *When a Teenager Rules over a City, Programmed for Politics?*

QUIZ 8 208

Key Words from Chapters 22–24

CHAPTER 25 210

Key Words: command, cruel, defeat, disgust, enemy, faint, greed, owe, surface, whisper

Readings: *The Many Peoples of Italy, Blackbeard's Last Home*

CHAPTER 26 218

Key Words: avoid, combine, demand, figure, fit, offer, press, provide, reach, store

Readings: *Taking Television in a New Direction, The Radio of Tomorrow— Today*

CHAPTER 27 226

Key Words: admire, attract, civilize, crop, remain, society, soil, steep, tame, voyage

Readings: *Much More than a Garden, Africa under Geography's Control*

QUIZ 9 234

Key Words from Chapters 25–27

CHAPTER 28 236

Key Words: advance, afford, case, discover, edge, manufacture, recent, satisfy, spill, stain

Readings: *Today's Man Is Looking Good, Cool Clothes*

CHAPTER 29 244

Key Words: common, detail, force, miss, multiply, object, particular, rapid, sort, value

Readings: *Seeing the World through Different Eyes, Which English Do You Speak?*

CHAPTER 30 252

Key Words: dive, fold, gentle, harvest, height, pipe, solid, steer, trade, wrap

Readings: *The Importance of Latin American Economies, Ikea Welcomed Around the World*

QUIZ 10 260

Key Words from Chapters 28–30

APPENDIX A: Understanding Parts of Speech 262

APPENDIX B: Spell and Grammar Checks 263

KEY WORD INDEX 277

TO THE TEACHER

Giving your students an excellent vocabulary doesn't have to be difficult. *Vocabulary Power* simplifies the process to make vocabulary acquisition effective and interesting.

THE LATEST RESEARCH

The Most Important Words

Research shows that it is possible but not probable for the human mind to learn 1,000 new words a year (Nation 2001). In light of this, it is no surprise that English language learners are often frustrated by their limited vocabulary. Even if they manage to learn 1,000 words a year, the words they acquire may not be those that they need for academic and professional success. *Vocabulary Power* solves this problem by teaching the words that are most worthy of their time and attention.

Of the 100,000+ words in the English language, only the 2,000 most frequent words (compiled in the General Service List) are necessary for students to understand at least 80% of daily conversation and writing (Nation 2002). If students know the 2,000 most frequent words in English, in conjunction with 570 high frequency academic words found on the Academic Word List (AWL), they may understand close to 90% of academic text (Nation 2001, Coxhead 2000). The combined knowledge of the General Service List (GSL) and the Academic Word List (AWL) will strengthen your students' ability to understand a textbook, follow an academic lecture, or read a newspaper with ease.

- **Vocabulary Power 1** teaches Low Intermediate students words from the GSL.
- **Vocabulary Power 2** teaches Intermediate students more challenging words from the GSL and words from the AWL.
- **Vocabulary Power 3** teaches Advanced students more challenging words from the AWL.

Effective Methodology

Vocabulary Power is different from most vocabulary books because it is based on research on memory. Memorizing a word often requires that it be encountered seven or more times. It is important that words are not simply seen on each occasion, but encountered in new contexts, retrieved and used (Nation 2001).

Vocabulary Power exposes students to each word in at least eight different contexts. This not only fixes new words in the memory, it offers learners a rich understanding of words. The eight different exposures follow a process approach, guiding the learner through the cognitive stages of noticing, retrieval, and generation. This approach teaches learners to not only recognize and understand a word, but also produce it.

HIGH INTEREST CONTENT

Vocabulary Power is unique because it makes vocabulary learning enjoyable. Examples are modern and realistic. The readings are adapted from articles in current newspapers, magazines, or online news sources on a variety of up-to-date topics. Students are encouraged to apply new words to their own lives, making vocabulary more relevant and useful.

CLASSROOM FRIENDLY FORMAT

Each chapter is organized as follows:

- **Words in Context:** understanding new words from context
- **Words and Definitions:** matching the words with their definition from the Longman Dictionary of American English
- **Comprehension Check:** checking comprehension of the words
- **Word Families:** expanding knowledge of the words with word families
- **Same Word, Different Meaning:** expanding knowledge of the words with multiple meanings
- **Words in Sentences:** using the words to complete sentences
- **Words in Collocations and Expressions:** understanding collocations and expressions featuring the words to improve memory and activate production
- **Words in a Reading:** using the words to complete a reading adapted from a current news article
- **Words in Discussion:** applying the words to real life with lively discussion questions
- **Words in Writing:** using the words in writing about a relevant topic

In addition:

- Ten Quizzes throughout the book make it easy for teachers and students to check the students' progress.
- The Grammar and Spell Check exercises and charts in the Appendix also provide extra practice with spelling and using the words.
- A complete Answer Key (for all exercises and quizzes) is provided in a separate booklet.

Vocabulary Power can be used as a supplement to reading, writing, grammar, or speaking classes. It can be used in class or assigned as homework. It can also be used as a self-study text. This flexibility makes the book an easy way to strengthen the academic core of a class.

REFERENCES

Coxhead, A. 2000. A new academic word list. TESOL Quarterly, 34(2000), 213–239.

Nation, P. 2001. Learning Vocabulary in Another Language. Cambridge University Press: Cambridge.

Nation, P. 2002. Managing Vocabulary Learning. SEAMEO Regional Language Centre: Singapore.

ACKNOWLEDGMENTS

I am grateful to the wonderful editorial team at Longman for their contributions to this series. In particular, I would like to thank Amy McCormick and Francoise Leffler. I also thank Longman for allowing me to use definitions, the pronunciation table, and transcriptions from the Longman Dictionary of American English. This book could not have been developed without the insights of students, so I would like to thank the students at Northeastern University who piloted these materials and gave me great feedback.

TO THE STUDENT

Do you want to improve your vocabulary, but don't know which words are most important to learn? Is studying vocabulary sometimes boring for you? Do you want to remember words easily, and know how to use them when speaking and writing? Do you need a better vocabulary to be ready for university? If you can answer "yes" to any of these questions, this is the book for you.

Which words are important to learn?

The English language has over 100,000 words, but you only need to know the 2,000 most common words (the General Service List) to understand 80% of daily conversation and reading. After this, learning a group of 570 special academic words (the Academic Word List) will increase your comprehension to almost 90% of academic speaking and reading. This book only teaches words from the General Service List. Whether you are preparing for academic work or simply wish to better your vocabulary, studying these words is an excellent use of your time.

How can I remember new words easily?

To remember a word, you need to see it used several times, in different ways. Every new word in this book is taught through eight different exercises. By the end of a chapter, every word will be a part of your memory.

How can I enjoy learning vocabulary?

Learning vocabulary should be interesting! This book can help you enjoy learning new words in four ways:

1. The examples of the words are modern and realistic. (You don't have to worry that you will sound old-fashioned or strange when you use a new word.)
2. The readings in the book come from newspapers, magazines, and online sources (such as the *New York Times* and *National Geographic*) and cover up-to-date topics like technology, music, and sports.
3. Special exercises show you common collocations (word combinations) and expressions to help you use the words in conversation and academic writing.
4. Engaging discussion questions about your opinions and your life give you the opportunity to use the words in interesting conversation.

Now that you understand how you can get a better vocabulary, you are ready to start *Vocabulary Power*.

ABOUT THE AUTHOR

Jennifer Recio Lebedev received degrees in Russian studies from Bryn Mawr and Middlebury Colleges. She began teaching English in 1996 in Moscow, Russia, where she also wrote several publications for EFL learners. Since returning to the United States in 2001, she has conducted teacher training courses and professional development seminars in addition to classroom teaching at a private language school in Boston.

WORDS IN CONTEXT

*Use the sentences to guess what each key word means. Choose the meaning that is closest to that of the key word in **bold**.*

1. **consider**
   /kənˈsɪdɚ/
   -verb

   • I need to **consider** all my choices before I can make a decision.
   • You have a beautiful voice. Have you ever **considered** performing on stage?

   Consider means . . .   ⓐ to think about   b. to question   c. to dream about

2. **feast**
   /fist/
   -noun

   • My friends cooked a **feast** for all of us to enjoy on my birthday.
   • The Frankola family and their many cousins shared a holiday **feast** of beef, turkey, potatoes, corn, salad, biscuits, and bread pudding.

   Feast means . . .   a. a party   b. a large meal   c. a special dish

3. **generous**
   /dʒɛnərəs/
   -adjective

   • Thank you for your help this week. You've been very **generous** with your time.
   • My grandparents were **generous** on my birthday. They gave me $50.

   Generous means . . .   a. willing to give   b. willing to give   c. unwilling to give
                          enough   more   much

4. **guilt**
   /gɪlt/
   -noun

   • When Ella broke her promise to help her mother, a feeling of **guilt** filled her.
   • Keeping secrets from others leaves me with a lot of **guilt**. It doesn't feel good.

   Guilt means . . .   a. a feeling of anger   b. a feeling of physical   c. a feeling you did
                                            weakness   something wrong

5. **load**
   /loʊd/
   -noun

   • Can you help me carry a **load** of groceries from the car?
   • We put bags of garbage outside. The garbage truck took away our **load** of trash.

   Load means . . .   a. a box   b. a large amount   c. half of something

6. **mean**
   /min/
   -adjective

   • Steve's **mean** words hurt my feelings.
   • Don't be **mean** to your little sister! Please tell her you're sorry.

   Mean means . . .   a. confusing   b. too loud   c. unkind

7. **occasion**
/əˈkeɪʒən/
-*noun*

- Bonnie lives in Hollywood. She's seen a movie star on more than one **occasion.**
- On several **occasions** I've asked for the teacher's help after class.

Occasion means . . .   a. way of doing something   b. a time   c. a problem

8. **proof**
/pruf/
-*noun*

- The police think that Dillon stole the money, but they have no **proof**.
- Scientists need **proof** to accept new ideas.

Proof means . . .   a. information to show the truth   b. a reason for an action   c. an answer to a problem

9. **settle**
/ˈsɛt̬l/
-*verb*

- Our father had to **settle** our fight over who would sit in the front seat of the car.
- After the divorce, the couple had to **settle** questions about the house and money.

Settle means . . .   a. to listen to   b. to help forget   c. to end an argument

10. **spirit**
/ˈspɪrɪt/
-*noun*

- Even though Elvis Presley is dead, his **spirit** lives on for many music fans.
- My grandmother was small in height, but big and strong in **spirit**. She loved life and lived hers well.

Spirit means . . .   a. the loudness or softness of someone's voice   b. the special parts of someone's personality   c. someone's body

WORDS AND DEFINITIONS

Match each key word with its definition.

1. _____load_____ a large amount of something that is carried

2. _____ willing to give more money, time, etc., than normal

3. _____ unkind or wanting to hurt others

4. _____ to end an argument or a bad situation

5. _____ to think about something very carefully

6. _____ the parts of someone's personality that make him or her special (people believe these special things live on after death)

7. _____ facts or information that show something is true

8. _____ a large meal for many people to celebrate a special event

9. _____ a time when something happens

10. _____ sadness and embarrassment because of a wrongdoing

COMPREHENSION CHECK

Choose the best answer.

1. Danesh **considered**

   a. sneezing.

   b. turning on the light in the living room.

   c. studying history or political science in college.

2. Which of the following is a **feast**?

   a. a small bowl of soup

   b. half a sandwich and some juice

   c. a whole chicken, potatoes, carrots, bread, and two apple pies

3. What was the reason for Lena's **guilt**?

   a. She helped her brother with his homework.

   b. She lied to her brother.

   c. Her brother didn't give her a birthday present.

4. Henri was very **generous** during my visit;

   a. he took me to the theater and paid for every dinner we had in a restaurant.

   b. he had little free time because of his work.

   c. he got so sick that he had to go to the hospital.

5. Jill has **proof** that she met a famous actor on vacation;

   a. she likes to make up such interesting stories.

   b. she showed me a photograph.

   c. I don't think she's lying.

6. What does a businessman wear on many **occasions**?

   a. a suit

   b. athletic shoes

   c. a T-shirt

7. A **mean** neighbor is likely to

   a. greet you with a smile.

   b. invite you to dinner.

   c. yell at your dog for no good reason.

8. We all remember my grandfather's strong **spirit**;

   a. he was a very tall man.

   b. his kindness and love for life made him a special man.

   c. no one had a voice louder than his.

9. The robber had a **load** of

   a. money and jewels.

   b. sports cars.

   c. an expensive painting.

10. You **settle** each of the following EXCEPT

   a. a conversation.

   b. an argument.

   c. a fight.

WORD FAMILIES

Now that you have studied the ten key words and their basic definitions, you are ready to learn words that belong to the same family as some of the key words. A word family includes words that look alike but have different functions (noun, verb, adjective, or adverb). Their meanings are related but different.

A. *Look at each model phrase and decide whether the word in **bold** is used as a noun, verb, adjective, or adverb.*

	NOUN	VERB	ADJECTIVE	ADVERB
1. feast				
• a holiday **feast**	✓			
• to **feast** with your family		✓		
2. generous				
• a **generous** person				
• known for your **generosity**				
3. guilt				
• feelings of **guilt**				
• a **guilty** face				
4. load				
• a **load** of boxes				
• will **load** suitcases on the plane				
5. occasion				
• on many **occasions**				
• call me **occasionally**				
6. proof				
• find **proof**				
• try to **prove** I'm right				

B. *Read the first half of each sentence and match it with the appropriate ending.*

___c___ 1. I broke my brother's camera; now I

_____ 2. The guests at the wedding will dance and

_____ 3. Anne says that she's a distant cousin to the Queen of England. I asked her to

_____ 4. Our parents gave a lot of their time to help us. We thank them for

_____ 5. My brother's taking a lot of things to college, so I'll help him

_____ 6. The Carlson family moved away, but they come and

a. their **generosity**.

b. **load** bags and boxes into the car.

c. feel **guilty**.

d. visit **occasionally**.

e. **feast** until the sun goes down.

f. **prove** it.

SAME WORD, DIFFERENT MEANING

Most words have more than one meaning. Study the additional meanings of **consider**, **generous**, **mean**, and **occasion**. Then read each sentence and decide which meaning is used.

a. **consider** *v.*	to think about something very carefully
b. **consider** *v.*	to think of someone or something in a special way
c. **generous** *adj.*	willing to give more money, time, etc. than normal
d. **generous** *adj.*	larger than the usual amount
e. **mean** *adj.*	unkind or wanting to hurt others
f. **mean** *v.*	to show that something has happened or will happen because of something else
g. **occasion** *n.*	a time when something happens
h. **occasion** *n.*	an important event or ceremony

___e___ 1. All pets need love and care; people should never be **mean** to animals.

_____ 2. Stella is the most **generous** person I know; she'll help anyone and everyone.

_____ 3. Roger gave his daughter a pearl necklace on the **occasion** of her 16th birthday.

_____ 4. My classmate is sick. That **means** I'll have to study for the test by myself.

_____ 5. The Evans family gave a **generous** amount of money to the museum.

_____ 6. Would you **consider** the idea of moving to New York?

_____ 7. My grandfather was a great storyteller. On many **occasions** he entertained the whole family.

_____ 8. I **consider** you among my closest friends.

WORDS IN SENTENCES

Complete each sentence with one of the words from the box.

consider	generosity	~~load~~	occasion	settle
feast	guilty	meant	prove	spirit

1. The movers will _____load_____ the furniture onto the truck for us.

2. On New Year's Eve my family gets together, and we _____ and party until dawn.

3. Can you _____ our argument? We can't agree on who's the best soccer player ever.

4. The little boy said he didn't eat the cookies, but his mother saw the _____ look on his face.

5. A wedding anniversary is a special _____.

6. Your _____ surprises me. You really didn't have to give so much.

7. The deep snow _____ we had to drive more slowly and carefully than usual.

8. Rhonda wanted to _____ to her parents that she could take care of herself.

9. Why do you think the book is terrible? Many _____ it to be a great work.

10. Many people's lives were touched by the princess; so even after her death her _____ lives on.

WORDS IN COLLOCATIONS AND EXPRESSIONS

Following are common collocations (word partners) and expressions with some of the key words. Read the definitions and then complete the conversations with the correct form of the collocations and expressions. Note two abbreviations used in the items below: **sb** = *somebody;* **sth** = *something.*

1. **consider**
   - **consider (sth) to be**   to think about someone or something in some way

2. **feast**
   - **feast on (sth)**   to eat a lot of food with great enjoyment

3. **guilty**
   - **feel guilty about (sth)**   to feel sad and embarrassed because you did something wrong

4. **load**
   - **load up on (sth)**   to get a lot of something

5. **occasion**
   - **on several occasions (on a number of occasions)**   several times or meetings

6. **spirit**
   - **(be) in high spirits**   to be happy and excited

1. ANNA: I love going to the town picnic every year.

    DALE: Who doesn't? Everyone comes to _____*feast on*_____ fried chicken, watermelon, and pies.

2. RENEE: What foods should we plan to take on our camping trip?

    HAL: I think we should _____ bottles of water and dry foods like nuts.

3. ROSE: Mike complains a lot about his neighbor's kids.

    ZACK: Mike says he doesn't like children in general, but I've seen him play happily with his nephews _____.

4. BART: What do you think about going to college in another country?

    MELANIE: Well, I _____ traveling _____ a form of education, so going to college in another country means you learn more than a tourist.

5. TOM: The whole school was _____ after our football team won the big game.

    BARBARA: Yeah. Even the teachers couldn't stop talking about how well our team played.

6. DAVID: Carol and George _____ leaving their new puppy home alone.

    TIFFANY: If it's only for two or three hours, that's not so bad.

WORDS IN READINGS

Read the two articles about food. Complete each one with words and expressions from the boxes.

THE FIRST NOODLES

Who were the first people to enjoy a meal of noodles, and just how far back do noodles go in history? The Italians, Arabs, and Chinese all _____consider_____ noodles _____to be_____ their
1
gift to the world of food. Naturally, someone is right, and someone is wrong. Finally, the work of
archeologists* _____ this old disagreement.
2

Chinese archeologists found a bowl of noodles near the Yellow River in northwestern China. They say it's 4,000 years old. That _____ the Chinese were _____ *lo mein*
                                      3   **4**
(a Chinese dish of noodles) as early as 2,000 B.C. There is no other _____ to show that
                                            5
others were making noodles before this time.

The Chinese believe that other countries learned about noodles through Marco Polo, the famous traveler. It's possible that he found this food when he visited China and then took it back to the Western world.

An archeologist (n.) is a person who studies very old societies by examining what is left of their buildings, tools, etc.

(Based on information in "It Wasn't All Bad." The Week, October 28, 2005.)

WHAT MEN AND WOMEN EAT

All people find comfort in food from time to time, but the experience is not the same for men and women. Cornell University studied what 277 men and women ate and found that choices of foods and the reasons for eating them were quite different.

Men are likely to eat a nice big steak or a(n) _____ serving of pasta after doing a job
                                           6
well-done. Men are already feeling good when they decide to eat their "comfort foods," and a steak
dinner is really a way to celebrate the happy _____.
                                          7

Women, on the other hand, choose less healthy foods. When they shop for comfort foods, they
_____ sweets like ice cream and cake. Another big difference is that men eat when
8
they're _____, but women like to eat when they're sad or lonely. Worse, women think
        9
about the calories* on their plate, so they often _____ eating their comfort foods.
                                                              10

A calorie (n.) is a unit for measuring the amount of energy a particular food can produce.

(Based on information in "The Gender Gap in Food Cravings." The Week, December 9, 2005.)

WORDS IN DISCUSSION

Apply the key words to your own life. Read and discuss the questions with a partner. Try to use the key words.

1. What do you **consider to be** a healthy snack?

   EXAMPLE

   *I love to eat popcorn. I eat it with salt and butter. That's not good, but I **consider** it **to be** healthier than a candy bar.*

2. Name something you often forget to do or decide not to do until later. Do you **feel guilty about** doing this?

3. You have $200 to spend on dinner with some friends. What will you **feast on**?

4. How can you try to **prove** that someone is lying about his or her age?

5. What's the easiest way to carry a **load** of books?

WORDS IN WRITING

Write a short answer (1–2 sentences) for each question. Try to use the key words.

1. When was the last time you were **in high spirits**?

   EXAMPLE

   *I was **in high spirits** for a whole week when my cousin visited me last month.*

2. A doctor gives you very sad news: you have only one year to live. What kind of changes does that **mean** for you?

3. Name a special **occasion** you like to celebrate every year.

4. Do you have brothers or sisters? If so, did your parents **settle** your fights? If not, do you think parents should **settle** arguments among their children?

5. Who is the most **generous** person you know? Give an example of his/her **generosity**.

Key Words

allow	cause	damage	raise	risk
attempt	cure	disease	record	shore

WORDS IN CONTEXT

*Use the sentences to guess what each key word means. Choose the meaning that is closest to that of the key word in **bold**.*

1. allow
/əˈlaʊ/
-verb

- I want to wear jeans to work, but my boss doesn't **allow** it.
- Smoking is not **allowed** in hospitals.

Allow means . . .   a. to understand   b. to try to stop   (c.) to let happen

2. attempt
/əˈtɛmpt/
-verb

- Joan wants to win, so she'll **attempt** to run faster than she ever has before.
- The child **attempted** to ride his bike without using his hands.

Attempt means . . .   a. to learn how to do   b. to try to do   c. to do well

3. cause
/kɔz/
-noun

- The police and fire departments looked for the **cause** of the fire.
- I'm sure the sour milk was the **cause** of my sickness.

Cause means . . .   a. something that stops an event from happening   b. something that makes an event happen   c. the most serious moment of an event

4. cure
/kyʊr/
-verb

- Sadly, my dog is sick with cancer, and no medicine can **cure** him.
- The doctors are working to **cure** her illness. We all hope she'll become well again.

Cure means . . .   a. to understand an illness   b. to make an illness go away   c. to become ill

5. damage
/ˈdæmɪdʒ/
-noun

- Oliver dropped the box, but there was no **damage** to the glasses inside.
- A lot of water came through the ceiling. The **damage** is quite bad.

Damage means . . .   a. a change that creates a bad smell   b. a change that makes something turn a different color   c. a change that makes something hurt or broken

6. disease
/dɪˈziz/
-noun

- Drinking unclean water can bring **disease** into a group of people.
- The child was born with a brain **disease**. The parents have asked many doctors to find a way to make their child healthy.

Disease means . . .   a. an illness   b. an accident   c. a strong pain

7. raise
/reɪz/
-verb

- When the teacher asks a question, we **raise** our hands to answer it.
- The child **raised** her eyes to the sky to watch the plane.

Raise means . . .   a. to open   b. to move from side to side   c. to move up

8. record
/ˈrɛkɚd/
-noun

- The school keeps **records** of all its students. They're shared only with teachers and parents.
- The hospital needed time to put all the health **records** on the computer.

Record means . . .   a. information written down   b. a list   c. a plan

9. risk
/rɪsk/
-noun

- Before you do dangerous activities like mountain climbing, you should understand all the **risks**.
- Tara knew that leaving her present job to find a new one was a **risk**, but she was so unhappy that she didn't care.

Risk means . . .   a. a big mistake   b. a bad possibility   c. a bad situation you cannot change

10. shore
/ʃɔr/
-noun

- The couple took a walk along the **shore**. They watched the sun set over the lake.
- The houses near the **shore** are more expensive than the ones farther from the ocean.

Shore means . . .   a. land near water   b. a wave of water   c. a road

WORDS AND DEFINITIONS

Match each key word with its definition.

1. _____shore_____ the land along a large area of water (an ocean or lake)

2. _____ a change, usually physical, that makes something hurt or broken

3. _____ to let someone do something or have something

4. _____ information about something that is written down for future use

5. _____ the chance that something bad may happen

6. _____ to make a person who is ill or hurt well again

7. _____ to move or lift something to a higher position

8. _____ an illness or something that makes you sick

9. _____ to try to do something

10. _____ a person, event, or thing that makes something happen

Choose the best answer.

1. A person with a **disease**
   a. has a healthy body.
   (b.) needs the help of medicine.
   c. looks for danger.

2. What would likely be a **cause** of sadness?
   a. making a small grammar mistake
   b. getting a new job with good pay
   c. losing your favorite pet

3. I **raised** my leg
   a. to step over the box in front of me.
   b. to sit down on the floor.
   c. to relax.

4. All of the following activities have some **risks** EXCEPT
   a. starting a new business.
   b. doing homework.
   c. not wearing a seatbelt in the car.

5. Alan **attempted** to find an answer to the problem;
   a. he closed his eyes and went to sleep.
   b. he took a long vacation to think about other things for a while.
   c. he talked with friends and read a lot of information on the Internet.

6. All of the following places must keep people's **records** EXCEPT
   a. a doctor's office.
   b. a night club.
   c. a police station.

7. Which of the following do all teachers **allow** in class?
   a. talking on your cell phone
   b. asking a question
   c. sleeping

8. The accident was bad; there was a lot of **damage** to Isis's car.
   a. Now she must find a good mechanic.
   b. She's happy with the color.
   c. She plans to take a road trip this weekend.

9. Which of the following has a **shore**?
   a. a sea
   b. a swimming pool
   c. a mountain

10. We try to **cure** people
    a. when they cry.
    b. when they're in trouble with the law.
    c. when they have illnesses.

WORD FAMILIES

Now that you have studied the ten key words and their basic definitions, you are ready to learn words that belong to the same family as some of the key words. A word family includes words that look alike but have different functions (noun, verb, adjective, or adverb). Their meanings are related but different.

A. *Look at each model phrase and decide whether the word in* **bold** *is used as a noun, verb, adjective, or adverb.*

	NOUN	VERB	ADJECTIVE	ADVERB
1. **attempt**				
• **attempted** to swim		✓		
• several **attempts**	✓			
2. **cause**				
• find the **cause**				
• to **cause** a fight				
3. **cure**				
• **cure** his illness				
• look for a **cure**				
4. **damage**				
• pay for the **damage**				
• to **damage** the painting				
5. **record**				
• must keep a **record**				
• is **recording** the information				
6. **risk**				
• understand the **risk**				
• will **risk** one's life				

B. *Read each sentence and match the word in* **bold** *with the correct definition.*

___b___ 1. Eve **damaged** most of her nails while she washed the dishes from the party.

_____ 2. Ty wasn't able to get to the top of the mountain, but he made a good **attempt**.

_____ 3. Juan **risked** all his money when he opened up his own hair salon.

_____ 4. What **caused** the terrible car accident? Maybe it was ice on the road.

_____ 5. In past centuries, many people died of illnesses before a **cure** was found.

_____ 6. The college **records** all of our grades and test scores.

a. to make something happen

b. to physically harm someone or something

c. to write information down so that it can be looked at in the future

d. a medicine or medical way to make a sick person well again

e. to put something in a situation in which it could be lost or harmed

f. an act of trying to do something

SAME WORD, DIFFERENT MEANING

*Most words have more than one meaning. Study the additional meanings of **raise** and **record**. Then read each sentence and decide which meaning is used.*

a. **raise** *v.*	to move or lift something to a higher position
b. **raise** *v.*	to become larger or higher in amount, number, or level
c. **raise** *v.*	to collect money so that you can use it to help people
d. **record** *n.*	information about something that is written down for future use
e. **record** *n.*	the fastest speed, longest distance, highest or lowest level, etc. ever

___c___ 1. The whole town worked together to **raise** money for a new park.

_____ 2. They **raise** the flag in front of the school every morning. They take it down in the evening.

_____ 3. Erik holds the school **record** for scoring the most points in a basketball game.

_____ 4. The lawyer studied the police **record** of his client.

_____ 5. The teacher **raised** the level of difficulty when she saw we were ready to learn more.

WORDS IN SENTENCES

Complete each sentence with one of the words from the box.

allow	caused	damaged	raised	risk
attempt	cure	~~disease~~	record	shore

1. _____*Disease*_____ killed everyone in the village.

2. Mei believes green tea is a(n) _____ for the common cold.

3. We sat on the _____ and watched the birds fly over the water.

4. Karina was very weak. Her _____ to stand up only made her more tired.

5. What's the world _____ for eating the most hot dogs at one time?

6. You can't leave now! I won't _____ it.

7. The store _____ its prices; it's become too expensive to shop there.

8. What _____ her anger? Do you know what happened?

9. Firefighters _____ their lives on the job.

10. I _____ my computer when I dropped it.

WORDS IN COLLOCATIONS AND EXPRESSIONS

Following are common collocations (word partners) and expressions with some of the key words. Read the definitions and then complete the conversations with the correct form of the collocations and expressions.

1. **allow**
   - **allow (sb) to**   to let someone do something or have something

2. **attempt**
   - **make an attempt to**   to try to do something

3. **cause**
   - **cause (sb/sth) to**   to make something happen, or to make a person do something

4. **cure**
   - **a cure for (sth)**   a way to make an illness go away

5. **record**
   - **set a (new) record (set the record for)**   to do something at the fastest speed, to go for the longest distance, to make it to the highest level, etc. ever

6. **risk**
   - **take a risk**   to take the chance that something bad may happen

1.   SON: Who's the best baseball player ever?

   FATHER: Well, Willie Mays _____*set*_____ more than one _____*record*_____. He was the first to hit 300 homeruns, and he finished his career with 660. All around he was a great player.

2.   PATIENT: How serious is my disease?

   DOCTOR: Well, I'm afraid it can be very serious, but thankfully there's _____ it.

3.   DAUGHTER: You never _____ me _____ do anything!

   MOTHER: You have more freedom than you know. My mother set even more rules than I do.

4.   JESSICA: Why are you in such a hurry?

   TIFFANY: Being late could _____ me _____ lose my job!

5.   STUDENT DRIVER: Is it okay to pass the car in front of us?

   DRIVING INSTRUCTOR: We're not in a hurry, and you're driving fast enough. Remember, drive safely and don't _____ if you don't have to.

6.   STUDENT 1:   How can we get the teacher to let us take the test on Monday instead of Friday?

   STUDENT 2:   I think we should _____ change her mind; we all need more time to study.

Read the two articles about sports. Complete each one with words and expressions from the boxes.

~~allow . . . to~~	caused	damage	shore	take a risk

RIVER SURFING

Surfing doesn't usually _____*allow*_____ a person _____*to*_____ ride a wave for very long.
                                    1

Ocean waves may travel hundreds of miles, but once they hit the _____ they only last for
                                                                            2

seconds. In northern Brazil, though, ten-minute rides are not uncommon. In fact, Brazilian star surfer

Alex "Picuruta" Salazar has had amazing rides of up to thirty-seven minutes, going for over seven

miles! How is this possible?

Science answers that question with something called a "tidal bore"—a wave that's _____
                                                                                            3

when water going out of a river hits with water running in from the ocean. Known to surfers as

pororoca, or "mighty noise," the tidal bore occurs around the new and full moons during the spring

and the fall.

Surfers _____ when they try to ride a bore; the waves are very powerful. The biggest
                4

bore in Brazil can be found in the Araguari, and its brown waters leave a lot of _____ as
                                                                                        5

the wave moves along the land. California surfer Gary Linden also points out that the Brazilian rivers

carry dangerous fish, such as piranhas. Even so, Linden says, "It's one of the greatest experiences ever."

(Based on information in "Surfing Brazil's Pororoca." National Geographic, May 2005.)

attempt	cure for	disease	raised	set a new record

POWERFUL WOMEN IN THE AIR

In 2002, 131 women skydivers jumped from planes and joined together as they fell through the air.

Three years later a group of 151 ladies _____. They needed eight aircraft and more than
                                                6

one try. On their eighteenth _____, they jumped and held on to one another for
                                    7

4.8 seconds. In doing so, they made history for what is known as female formation skydiving.

Team leader Kate Cooper noted how special the group was. Not only did they come from fifteen

different countries, they were also from different professions—from mothers to lawyers.

Cooper explained that the women had a good reason to make this jump. Their actions received a lot of

attention, and they used this attention to help City of Hope, a center for cancer in California. The skydiving

event _____ close to $500,000 to help find a(n) _____ the _____.
        8   **9**   **10**

These powerful, intelligent, [and] amazing women "worked together for a common good."

(Based on information in "It Wasn't All Bad." The Week, October 21, 2005.)

WORDS IN DISCUSSION

Apply the key words to your own life. Read and discuss the questions with a partner. Try to use the key words.

1. What's something your parents didn't **allow** you **to** do when you were younger?

   EXAMPLE

   *My parents never **allowed** me to go to bed very late, especially on a school night.*

2. Name a terrible **disease** in the world today. Is there a **cure for** it?

3. You just noticed you lost your wallet. How will you **attempt** to find it?

4. Do you **record** movies or TV shows?

5. Do you know a joke that **causes** you **to** laugh whenever you hear it? Tell the joke to another person.

WORDS IN WRITING

Write a short answer (1–2 sentences) for each question. Try to use the key words.

1. Would you like to live near the ocean **shore**, or would you choose a cabin in the mountains instead?

   EXAMPLE

   *I'm from a warm country, so I think I'd like to live near the ocean **shore**. Also, it must be lonely in the mountains.*

2. Do you take good care of everything you own, or do you easily **damage** things?

3. Are you the kind of person who likes to **take a risk**?

4. Name at least two places that have **records** on you. Do you care if others look at this information?

5. For what organization would you be willing to help **raise** money? Explain.

Key Words

coast	contain	effect	public	skill
compare	develop	experiment	sense	system

▌WORDS IN CONTEXT

*Use the sentences to guess what each key word means. Choose the meaning that is closest to that of the key word in **bold**.*

1. coast
/koʊst/
-noun

- The states of Washington, Oregon, and California are on the Pacific **coast**.
- The road ran along the **coast**, so as we drove, we were able to see the water.

Coast means . . . (a.) land by an ocean b. a group of mountains c. a long and busy road

2. compare
/kəmˈpɛr/
-verb

- Parents shouldn't **compare** their children; each child is special in his or her own way.
- The family **compared** the two houses and decided to buy the bigger one.

Compare means . . . a. to try to make two things the same b. to study the differences between two things c. to prefer one thing to another

3. contain
/kənˈteɪn/
-verb

- The package from home **contained** sweaters, books, and a note from my grandma.
- I prefer homemade soups. Canned soups **contain** too much salt.

Contain means . . . a. to have many parts b. to have something inside c. to make use of

4. develop
/dɪˈvɛləp/
-verb

- Many believe that yoga **develops** the mind as well as the body.
- Greg and I worked at the same office for a year before our friendship began to **develop**.

Develop means . . . a. to grow b. to begin c. to test

5. effect
/ɪˈfɛkt/
-noun

- My essay discusses the good and bad **effects** of television on children.
- I saw the **effects** of Roy's hard schedule; he was tired, underweight, and unhappy.

Effect means . . . a. something that causes an illness b. something that helps you learn c. something that happens because of another thing

6. experiment
/ɪkˈspɛrəmənt/
-noun

- Some **experiments** use animals to study new medicines.
- Scientist Alexander Graham Bell's **experiments** with the telegraph helped him create the first telephone.

Experiment means . . . a. a scientific test b. a personal plan c. a medical building

7. public
/ˈpʌblɪk/
-adjective

- The president's address and salary are **public** knowledge.
- Any changes to the law should be for the **public** good.

Public means . . .   a. relating to all   b. relating to all   c. relating to all
                              people   journalists   politicians

8. sense
/sɛns/
-noun

- Erin didn't have the **sense** to stay away from the angry dog, and it bit her.
- Good **sense** tells you to dress warmly when it's snowing.

Sense means . . .   a. good behavior   b. good understanding   c. good information

9. skill
/skɪl/
-noun

- The chess champion tested his **skills** against the computer.
- The **skills** of an artist grow stronger with time.

Skill means . . .   a. ability   b. understanding   c. enjoyment

10. system
/ˈsɪstəm/
-noun

- The library's computer **system** was put together very well. It's clear and easy to use.
- The city needs a better subway **system**. It's confusing to have so many lines.

System means . . .   a. a set of connected   b. a group of workers   c. a station
                              parts

WORDS AND DEFINITIONS

Match each key word with its definition.

1. _____develop_____ to grow into something bigger or stronger

2. _____ to have something inside, or to have something as a part

3. _____ to study two or more things and see the differences or similarities

4. _____ a set of connected parts that work together as a single unit

5. _____ an ability to do something very well, especially because you have learned and practiced it

6. _____ a scientific test done to show a reaction or prove an idea

7. _____ a good understanding and ability to make decisions

8. _____ something that happens because of another thing, or a reaction to someone or something

9. _____ the land next to the ocean

10. _____ relating to all the ordinary people in a country or city

Choose the best answer.

1. Conrad **compared** cities
   a. and enjoyed visiting both.
   (b.) to decide where he should live after college.
   c. because he found a new job.

2. Whose job is it to care for **public** safety?
   a. the police
   b. a lawyer
   c. a parent

3. The scientist did an **experiment**
   a. to prove the dangers of the new medicine.
   b. because his understanding of the new medicine was correct.
   c. when the results were already clear.

4. Which famous city is on the **coast**?
   a. Moscow, Russia
   b. Sydney, Australia
   c. Washington, D.C.

5. Which of the following is a stereo **system**?
   a. rock, jazz, and classical music
   b. CDs and cassettes
   c. CD player, radio, speakers

6. At the post office, they asked me if the box I wanted to send **contained**
   a. any dangerous materials or items.
   b. an address.
   c. enough stamps.

7. Which of the following is an **effect** of exercising?
   a. You have no time to play sports or go to the gym.
   b. You want to be healthy.
   c. You look and feel good.

8. Your musical talent will **develop**
   a. with a good singing coach.
   b. at tonight's concert.
   c. a lot of money.

9. My little nephew doesn't have the **sense**
   a. to stay away from the hot oven.
   b. to read long words.
   c. to stay home alone.

10. Which of the following is a **skill**?
    a. how tall you are
    b. how well you write
    c. how early you wake up

WORD FAMILIES

Now that you have studied the ten key words and their basic definitions, you are ready to learn words that belong to the same family as some of the key words. A word family includes words that look alike but have different functions (noun, verb, adjective, or adverb). Their meanings are related but different.

A. *Look at each model phrase and decide whether the word in **bold** is used as a noun, verb, adjective, or adverb.*

	NOUN	VERB	ADJECTIVE	ADVERB
1. **compare**				
• to **compare** two artists		✓		
• need a **comparison**	✓			
2. **contain**				
• **contains** no new information				
• close the **container**				
3. **develop**				
• must **develop** one's talent				
• can the **development** of your skills				
4. **experiment**				
• a science **experiment**				
• can **experiment** with different materials				
5. **public**				
• **public** knowledge				
• will speak to **the public**				
6. **sense**				
• to use good **sense**				
• quickly **sense** her anger				

B. *Read each sentence and match the word in **bold** with the correct definition.*

___e___ 1. The president should know the views of the **public**.

_____ 2. Sara put the cookies in the **container**.

_____ 3. The teacher took pleasure in his students' **development**.

_____ 4. Animals run away if they **sense** danger.

_____ 5. Chefs like to **experiment** in the kitchen.

_____ 6. To show how different I was from my brother I used a **comparison**.

a. something such as a box, a bowl, a bottle, etc. that can be filled with something

b. to feel something is true without someone telling you so

c. the act of studying two or more things to see the differences or similarities

d. the act of becoming bigger, stronger, or more advanced

e. all the people in a country or city

f. to try using new things to see how good they are or how good they work

SAME WORD, DIFFERENT MEANING

Most words have more than one meaning. Study the additional meanings of **develop**, **public**, and **sense**.
Then read each sentence and decide which meaning is used.

a.	**develop** v.	to grow or change into something bigger or stronger, or to make someone or something do this
b.	**develop** v.	to make a new idea or item for sale better by working on it for a long time
c.	**public** adj.	relating to all the ordinary people in a country or city
d.	**public** adj.	can be used by anyone
e.	**sense** n.	a good understanding and ability to make decisions
f.	**sense** n.	a feeling about something

_f_ 1. The beginning of the trip was filled with a **sense** of excitement.

___ 2. I never ate a lot of vegetables in the past, but over the past few years I've **developed** a greater liking for tomatoes, mushrooms, and peppers.

___ 3. The post office is a **public** building.

___ 4. The teacher liked my ideas, but asked me to **develop** them. I'll have to work on my essay over the weekend.

___ 5. News about the closing of the factory caused **public** worry.

___ 6. Marianne showed good **sense** when she chose not to drive in the thick fog.

WORDS IN SENTENCES

Complete each sentence with one of the words from the box.

coast	~~container~~	effect	public	skill
comparison	develop	experiment	sense	system

1. I can save the leftover food inside this _____container_____.

2. The _____ stood outside the palace; they wanted to share their king's sad loss of his wife and their queen.

3. A(n) _____ of cell phones shows that this model is the best.

4. When I _____ with my writing, I sometimes surprise myself with the results.

5. If we take a drive to the _____, we can have a picnic by the water.

6. You said you're fine, but I can _____ your unhappiness. What's wrong?

7. It doesn't take much _____ to make toast.

8. The _____ of highways is very easy to use and saves time.

9. The company must _____ its line of computers to help its sales.

10. The summer rain had the _____ of cooling everything off.

WORDS IN COLLOCATIONS AND EXPRESSIONS

Following are common collocations (word partners) and expressions with some of the key words. Read the definitions and then complete the conversations with the correct form of the collocations and expressions.

1. **coast**
   - **from coast to coast**   across all of the U.S.

2. **compare**
   - **compare (sb/sth) with**   to say that something or someone is different or worse than another

3. **develop**
   - **develop from**   to change into something bigger or stronger, or to make someone or something do this

4. **effect**
   - **create the effect of**   to create an idea or feeling (often used in art)

5. **experiment**
   - **experiment with**   to try using different ideas, materials, etc. in order to find out how good they are

6. **sense**
   - **sense of humor**   the ability to understand and enjoy things that are funny, or to make people laugh

1.   NILES: What instruments do you play?

   ZACK: I've been playing the piano for years, but I also like to _____*experiment*_____ a little _____*with*_____ the guitar.

2. ROOMMATE 1:   I worry about George. Sometimes I think he has no _____.

   ROOMMATE 2:   He takes life too seriously. We need to make him laugh more.

3.   MIKA: Are there really that many fast-food restaurants in the U.S.?

   DAVE: Yes. You can find them _____.

4. ART STUDENT: How can I show rain? White paint will just cover everything.

   INSTRUCTOR: You can _____ rain by painting white lines on a blue-gray sky.

5. CO-WORKER 1:   Our manager really listens to what we think.

   CO-WORKER 2:   It's true; and she has the ability to _____ a great plan _____ a simple suggestion.

6.   TOM: It must be great to have a brother. I'm an only child.

   JOE: Sometimes, but I hate it when people _____ me _____ my older brother. They always tell me how great he was on the football field and ask me why I don't play.

WORDS IN READINGS

Read the two articles about art. Complete each one with words and expressions from the boxes.

compare . . . with	~~developed from~~	skill
create the effect of	experimented with	

THE VAN GOGH DRAWINGS

Vincent Van Gogh's career as an artist lasted for more than ten years, and his most famous works are his paintings. Many people are not familiar with his drawings. They do not know that Van Gogh's painting <u>developed from</u> what he did with pen and ink.
1

"Vincent Van Gogh: The Drawings" is a show of over 100 works. The collection also has a few paintings so that art lovers can _____ the Dutchman's oil paintings _____
2

his work with ink. For example, in one painting of the sea, he used drops of white paint on the picture to _____ foam* on top of a wave. The artist did something similar in his drawings by
3

making different kinds of marks with his pen.

Van Gogh _____ pen marks like a musician mixes sounds to get music. He learned
4

that he could make his marks light or dark, close together or far apart, in circles or waves, and more. The world knows that as the years passed, Vincent Van Gogh's mind became more and more ill, but he still had an artist's _____ and control to put life on paper.
5

*Foam *(n.) is a lot of very small bubbles on top of water, soup, a drink, etc.*

(Based on information in Mark Stevens, "Scribble Scribble: How Van Gogh Rendered His Flickery World in the Hard Lines of Pen and Ink." New York Magazine online, October 24, 2005.)

contained	from coast to coast	public	sense of	system

THE MAN WHO LOVED TO BUILD PARKS

In 1893, the *Garden and Forest* magazine called Frederick Law Olmsted the best artist of the New World. Today few know his name, but thousands enjoy Olmsted's work _____ because he
6

was the dreamer behind many of North America's _____ parks.
7

As a young man, Olmsted visited England with his brother. There they hiked through Wales and the Midlands. Then Olmsted visited a large park in the city of Birkenhead and was surprised by all the loveliness it _____. Olmsted later gave the same _____ quiet beauty to the
8   9

people of New York City by creating Central Park.

Olmsted also made a name for himself as an author and journalist. One of his books was about the trip he took with his brother. Still, his greatest works are in the open air, not on paper: a park _____ for Boston, an island park for Chicago, a mountain park for Montreal, and a

10
parkway* in Buffalo, just to name a few.

Olmsted should be remembered. He gave North America the art called landscape architecture, and through his art he gave people beauty in their everyday lives.

*A parkway (n.) is a wide road in or around a city, usually with grass or trees in the middle or along the sides.

(Based on information in John G. Mitchelle, "Frederick Law Olmsted's Passion for Parks." National Geographic, March 2005.)

▌WORDS IN DISCUSSION

Apply the key words to your own life. Read and discuss the questions with a partner. Try to use the key words.

1. Name an important **skill** that you have.

   EXAMPLE

   *I can play the flute. Maybe this **skill** doesn't seem important, but music makes me happy.*

2. Do you own a stereo **system**?

3. Do you live near a **public** park? Where's the nearest **public** park?

4. You're visiting the United States. Would you like to drive **from coast to coast**? Who would you take with you and what cities would you like to see?

5. How does English **compare** to your language?

▌WORDS IN WRITING

Write a short answer (1–2 sentences) for each question. Try to use the key words.

1. What are some **effects** of watching television?

   EXAMPLE

   *I think TV is helpful and interesting, especially in English. One **effect** is a better understanding of the language.*

2. Can a friendship **develop from** a business relationship?

3. Do your drawers at home **contain** things you don't need? Why do you keep these things?

4. Do you ever **experiment with** cooking?

5. Do you think you have a good **sense of humor**? Do others in your family have a similar **sense of humor**?

QUIZ 1

PART A

Choose the word that best completes each item and write it in the space provided.

1. The child _____*attempted*_____ to climb the tall tree, but got too scared halfway up.
   - a. attempted
   - b. compared
   - c. settled
   - d. developed

2. Our boss does not _____ us to send or receive personal e-mail messages.
   - a. consider
   - b. allow
   - c. contain
   - d. settle

3. The baseball player _____ his arm high in the air to catch the ball.
   - a. developed
   - b. allowed
   - c. compared
   - d. raised

4. Everyone knows who robbed the store. The video camera gave _____.
   - a. guilt
   - b. proof
   - c. sense
   - d. damage

5. The teacher took a moment to _____ our suggestion.
   - a. consider
   - b. allow
   - c. contain
   - d. settle

6. She looked at the box and tried to guess what it _____.
   - a. developed
   - b. contained
   - c. sensed
   - d. considered

7. The factory had a good _____ for making TVs; each worker knew his or her part.
   - a. cure
   - b. sense
   - c. feast
   - d. system

8. There are many medicines, but sometimes there is no _____ for an illness.
   - a. proof
   - b. skill
   - c. spirit
   - d. cure

9. Youngho has good speaking _____; he speaks clearly and confidently.
   - a. records
   - b. skills
   - c. systems
   - d. cures

10. The boss had to _____ the disagreement among the workers.
   - a. consider
   - b. develop
   - c. contain
   - d. settle

PART B

*Read each statement and write **T** for true or **F** for false in the space provided.*

__F__ 1. A swimming pool has a **shore**.

_____ 2. The **effect** of a mistake is what happens because of the mistake.

_____ 3. Driving too fast during bad weather is a **risk**.

_____ 4. Eating all the pie yourself and not sharing it is a **generous** act.

_____ 5. A **disease** improves your health.

_____ 6. Stores give away free clothes on many **occasions**.

_____ 7. **Guilt** often makes people say they're sorry.

_____ 8. An elderly person can feel young in **spirit**.

_____ 9. If there is **damage** to your cell phone, you may not be able to use it.

_____ 10. The **cause** of a problem is something that helps you to fix it.

PART C

Each situation shows the meaning of one of the key words. Write the appropriate key word next to the situation. Use the clues in italics.

coast	develop	feast	mean	record
compare	~~experiment~~	load	public	sense

1. The *scientist* did several *tests* on the new drug. _____experiment_____

2. The teacher kept *information* on each student's performance. _____

3. My guitar teacher really helped me to *get stronger* and really *grow* as a musician. _____

4. These are the views of *the ordinary people*. _____

5. Troy showed no *understanding* of how to take care of a cut. He didn't even know he should wash the dirt away with water. _____

6. I like both artists, but if you *study* their work, you can see that the first has more talent and chooses more unusual subjects. _____

7. I don't want to be *unkind*, but sometimes telling the truth hurts others. _____

8. The student had to *carry a large number* of books. _____

9. We cooked *a large meal* to *celebrate* Jihyun's return. _____

10. Our trip from Maine to Florida let us see all the states *next to the* Atlantic *Ocean*. _____

Key Words

bold	creature	exist	rise	shallow
certain	degree	pattern	serve	stick

WORDS IN CONTEXT

*Use the sentences to guess what each key word means. Choose the meaning that is closest to that of the key word in **bold**.*

1. **bold**
   /boʊld/
   -adjective

   • The chess player made a **bold** move; he believed he would win.
   • Dana asks **bold** questions in class. She's never afraid to ask anything.

   Bold means . . .   a. not careful   ⓑ confident   c. rude

2. **certain**
   /ˈsɚtˀn/
   -adjective

   • Are you **certain** that you know the way? I think we're lost.
   • Chen Li is not **certain** about changing jobs; he needs more time to make a decision.

   Certain means . . .   a. completely sure   b. confused   c. very tired

3. **creature**
   /ˈkritʃɚ/
   -noun

   • Who or what were the first **creatures** on Earth?
   • The boy studied the tiny **creature** on the ground. It was an insect of some kind.

   Creature means . . .   a. a wild animal   b. a dinosaur   c. any living thing

4. **degree**
   /dɪˈgri/
   -noun

   • Thirty **degrees** Fahrenheit is cold weather.
   • Each corner of the room is a 45-**degree** angle.

   Degree means . . .   a. the temperature   b. a system for counting   c. a measurement

5. **exist**
   /ɪgˈzɪst/
   -verb

   • The problem of homeless animals **exists** in many large cities.
   • When I was a child, I thought that a monster **existed** under my bed.

   Exist means . . .   a. to be real   b. to hide   c. to change

6. **pattern**
   /ˈpæt̮ɚn/
   -noun

   • There's a **pattern** in my cat's behavior. Koko likes to eat and then nap in the sun.
   • You can learn speech **patterns** by listening to people talk on the radio or TV.

   Pattern means . . .   a. the feelings of a person or animal   b. the things a person or animal prefers   c. the regular way something is done

7. **rise**
/raɪz/
-verb

- It's cool in the morning, but later in the day the temperature **rises**.
- Gas prices **rose**, and we tried to use the car less often.

Rise means . . .   a. to stay the same   b. to become too high   c. to increase

8. **serve**
/sɚv/
-verb

- The waitress **served** everyone their meal with a big smile.
- My mother puts dishes on the table, and everyone **serves** themselves.

Serve means . . .   a. to prepare a meal   b. to give food   c. to clean up
                                              or drinks

9. **shallow**
/ˈʃælou/
-adjective

- The father let his young daughter swim in the **shallow** end of the pool.
- The river was too **shallow** for the big ship to travel on it.

Shallow means . . .   a. calm or not moving   b. not deep   c. narrow

10. **stick**
/stɪk/
-verb

- Why don't you **stick** a piece of tape on the box to keep it closed?
- The candy is good, but it **sticks** to my fingers and it's hard to get off.

Stick means . . .   a. to put or be put   b. to close or be   c. to break or be broken
                        on something   closed

▌WORDS AND DEFINITIONS

Match each key word with its definition.

1. ____*creature*____ any living thing except plants (animal, fish, insect, etc.)

2. _____ not deep, measuring only a short distance from top to bottom

3. _____ completely sure

4. _____ the regular way in which something happens or is done

5. _____ to be real or alive

6. _____ to put something on another thing by connecting or gluing, or to be put on something this way

7. _____ to increase in number, amount, or quality

8. _____ to give someone food or drinks as part of a meal

9. _____ showing that you are confident and willing to take risks

10. _____ a measurement of temperature or the size of an angle (the space between two lines that meet or cross each other)

Choose the best answer.

1. At a restaurant, they **serve**
   a. a check.
   (b.) warm meals.
   c. forks, knives, and spoons.

2. We do NOT use **degrees** to measure
   a. an athlete's running speed.
   b. a sick person's temperature.
   c. the angles of a triangle.

3. If an animal **exists**, then
   a. it is too dangerous to keep as a pet.
   b. you can only read about it in books.
   c. you might see one in nature.

4. Antonio is **bold**;
   a. he gets nervous about trying something new at work.
   b. he's a good businessman because he takes chances.
   c. he learns by reading and talking to others.

5. If Gosha is **certain** of his answer on a test, how sure is he that his answer is correct?
   a. less than 50%
   b. 50%
   c. 100%

6. Which of the following is **shallow**?
   a. a deep swimming pool
   b. a tall glass of water
   c. a small saucer of milk

7. Which of the following CANNOT **rise**?
   a. the number of students at your school
   b. the price of a hot lunch at the school cafeteria
   c. the rules for how students can dress at your school

8. The largest **creature** on this planet is
   a. Asia.
   b. the Atlantic Ocean.
   c. the blue whale.

9. As a guest in our home, Shizuko learned the **patterns** of American family life and
   a. made many of our practices her own.
   b. asked us how to say or write them correctly.
   c. took the recipes back to Japan to share with her family.

10. What can easily **stick** to the bottom of your shoe?
    a. a banana peel
    b. bubble gum
    c. snow

WORD FAMILIES

Now that you have studied the ten key words and their basic definitions, you are ready to learn words that belong to the same family as some of the key words. A word family includes words that look alike but have different functions (noun, verb, adjective, or adverb). Their meanings are related but different.

A. *Look at each model phrase and decide whether the word in **bold** is used as a noun, verb, adjective, or adverb.*

	NOUN	VERB	ADJECTIVE	ADVERB
1. bold				
• a **bold** plan			✓	
• speak **boldly**				✓
• his **boldness**	✓			
2. uncertain				
• be **certain** about your decision				
• speak with **certainty**				
• feel **uncertain**				
3. exist				
• where they **exist**				
• the **existence** of ghosts				
4. stick				
• to **stick** two pieces together				
• wash your **sticky** hands				

B. *Read each sentence and match the word in **bold** with the correct definition.*

__f__ 1. After eating bread with honey, my lips felt **sticky**.

_____ 2. Tia decided to forget all her fears about performing and **boldly** walked on stage.

_____ 3. Scientists become excited about the **existence** of rare plants.

_____ 4. The president could not say with **certainty** that his plan would work.

_____ 5. Reporters can't be afraid of asking too many questions; **boldness** is part of the job.

_____ 6. On my first day of school, I was **uncertain** about finding my first class.

a. the state of being completely sure about something

b. not completely sure

c. the state of being real or alive

d. the quality of being confident and willing to take risks

e. in a way that shows you are confident and willing to take risks

f. made of or covered with a substance that sticks to things

SAME WORD, DIFFERENT MEANING

Most words have more than one meaning. Study the additional meanings of **bold**, **degree**, **rise**, and **stick**. Then read each sentence and decide which meaning is used.

a.	**bold** *adj.*	showing that you are confident and willing to take risks
b.	**bold** *adj.*	very clear and strong or bright (said of writing, shapes, or colors)
c.	**degree** *n.*	a measurement of temperature or the size of an angle (the space between two lines that meet or cross each other)
d.	**degree** *n.*	the level or amount of something, especially ability
e.	**rise** *v.*	to increase in number, amount, or quality
f.	**rise** *v.*	to physically move up
g.	**stick** *v.*	to put something on another thing by connecting or gluing, or to be put on something this way
h.	**stick** *n.*	a long thin piece of wood that has fallen or been cut from a tree

_b_ 1. The Polish flag is simple yet **bold** with a white stripe on top and a red one on the bottom.

____ 2. Flying a large plane takes a high **degree** of skill.

____ 3. The cost of houses in our town is **rising**.

____ 4. Children can be very **bold** when they don't understand enough to be afraid.

____ 5. I love to watch the sun **rise** over the ocean.

____ 6. The builders carefully measured the **degree** of the stairs to the floor.

____ 7. To keep the fire burning, we need to add some dry **sticks**.

____ 8. I **stuck** a note for my roommate on the refrigerator door before I left.

WORDS IN SENTENCES

Complete each sentence with one of the words from the box.

boldly	degree	pattern	serves	sticky
~~creatures~~	existence	rise	shallow	uncertain

1. Dinosaurs were the largest ____creatures____ to walk the Earth.

2. Fred was _____ about buying a new car. Should he spend less on a used one?

3. The students _____ asked their new teacher how much experience he had.

4. The holes in the road are _____, but they still make the car shake a lot.

5. This is too easy for me to read. I need a book with a higher _____ of difficulty.

6. I used glue to fix the drawer, and now my fingers are _____.

7. Sadly, not many giant panda bears are left in _____.

8. We watched the ducks _____ out of the water and fly away.

9. The hotel _____ breakfast from 7:00 A.M. to 9:00 A.M.

10. The police found a similar _____ in the three bank robberies. This helped them catch the robber when he tried to steal money from a fourth bank in the same way.

WORDS IN COLLOCATIONS AND EXPRESSIONS

Following are common collocations (word partners) and expressions with some of the key words. Read the definitions and then complete the conversations with the correct form of the collocations and expressions.

1. certain	
• **certain (people, things, etc.)**	used to speak of someone or something you won't name or describe
2. degree	
• **to what degree**	to what level or amount of something
3. serve	
• **serve as**	to be used for something specific
4. stick	
• **stick (sth) on**	to put something on another thing, or stay connected or glued to another thing
• **stick together**	to continue to help someone and keep each other company
• **stick with**	to continue doing something and make no changes

1. JAN: How are your guitar lessons going?

   HAL: My fingers hurt from learning to play, but I'm going to _____*stick with*_____ it.

2. VINCE: The kitchen table can _____ a desk until we buy more furniture.

   PIPER: That's fine with me. It's big enough for both of our computers.

3. BONNIE: Thanks for being here today. I really needed some company.

   DIANE: Good friends always _____. Call me anytime if you have a problem.

4. GLEN: Do people at work know you used to be a ballet dancer?

   CLARA: No. There are _____ topics I don't discuss with my new co-workers.

5. STUDENT: Can our essay be about any problem people face today?

   TEACHER: Any problem shared by people in general. I want you all to answer two questions: _____ can politicians help the public? How much help should be free?

6. MAURICE: Why did your letter come back in the mail?

   KIM: The stamp was old, so it didn't _____ the envelope very well. I guess it fell off.

WORDS IN READINGS

Read the two articles about wildlife. Complete each one with words and expressions from the boxes.

~~creatures~~	degree	serve as	shallow	stick

SMART ENOUGH TO USE TOOLS

Which apes* are the smartest? After humans, many think of chimpanzees as intelligent

___creatures___ . People often see gorillas, though, as being big, strong, yet not so smart. New

1

findings suggest that this view may not be correct. The truth lies in the gorillas' ability to use tools.

In the past, there were only four members of the "tool club": humans, chimpanzees, bonobos,

and orangutans. For example, chimpanzees can open nuts with a rock and get insects with a

_____ . What does the use of tools tell us? The greater the use of tools, the higher the

2

_____ of intelligence.

3

So why are gorillas now a part of the tool club? Thomas Breuer of the Wildlife Conservation

Society took a team into the Republic of Congo and noted three activities performed by gorillas with a

piece of wood: to see if the water was _____ enough to cross, to lean on while digging for

4

food, and to _____ a bridge over a puddle**. Maybe gorillas have just as much intelli-

5

gence as other tool users.

*An ape (n.) is a large monkey without a tail or with a very short tail.

**A puddle (n.) is a small pool of water on a road, path, etc. often caused by rain.

(Based on information in "Gorillas Join the Tool Club." The Week, October 21, 2005.)

bold	certain	exist	patterns	rise

LITTLE KNOWN FACTS ABOUT THE KILLER WHALE

The orca, or killer whale, is not really a whale at all. It belongs to the dolphin family. This is one of

several interesting facts people often forget or just don't know.

Killer whales have a small relative called the pygmy killer whale, or *Feresa attenuata*. Scientists are

not _____ how many of these small whales _____ , but the pygmy killer

6 7

whale is sometimes seen when caught by accident or when one comes up on a beach and cannot

move back into the water. The pygmy looks more like a dolphin. It is mostly black, without the

_____ black-white-and-gray coloring of the large killer whale.

8

Other interesting facts can be learned by studying the killer whale's eating _____.
9
Orcas have learned to catch food on land, though they live in the water. If a seal is on a piece of
ice, a group of swimming whales can make a quick turn in front of the seal, and this creates a strong
wave that pushes the seal into the water. Also, one whale can _____ out of the water and
10
land on the piece of ice; the seal slides down into the water for the other whales to eat. These are just
two of many clever ways orcas can turn a seal or sea lion into a meal.

(Based on information in David O'Connor, "Did You Know? A Killer Whale Treble." National Geographic online, April 2005.)

WORDS IN DISCUSSION

Apply the key words to your own life. Read and discuss the questions with a partner. Try to use the key words.

1. Can you describe your sleep **pattern**?

   ### EXAMPLE

   *I like to go to bed late. I fall asleep after midnight, and I wake up around nine o'clock in the morning. But this is only my **pattern** when I don't work.*

2. Have you ever gone swimming in deep water, or do you only swim in **shallow** water?

3. When was the last time you stopped to watch the sun **rise**?

4. What do you think is the most interesting **creature** in the sea?

5. In your country, who **serves** whom at the dinner table?

WORDS IN WRITING

Write a short answer (1–2 sentences) for each question. Try to use the key words.

1. **To what degree** do you trust other people?

   ### EXAMPLE

   *I don't trust everyone. I have a few close friends, and I trust them **to a high degree**.*

2. Are you **bold** or shy? When was the last time you acted **boldly**?

3. Do you often change your mind, or do you usually **stick with** a decision?

4. Do you think **certain** languages are easier to learn than others? Explain.

5. Do you think life **exists** on other planets?

Key Words

doubt	habit	improve	origin	result
gain	handle	lead	reduce	reward

▌WORDS IN CONTEXT

*Use the sentences to guess what each key word means. Choose the meaning that is closest to that of the key word in **bold**.*

1. **doubt**
   /daʊt/
   -noun

   • We have no **doubt** that our team will win. We haven't lost a game all season.
   • I have many **doubts** about going to a new school. Will I like it there? Are the teachers good? Will I be able to make new friends?

   Doubt means . . .
   a. a feeling of being upset
   b. a wish to change things
   c. a feeling of being unable to believe ⓒ

2. **gain**
   /geɪn/
   -verb

   • Why do you want to change jobs? What do you hope to **gain**?
   • Frances **gained** business experience by working in her family's grocery store.

   Gain means . . .
   a. to lose something
   b. to get something
   c. to ask for something

3. **habit**
   /ˈhæbɪt/
   -noun

   • I bite my nails when I worry; it's a bad **habit**.
   • We're trying to make a **habit** of cooking healthy meals every night.

   Habit means . . .
   a. a regular action
   b. a small mistake
   c. an action that surprises others

4. **handle**
   /ˈhændl/
   -verb

   • There were too many phone calls to **handle**. The secretary did the best she could.
   • The lesson was difficult to teach, but Mr. Gleason **handled** it well.

   Handle means . . .
   a. to answer
   b. to take correct action
   c. to become confused

5. **improve**
   /ɪmˈpruv/
   -verb

   • I feel comfortable speaking in English, but I need to **improve** my grammar.
   • Frank has been practicing hard on the piano. His playing has really **improved**.

   Improve means . . .
   a. to make or get better
   b. to study
   c. to correct or be corrected

6. **lead**
   /lid/
   -verb

   • I work at a restaurant. My job is to greet people and **lead** them to their tables.
   • The new student was lost, so I **led** him to his next class.

   Lead means . . .
   a. to give directions
   b. to choose something for someone
   c. to show the way

7. **origin**
/ˈɔred ʒɪn,ˈar-/
-noun

- Mr. Poulos loves to explain the Greek **origin** of many English words.
- The **origin** of hot dogs is either Frankfurt-am-Main or Coburg, Germany.

Origin means . . .   a. the place something   b. the way something   c. the place where
comes from   is created   something is used

8. **reduce**
/rɪˈdus/
-verb

- There's going to be a big sale tomorrow. The store will **reduce** all prices by 40%.
- The doctor told me that I need to **reduce** the amount of salt in my diet.

Reduce means . . .   a. to make smaller or   b. to replace   c. to keep the same
less

9. **result**
/rɪˈzʌlt/
-noun

- My mistake was the **result** of poor attention. I need to be more careful.
- Uncle Roy loves to say that a good life is the **result** of hard work and a little luck.

Result means . . .   a. something you   b. something that   c. something that
must fix   happens because of   creates a problem
something else

10. **reward**
/rɪˈwɔrd/
-noun

- The man gave me a **reward** of $25 for finding his lost dog.
- My parents often gave me a small **reward** when I got 100% on a test in school.

Reward means . . .   a. a present to say   b. something you get   c. money that you give
thank you   for doing something   to help someone
good

WORDS AND DEFINITIONS

Match each key word with its definition.

1. ___handle___ to take correct action in a situation

2. _____ a feeling of being unable to trust or believe

3. _____ to show the way by going first

4. _____ something that happens or exists because of something else

5. _____ to become better, or to make something better

6. _____ to become smaller or less, or to make something do this

7. _____ to get or win something important or useful

8. _____ something given, especially money, for doing something good

9. _____ something you do regularly

10. _____ the situation or place from which something comes, or where it began to exist

COMPREHENSION CHECK

Choose the best answer.

1. If it's my **habit** to brush my teeth after every meal,

   a. the dentist tells me to take better care of my teeth.

   b. the dentist is pleased each time he looks at my teeth.

   c. I don't carry an extra toothbrush with me to school.

2. Each of the following practices can **improve** your vocabulary EXCEPT

   a. reading books, magazines, and other texts.

   b. writing down new words you hear and then checking their meanings in a dictionary.

   c. always using the same words because they are very familiar.

3. Which of the following is the **result** of a rain shower?

   a. dark clouds in the sky

   b. umbrellas

   c. wet ground

4. If I want to know the **origin** of my name,

   a. I want to know where it came from and what it means.

   b. I want to know why my parents chose it for me.

   c. I want to know how popular it is.

5. A feeling of **doubt** can make you feel

   a. very confident.

   b. certain that you've answered a question correctly.

   c. unsure about trusting another person's promise to you.

6. Derek gave his dog a **reward** because

   a. it made a mess on the carpet.

   b. it brought him his slippers when he asked for them.

   c. its barking woke him up very early in the morning.

7. If I **gain** time for a project,

   a. I must rush to finish it.

   b. I can use the extra time to do a better job.

   c. I need to make a schedule.

8. Each of the following situations are reasons to **lead** another person EXCEPT if

   a. the person is blind.

   b. the person is lost.

   c. the person knows the way better than you do.

9. If Heather's brother can **handle** responsibility,

   a. she can ask him to take care of her plants and mail while she's away.

   b. she knows he'll forget any instructions she gives.

   c. she can't trust him with the care of her cat.

10. You can **reduce** noise by

    a. screaming through an open window.

    b. turning down the stereo and closing your doors and windows.

    c. using the phone on the bus or train.

WORD FAMILIES

Now that you have studied the ten key words and their basic definitions, you are ready to learn words that belong to the same family as some of the key words. A word family includes words that look alike but have different functions (noun, verb, adjective, or adverb). Their meanings are related but different.

A. *Look at each model phrase and decide whether the word in **bold** is used as a noun, verb, adjective, or adverb.*

	NOUN	VERB	ADJECTIVE	ADVERB
1. **doubt**				
• be in **doubt**	✓			
• cannot **doubt**		✓		
2. **improve**				
• to **improve** your handwriting				
• make an **improvement**				
3. **lead**				
• will **lead** a group of tourists				
• choose a **leader**				
4. **origin**				
• place of **origin**				
• the **original** plan				
5. **result**				
• look at the **result**				
• will **result** in happiness				
6. **reward**				
• get a **reward**				
• to **reward** you with money				

B. *Read the first half of each sentence and match it with the appropriate ending.*

<u> c </u> 1. We hope the business meeting

_____ 2. I want a job that's going to

_____ 3. This painting is only a copy of the artist's work;

_____ 4. After five days in the hospital, Grandma's health finally began to show

_____ 5. We are lost, and I'm beginning to

_____ 6. We learned about Salzburg's history from

a. the **original** was lost in a fire.

b. our tour **leader**.

c. will **result** in an agreement that pleases both companies.

d. **doubt** that we'll find our way back home again.

e. **reward** me with more than just money.

f. some **improvement**.

SAME WORD, DIFFERENT MEANING

Most words have more than one meaning. Study the additional meanings of **lead**, **original**, and **result**. Then read each sentence and decide which meaning is used.

a.	**lead** *v.*	to show the way by going first
b.	**lead** *v.*	to be in charge or control of something, especially an activity or group of people
c.	**original** *adj.*	first or earliest
d.	**original** *adj.*	completely new and different
e.	**result** *n.*	something that happens or exists because of something else
f.	**result** *n.* *(usually plural)*	the answers that you get from a scientific or medical study or test

_c_ 1. The **original** McDonald's restaurant opened in 1948 in San Bernardino, California.

_____ 2. I **led** our houseguest to her room and showed her where the bathroom was along the way.

_____ 3. My cold was the **result** of going for a walk with wet hair in cool weather.

_____ 4. Few movies today are very **original**; mostly they take ideas from books or older films.

_____ 5. The same music teacher has **led** the school choir for seven years.

_____ 6. The teacher promised to give us our test **results** on Monday.

WORDS IN SENTENCES

Complete each sentence with one of the words from the box.

doubt	habits	improvement	original	results
gain	handled	~~leader~~	reduce	rewarded

1. The police are looking for the _____leader_____ of the gang.

2. Why do you _____ that we can finish the job on time?

3. The _____ plan was to fly to New York, but we drove instead.

4. The store owner _____ the angry customer's complaint.

5. Mark will be a good lawyer, but he still needs to _____ experience.

6. The _____ of the medical test showed that Cal had heart problems.

7. The mayor worked hard to _____ the number of people without jobs.

8. The mother _____ the boy with a cookie.

9. My uncle says he'll never marry because he doesn't want to change his _____.

10. My teacher said she sees _____ in my writing. I'm happy about that.

WORDS IN COLLOCATIONS AND EXPRESSIONS

Following are common collocations (word partners) and expressions with some of the key words. Read the definitions and then complete the conversations with the correct form of the collocations and expressions.

1. **doubt**
   - **doubt yourself**   to not trust or believe in yourself
2. **gain**
   - **gain weight**   to increase in weight
3. **habit**
   - **break the habit of**   to stop doing something that is bad for your health
   - **have the habit of**   something you do regularly
4. **handle**
   - **get a handle on (sth)**   to get control of something; to bring to order
5. **lead**
   - **lead to**   to make something happen or exist as a result of something else

1. GINA: Do you know you _____*have the habit of*_____ tapping your foot when you're worried?

    SAMILLA: Yeah, my mother's always telling me not to do this. I can't help it.

2. COACH: You need to _____ your anger. Don't let your feelings control you.

    ATHLETE: I'll try.

3. FATHER: You _____ too often. You're a smart person. I trust you to make good decisions.

    SON: Thanks, Dad. I guess I needed to hear that.

4. OLIVIA: Your brother sure got bigger. I remember him being thinner.

    LAURA: Yeah, he started playing hockey a few years ago. That's when he also started working out at the gym in order to _____. He's all muscle!

5. WORKER 1: Let's take a coffee break.

    WORKER 2: A break sounds great, but I'll have juice instead. I'm trying to _____ drinking so much coffee every day. The doctor told me it's not good.

6. PAUL: Since when do you smoke? I don't have to tell you all the problems smoking can _____, do I? From bad breath and yellow teeth to lung cancer!

    LIBBY: I know. It's an awful habit.

Read the two articles about health and fitness. Complete each one with words and expressions from the boxes.

gained	habits	improve	~~results~~	reward

SMALL CHANGES MAKE A DIFFERENCE

There are people who are crazy about their health, and they work out all the time. The good news is that you don't have to live at the gym to be in good shape. New findings prove that just a little exercise done regularly can give great _____*results*_____ . Scientist James Hill of the University
  1
of Colorado suggests that fifteen, twenty, or thirty minutes of walking each day is enough to

_____ your health.
  2

Hill's study looked at the health and exercise _____ of more than 5,000 middle-aged
  3
and elderly people in the United States. One group exercised five times a week for about thirty

minutes. Their _____: living 1.4 years longer. A second group chose to do harder
  4
activities like running or swimming. These people _____ up to 3.7 years of extra life.
  5

What can you learn from the study? Just a small amount of regular exercise helps you stay fit and live longer.

(Based on information in "Walk the Walk." The Week, December 2, 2005.)

doubt yourself	get a handle on	leads to	origin	reduces

WHAT TO DO WHEN YOU'RE STRESSED

When there's a lot of work to do, do you push yourself to finish it? Psychologist Susan Fletcher

explains that stress* _____ our mind's ability to think, so trying to work longer hours in
  6
order to _____ the situation will not make stress go away. Most likely you will do a poor
  7
job because you cannot think well. It's better to take a break, says Dr. Stephen Hines of the Methodist Dallas Medical Center. He believes that even three to five minutes can help. After a short rest, you'll be able to get back to your work with better attention and energy.

That's good advice because stress is harmful.** As it grows, you lose confidence. This

_____ other problems: if you _____, you cannot make good decisions,
  8   9
or the decisions you make don't feel right.

Stress (n.) is a feeling of worry caused by difficulties in your life. Being stressed means feeling worried because of such difficulties.

**Harmful (adj.) means causing damage or likely to hurt.*

What's the _____ of all this stress? Dr. Hines states that a loss of control or a loss of
    10
order creates most of the stress we feel. The best way to fight it is to get enough exercise, enough sleep,
and good foods. You should also have your own safe way of relaxing: shopping, reading, or listening to
music, to name a few examples.

*(Based on information in Sophia Dembling, "The Do's and Don'ts of Tackling Stress." The Dallas Morning News online,
January 10, 2006.)*

▌WORDS IN DISCUSSION

Apply the key words to your own life. Read and discuss the questions with a partner. Try to use the key words.

1. Do you ever **reward** yourself for a job well-done? Explain.

   EXAMPLE

   *I like to **reward** myself with good food like a shrimp dinner. Sometimes I also buy something
   small such as a new CD.*

2. What kinds of foods make most people **gain weight**?

3. What do you hope will be the **result** of learning English?

4. What do you **have the habit of** doing when you're nervous?

5. Do you need to **reduce** your personal spending? Explain.

▌WORDS IN WRITING

Write a short answer (1–2 sentences) for each question. Try to use the key words.

1. Name a time you **doubted yourself**, but in the end everything turned out just fine.

   EXAMPLE

   *When I came to England to study, I worried about doing everything in English. But now I know
   there was no need to **doubt myself** because I'm doing all right.*

2. When you get really upset, what do you do to **get a handle on** your emotions?

3. Name a famous **leader** in your country. What is this person famous for?

4. Do you know the **origin** of your name? Do you think it's a very **original** name?

5. Have you seen any **improvements** in your English? How are you trying to **improve** your
   English?

WORDS IN CONTEXT

Use the sentences to guess what each key word means. Choose the meaning that is closest to that of the key word in **bold**.

1. **admit**
   /əd'mɪt/
   -verb

   • Garry can't fix the car by himself, but he won't **admit** that he needs help.
   • You've been looking at the map for a long time. **Admit** it. We're lost, right?

   Admit means . . .   (a.) to say something is true   b. to laugh about something   c. to be worried about something

2. **beam**
   /bim/
   -noun

   • A **beam** of morning sunlight came through the window and woke me up.
   • The **beam** of our car's headlights did little to help us see in the fog.

   Beam means . . .   a. a light bulb   b. a line of light   c. a natural form of light

3. **board**
   /bɔrd/
   -noun

   • The teacher wrote the answer on the **board** for the class to see.
   • We put our chess pieces on the **board** and started to play a new game.

   Board means . . .   a. a piece of paper for writing   b. a hard flat piece of material that has a special use   c. the part of a computer that shows words and pictures

4. **crime**
   /kraɪm/
   -noun

   • The police work hard to stop **crime** in the city.
   • The man was guilty of many **crimes**: he stole everything from clothes to cars.

   Crime means . . .   a. dangerous person   b. a serious accident   c. activity against the law

5. **destroy**
   /dɪ'strɔɪ/
   -verb

   • We keep important documents in a safe; a flood or fire cannot **destroy** them.
   • The great earthquake of 1906 **destroyed** much of San Francisco.

   Destroy means . . .   a. to damage something badly   b. to lose something important   c. to make a big change to something

6. **disturb**
   /dɪ'stɚb/
   -verb

   • Lance is working on the computer. He asked us not to **disturb** him.
   • My dog's loud snoring **disturbed** my sleep.

   Disturb means . . .   a. to help someone do something   b. to stop what someone is doing   c. to copy what someone is doing

7. faith
/feɪθ/
-noun

- My parents' **faith** in me gives me the strength to make hard decisions by myself.
- We have a good soccer team, and our fans always have **faith** that we will win.

Faith means . . .   a. a dream   b. love   c. a belief

8. population
/ˌpapyəˈleɪʃən/
-noun

- China has the largest **population** with about 1.3 billion people.
- A city's **population** is tied to the economy; where there are jobs there are people.

Population means . . .

a. the number of people living in an area
b. the number of people with jobs
c. the amount of land in a city or country

9. ripe
/raɪp/
-adjective

- We can't eat these green bananas; they're not **ripe** yet.
- The tomatoes will soon be **ripe** for picking.

Ripe means . . .   a. ready to eat   b. at a good price   c. big enough

10. warn
/wɔrn/
-verb

- The weather report **warned** people in the city to prepare for a bad storm.
- They always **warn** parents to keep medicine bottles away from small children.

Warn means . . .

a. to explain good habits
b. to teach important skills
c. to tell someone about a possible danger

WORDS AND DEFINITIONS

Match each key word with its definition.

1. _____beam_____ a line of light shining from something

2. _____ to damage something very badly, so that it cannot be used or no longer exists

3. _____ the number of people or animals living in an area, country, etc.

4. _____ ready to eat

5. _____ a flat piece of wood, plastic, or other hard material that has special use

6. _____ to agree or say that something is true, especially if you did something wrong

7. _____ a strong belief that someone or something can be trusted to be right or to do the right thing

8. _____ to tell someone that something bad or dangerous may happen, so that s/he can stop it from happening or prepare for it

9. _____ activity that breaks the law

10. _____ to stop what someone is doing by making a noise, asking a question, etc.

Choose the best answer.

1. If fruit is **ripe**,
   a. it's best to throw it away.
   b. you should wait a few days before eating it.
   c. you can enjoy eating it today.

2. Karen **disturbed** the lecture by
   a. quietly taking notes.
   b. asking too many questions.
   c. not listening carefully.

3. Who is **warning** another person?
   a. Waverly: "Would you please be more quiet?"
   b. Seth: "Tell me what you think of my essay."
   c. Lara: "If you eat too much too fast, you'll make yourself sick."

4. Which of the following gives a **beam**?
   a. a flashlight
   b. a stove
   c. a window

5. I have **faith** in Hayden;
   a. he'll work hard to do a good job on this project.
   b. he'll likely quit if this project gets too hard.
   c. he's never done anything like this project before.

6. Shanna **admitted** the truth;
   a. she told the teacher she cheated on the test.
   b. you never know when she's lying.
   c. she was careful not to let anyone learn her secret.

7. What can **destroy** a vegetable garden?
   a. a light rain
   b. a small fence
   c. a hungry rabbit

8. You will NOT likely find a **board**
   a. in a classroom.
   b. near a swimming pool.
   c. in a glove.

9. Which of the following actions is a **crime**?
   a. giving money to a homeless person
   b. killing another person
   c. not going to work

10. To record the **population** of dolphins in these waters, scientists
    a. give a number to each animal.
    b. use sign language to communicate with the animals.
    c. feed the animals.

WORD FAMILIES

Now that you have studied the ten key words and their basic definitions, you are ready to learn words that belong to the same family as some of the key words. A word family includes words that look alike but have different functions (noun, verb, adjective, or adverb). Their meanings are related but different.

A. *Look at each model phrase and decide whether the word in **bold** is used as a noun, verb, adjective, or adverb.*

	NOUN	VERB	ADJECTIVE	ADVERB
1. crime				
• saw a **crime**	✓			
• find a **criminal**	✓			
2. destroy				
• to **destroy** her dream				
• see much **destruction**				
3. faith				
• a strong **faith**				
• a **faithful** son				
• to visit **faithfully**				
4. warn				
• must **warn** everyone				
• to give a **warning**				

B. *Read each sentence and match the word in **bold** with the correct definition.*

___c___ 1. The **destruction** from the war was truly terrible.

_____ 2. My dog greets me **faithfully** every evening with a loud bark.

_____ 3. The police officer didn't give me a ticket for speeding, just a **warning** to drive more safely.

_____ 4. Grandpa was a **faithful** husband and friend to Grandma; he cared for her during her illness and was with her when she died.

_____ 5. The **criminal** was sent to jail for 25 years.

a. not changing your feelings towards someone or something and continuing to show your care

b. something that prepares you for something bad or dangerous that might happen

c. the act or process of damaging something

d. done in a way that shows you still care and things remain the same

e. someone who is shown to be guilty of a crime

SAME WORD, DIFFERENT MEANING

*Most words have more than one meaning. Study the additional meanings of **beam**, **disturb**, **faith**, and **ripe**. Then read each sentence and decide which meaning is used.*

a.	**beam** *n.*	a line of light shining from something
b.	**beam** *v.*	to send out energy, light, radio, or television signals, etc.
c.	**disturb** *v.*	to stop what someone is doing by making a noise, asking a question, etc.
d.	**disturb** *v.*	to make someone feel worried or upset
e.	**faith**	a strong belief that someone or something can be trusted to be right or do the right thing
f.	**faith** *n.*	a religion
g.	**ripe** *adj.*	ready to eat
h.	**ripe** *adj.*	to be ready for something to happen, or to exist in such a way that some kind of event or action can easily take place

_c_ 1. The secretary took a message from the caller; she didn't want to **disturb** her boss's meeting.

____ 2. A **beam** of moonlight helped me find my way across the dark room.

____ 3. The city is **ripe** for change; new businesses are welcome.

____ 4. The radio station **beamed** the new talk show across the country.

____ 5. I have **faith** in Ian's ability to become a good lawyer.

____ 6. I don't like to watch scary movies with lots of killing. They **disturb** me for days.

____ 7. Job interviewers shouldn't ask questions about religion. They cannot ask what **faith** you practice.

____ 8. **Ripe** lemons are bright yellow and a little soft when you squeeze them.

WORDS IN SENTENCES

Complete each sentence with one of the words from the box.

admit	board	destruction	faithful	ripe
~~beam~~	criminal	disturbs	population	warning

1. A radio station can _____ _beam_ _____ a signal across the ocean.

2. The police questioned the man, but he didn't _____ to the robbery.

3. Joe's unusually quiet today, and that _____ me. Something must be wrong.

4. My doctor has given me more than one _____ about my poor diet.

5. I need to slice the cheese. Do you have a cutting _____?

6. Pukekura is a very small town in South Westland, New Zealand with a _____ of two.

7. The _____ from the famous Chicago fire of 1871 was so great that a third of the city was lost. The people rebuilt their city with stone and brick.

8. This neighborhood is _____ for crime. Unlocked doors and dark streets invite robbers.

9. I own every book that author has written. I must be his most _____ reader.

10. Mother says that in my dark clothes and sunglasses I look like a(n) _____.

■ WORDS IN COLLOCATIONS AND EXPRESSIONS

Following are common collocations (word partners) and expressions with some of the key words. Read the definitions and then complete the conversations with the correct form of the collocations and expressions.

1. **admit**	
• **admit that** (*also* **admit to**)	to agree or say that something is true, especially if you did something wrong
2. **board**	
• **get on board**	to get on a plane, ship, train, etc. in order to travel somewhere
3. **population**	
• **the general population**	all the people living in an area
4. **ripe**	
• **ripe for**	to be ready for something to happen
5. **warn**	
• **warn (sb) that/ warn (sb) about**	to tell someone that something bad or dangerous may happen, so that s/he can stop it from happening
• **give a warning about (sth)**	to warn someone about something

1. LETTY: Did you enjoy your cruise?

   ARIEL: Oh, yes! As soon as you _____*get on board*_____, it's like living in a palace.

2. JOURNALIST 1: The new plan is making everyone talk, and some are very much against it.

   JOURNALIST 2: Well, the president believes that the country is _____ political change.

3. ELDERLY WOMAN: I remember times when you couldn't find an empty seat in this library.

   LIBRARIAN: With the use of the Internet, _____ no longer has a need for libraries.

4. SON: Is it really so bad if I forget to brush my teeth at night?

   MOTHER: Dentists _____ not brushing your teeth at least twice a day will give you cavities.

5. DAUGHTER: Why doesn't Grandpa ask for more help?

   FATHER: It's hard for him to _____ he has trouble remembering things.

6. WIFE: Why did the doctor tell me so much information? It just confuses and scares me.

   HUSBAND: Hospitals must _____ the dangers of surgery, but most surgeries happen without any problems.

WORDS IN READINGS

Read the two articles about crime. Complete each one with words and expressions from the boxes.

admits that	criminals	disturb
~~crime~~	destroyed	faith

A DARKNESS IN GERMAN SOCCER

One German reporter wrote: "There's nothing in life more important than soccer." So when referee[*] Robert Hoyzer brought _____*crime*_____ into this sport, the whole country was hurt. Hoyzer

<u>1</u>

worked in the Bundesliga, the country's professional soccer league, and he now _____ he

<u>2</u>

fixed[†] five games to make money—almost $80,000—from Croatian crime leaders. Hoyzer gave the

names of the _____ he worked for, but his honesty comes too late: he'll be in prison[‡] for

<u>3</u>

two and a half years.

Sadly, the darkness Hoyzer brought to the sport will last much longer than the time he'll spend in prison. In the past, Germans trusted their referees to make good decisions; Hoyzer's actions

_____ this _____. Now many Germans will watch soccer games, and one

<u>4</u>   <u>5</u>

question will _____ them: Are the referees being fair?

<u>6</u>

[*]*A referee (n.) is someone who makes sure that the rules are followed during a game in sports.*

[†]*To fix (v.) is to make dishonest plans and/or agreements to get the results s/he wants.*

[‡]*A prison (n.) is a large building where people are kept as a punishment for a crime.*

(Based on information in Wolfgang Roth, "A Dirty Ref Belongs behind Bars." The Week, December 2, 2006.)

beams	ripe for	warn that
get on board	the general population	warnings

SAFETY FOR COLLEGE STUDENTS

Police on American college campuses[*] are giving a clear message: there's safety in numbers. Yale University, for example, sends e-mail to students telling them that it's best to walk with friends or

_____ the college's free buses when possible. They also _____ talking on the

<u>7</u>   <u>8</u>

cell phone or listening to music while walking can take your attention away from what's around you.

Why all this worry about safety? It's true that crime on college campuses is lower than in

_____, but colleges by nature are _____ danger: doors and windows are

<u>9</u>   <u>10</u>

left open, phone numbers and room numbers are easily shared with new friends, and parties can easily

make students less careful than they should be.

[*]*A campus (n.) is the land or buildings of a college.*

College police aren't stopping with e-mail _____. Johns Hopkins University spent $500,000 on cameras, and the University of Bridgeport in Connecticut gave each student a personal alarm locator (PAL), which _____ a radio signal to campus police, telling them where you are if you find yourself in danger. Many other schools have created a "buddy** program" for walking across a dark campus.

The government is also helping to keep students safe. There's a law that says colleges must share information about crime on campus with its students each year. As one woman says, it's all about knowing and understanding.

**A buddy (n.) (informal) is a friend.

(Based on information in William Yardley, "Finding Safety in Numbers." New York Times, January 8, 2006.)

▌WORDS IN DISCUSSION

Apply the words to your own life. Read and discuss the questions with a partner. Try to use the key words.

1. Can you easily **admit** that you're wrong?

   ### EXAMPLE

   *Sure. I always **admit** my mistakes. I even laugh at them.*

2. Do you know the **population** of your hometown?
3. What's your favorite fruit? How do you know when it's **ripe**?
4. What kind of weather can cause terrible **destruction**?
5. Name something many parents **give warnings about**.

▌WORDS IN WRITING

Write a short answer (1–2 sentences) for each question. Try to use the key words.

1. Does anything **disturb** your sleep or do you usually sleep deeply?

   ### EXAMPLE

   *I sleep deeply. Loud noises don't **disturb** me.*

2. Do you like to see **beams** of sunlight when you wake up in the morning? Or do you keep it dark?
3. Are you usually on time to **board** planes, trains, and buses?
4. Name a person or place that's well-known for **crime.**
5. Who is your **faithful** friend? How long have you known this person?

QUIZ 2

PART A

Choose the word that best completes each item and write it in the space provided.

1. What is 98.6 _____*degrees*_____ Fahrenheit in Celsius?
   - a. boards
   - b. degrees
   - c. creatures
   - d. habits

2. I have _____ that you'll do well on the exam. You've prepared well.
   - a. crime
   - b. result
   - c. origin
   - d. faith

3. We need a thick, flat _____ to make a seat for our tree swing.
   - a. board
   - b. faith
   - c. pattern
   - d. habit

4. The cats _____ the furniture with all their scratching.
   - a. improved
   - b. destroyed
   - c. warned
   - d. handled

5. Most people agree that the _____ of hamburgers is Hamburg, Germany.
   - a. crime
   - b. result
   - c. origin
   - d. faith

6. Are you _____ we have enough food for the party?
   - a. shallow
   - b. certain
   - c. ripe
   - d. bold

7. Are you pleased with the _____ of all the changes we made?
   - a. patterns
   - b. results
   - c. origins
   - d. creatures

8. Our aunt _____ us how dangerous it was to pick and eat unfamiliar mushrooms.
   - a. admitted
   - b. destroyed
   - c. warned
   - d. disturbed

9. Our biology teacher says it's useful to study all _____, both big and small.
   - a. boards
   - b. degrees
   - c. creatures
   - d. crimes

10. It's my sister's _____ to write in her journal at the end of every day.
   - a. board
   - b. reward
   - c. crime
   - d. habit

PART B

*Read each statement and write **T** for true or **F** for false in the space provided.*

____T____ 1. If my brother **handled** a problem, he took correct action to fix it.

_____ 2. When an activity has a **pattern**, you know what will happen next.

_____ 3. If you **gain** money, you become poorer.

_____ 4. A **bold** person has little confidence.

_____ 5. An honest person **admits** a wrongdoing.

_____ 6. If I want to **lead** you, I'm asking you to follow.

_____ 7. If you can **reduce** the difficulties in your life you'll be happier and healthier.

_____ 8. When prices **rise**, customers save money.

_____ 9. Whales cannot swim in very **shallow** water.

_____ 10. Loud noises can **disturb** your sleep.

PART C

Each situation shows the meaning of one of the key words. Write the appropriate key word next to the situation. Use the clues in italics.

beam	doubt	improve	reward	serve
crime	exist	population	~~ripe~~	stick

1. I can tell if a melon is *ready to eat* by its smell. ____ripe____

2. The teacher *gave* us an evening without homework for the *good job* we all did on yesterday's test. _____

3. Mandy *gave* each of her guests a big piece of pie at the end of the *meal*. _____

4. The *line of light* from the flashlight was bright enough to let us see the path. _____

5. I was *unable to believe* that I had the winning ticket. _____

6. We used glue to *attach* the colored paper to the plain box. _____

7. Practice and experience helps you *get better* at almost any job. _____

8. There are *real* plants and fish that *live* at the very bottom of the ocean. _____

9. Always lock your doors. People can *break laws* in your own neighborhood. _____

10. *How many* bald eagles are left in North America? _____

blow	duty	inquire	pity	proper
compose	exact	miserable	probable	sympathetic

WORDS IN CONTEXT

*Use the sentences to guess what each key word means. Choose the meaning that is closest to that of the key word in **bold**.*

1. **blow**
/bloʊ/
-verb

• A strong wind often **blows** near the ocean shore.

• The fan **blew** cooler air into the classroom.

Blow means . . .   a. to hold air in one place   (b.) to move air   c. to change the air temperature

2. **compose**
/kəm'poʊz/
-verb

• The musicians that **compose** the band met one another in high school.

• Red, orange, yellow, green, blue, and purple **compose** the colors of a rainbow.

Compose means . . .   a. to perform together   b. to help one another   c. to come together to make something

3. **duty**
/'duṭi/
-noun

• Nao believes it is her **duty** as a daughter to care for her aging parents.

• It is everyone's **duty** to keep our neighborhood clean.

Duty means . . .   a. something people make you do   b. something you like to do   c. something you feel you must do

4. **exact**
/ɪg'zækt/
-adjective

• I don't know Carey's **exact** age, but I believe he's in his late forties.

• When you're baking, you need to use **exact** amounts and temperatures.

Exact means . . .   a. correct   b. more than usual   c. nearly correct

5. **inquire**
/ɪn'kwaɪɚ/
-verb

• Sharon called the school to **inquire** about Chinese language lessons.

• It's best to write a letter if you want to **inquire** about a job.

Inquire means . . .   a. to ask about something   b. to pay for a service   c. to explain something

6. **miserable**
/'mɪzərəbəl/
-adjective

• Raisa felt **miserable** because she couldn't find her lost dog.

• I was far from friends and family, so I was **miserable** during the holiday.

Miserable means . . .   a. very sick   b. very unhappy   c. very tired

7. **pity**
   /ˈpɪt̮i/
   -noun

   - Vance is upset about losing his job, but he doesn't want anyone's **pity**.
   - Les can be very mean, but I have **pity** for him because he has no friends.

   Pity means . . . a. the need to hurt someone   b. a feeling of being sorry for someone   c. the act of helping someone

8. **probable**
   /ˈprabəbəl/
   -adjective

   - It's quite **probable** that Heather will win; she's a strong player.
   - Ice on the road is the **probable** cause of the accident, but the police need to consider other explanations as well.

   Probable means . . .   a. uncertain   b. almost certain   c. certain

9. **proper**
   /ˈprapɚ/
   -adjective

   - Please don't say *I ain't*. It's not **proper** grammar.
   - My father is very organized. He believes everything has its **proper** place.

   Proper means . . .   a. correct   b. normal   c. clean

10. **sympathetic**
    /ˈsɪmpəˈθɛt̮ɪk/
    -adjective

    - My nephew loves animals, and he is very **sympathetic** to homeless cats and dogs; he helps them whenever he can.
    - We all felt **sympathetic** toward Cade when his father died. It hurts to lose a loved one.

    Sympathetic means . . .   a. showing that you understand and care   b. showing interest   c. showing strength or control

WORDS AND DEFINITIONS

Match each key word with its definition.

1. _____duty_____ something that you have to do because you think it is right

2. _____ to come together with other things or people to make something

3. _____ a feeling of being sorry for someone who is hurt or unhappy

4. _____ to move with or be moved by speed or power (said of wind or air)

5. _____ to ask someone for information

6. _____ very unhappy, especially because you are lonely or sick

7. _____ correct or right for a situation

8. _____ likely to happen, exist, or be true

9. _____ correct and having all the pieces of information needed

10. _____ showing that you understand and care for someone who is sad, hurt, lonely, etc.

COMPREHENSION CHECK

Choose the best answer.

1. You feel **sympathy** for
   a. the elderly man who is very healthy at the age of 90.
   b. the elderly man who visits his grandchildren once a week.
   c. the elderly man who is often ill and receives no visitors.

2. The three brothers **compose** a circus act;
   a. they buy tickets to the circus every year.
   b. Genya works in Russia, Kolya works in China, and Dima works in the U.S.
   c. people come from all over to see them perform together.

3. I feel **pity** for Jess because he
   a. loves to play soccer, and his broken leg will keep him out of the big game.
   b. is the best soccer player on the team.
   c. often gets angry and yells back at the coach.

4. We don't have **exact** directions to the stadium,
   a. but we know the general direction and I'm sure there'll be signs.
   b. and we marked the way from beginning to end on the road map.
   c. so we should have no problems finding it.

5. Each of the following are **probable** causes for a bad night of sleep EXCEPT
   a. you watched a scary movie before bedtime.
   b. you had a terrible fight with a close friend earlier today.
   c. you took a warm bath and read a favorite book before bedtime.

6. It was my **duty** to look after my younger sister;
   a. I knew she needed me.
   b. my parents paid me to do this.
   c. she could take care of herself.

7. Aunt Lia often **inquires** about school and my friends;
   a. I don't like all the advice she gives.
   b. I don't know why she complains so much.
   c. I like how she wants to know more about my life.

8. Wind can cause each of the following actions EXCEPT
   a. **blow** a door open.
   b. **blow** leaves across the grass.
   c. **blow** the radio on.

9. Mimi bought the **proper** shoe size;
   a. the new shoes made her feet hurt.
   b. the new shoes were comfortable and looked good.
   c. she liked the bigger size because she could wear an extra pair of socks.

10. What can make you feel **miserable**?
    a. bad news
    b. a helpful English lesson
    c. a gift from a friend

▌WORD FAMILIES

Now that you have studied the ten key words and their basic definitions, you are ready to learn words that belong to the same family as some of the key words. A word family includes words that look alike but have different functions (noun, verb, adjective, or adverb). Their meanings are related but different.

A. *Look at each model phrase and decide whether the word in **bold** is used as a noun, verb, adjective, or adverb.*

	NOUN	VERB	ADJECTIVE	ADVERB
1. exact				
• the **exact** time			✓	
• must be **exactly** right				✓
2. pity				
• to feel **pity** for the sick children				
• no need to **pity** me				
3. probable				
• a **probable** cause				
• to be **probably** correct				
4. proper				
• the **proper** size				
• to fit it **properly**				
5. sympathize				
• a **sympathetic** look				
• feel deep **sympathy**				
• to **sympathize** with others				

B. *Read the first half of each sentence and match it with the appropriate ending.*

___b___ 1. I had to return the second can of paint because it

_____ 2. As the rain came down harder, I

_____ 3. I'm sorry you broke your arm; I

_____ 4. Uncle Ed reads the newspaper every day, so he

_____ 5. The whole neighborhood

_____ 6. I have a long last name, and many people

a. can't write or say it **properly**.

b. wasn't **exactly** the same color as the first.

c. felt **sympathy** for the family whose home burned down.

d. **probably** knows the answer to your question about politics.

e. **pitied** the people without umbrellas.

f. **sympathize** with you. I broke mine two years ago.

SAME WORD, DIFFERENT MEANING

*Most words have more than one meaning. Study the additional meanings of **blow**, **compose**, and **proper**. Then read each sentence and decide which meaning is used.*

a. **blow** *v.*	to move with or be moved by speed or power (said of wind or air)
b. **blow** *v.*	to send air out through your mouth
c. **blow** *n.*	a hard hit with a hand, tool, etc.
d. **compose** *v.*	to come together with other things or people to make something
e. **compose** *v.*	to put sounds, words, colors, or pictures together to create music, writing, or art
f. **proper** *adj.*	correct or right for a situation
g. **proper** *adj.*	correct behavior within a group of people

__e__ 1. The artist **composed** an interesting work of art from pieces of metal and glass.

_____ 2. We didn't have the **proper** tools to fix the sink.

_____ 3. I watched the wind **blow** the clouds across the sky.

_____ 4. Is it **proper** to call your professor by his or her first name?

_____ 5. I **blew** on my finger after burning it on the iron.

_____ 6. The smartest students **compose** the school's chess club.

_____ 7. Surprisingly, the smaller boxer gave a strong **blow** to the other man's chin and won the match.

WORDS IN SENTENCES

Complete each sentence with one of the words from the box.

blow	duty	~~inquire~~	pity	properly
composed	exactly	miserable	probably	sympathetic

1. I'm calling to _____inquire_____ about your yoga classes.

2. Mozart _____ his first piece of music around the age of four.

3. It will _____ rain tomorrow, so we should take our umbrellas and raincoats.

4. The woman gave a hard _____ to the robber's head with a frying pan.

5. It is everyone's _____ to care for nature by not wasting water, paper, or electricity.

6. My teacher was _____ when I explained that my illness made it difficult for me to prepare for the exam.

7. You have to put the lid on the container _____ . If you don't, the food inside will go bad.

8. Arlene felt _____ because she was not able to go to her best friend's wedding.

9. You don't have to explain how to find the stadium; I know _____ how to get there.

10. Dana decided not to get married to Jeff. I _____ her parents, who already spent so much money on the preparations.

WORDS IN COLLOCATIONS AND EXPRESSIONS

Following are common collocations (word partners) and expressions with some of the key words. Read the definitions and then complete the conversations with the correct form of the collocations and expressions.

1. **blow**
   - **a (terrible) blow to (sth or sb)**   an event that makes you very unhappy or surprises you

2. **compose**
   - **be composed of**   to be formed from a group of parts

3. **duty**
   - **your duty to (do sth)**   something that you have to do because you think it is right

4. **pity**
   - **It's a pity (that)**   It's sad or too bad (that)

5. **probable**
   - **be highly probable (that)**   likely to happen, exist, or be true

6. **proper**
   - **proper (for sb) to (do sth)**   correct for someone to do something

1. SCOTT: Why isn't Lana going to college? I thought she wanted to be a lawyer.

   RYAN: Lana says that right now it's her _____*duty to*_____ help with the family business.

2. SALLY: Joan said her parents are upset with her, but she didn't explain why.

   NICK: Her decision to quit college was _____ her parents.

3. TOBY: How is glass made? What is it _____?

   TEACHER: Who can answer Toby's question? Let's see what you already know.

4. RASHIM: _____ you weren't feeling well last night. You missed a great concert.

   SAM: So I heard. Did you give my ticket to someone else?

5. TAMMI: You said some things were confusing in Japan. Can you give me an example?

   DALE: For one thing, I didn't know if it was _____ for a guest _____ refuse a dish that the hosts offer.

6. WIFE: This country needs a female leader! I just don't think the men will let that happen.

   HUSBAND: Well, more and more women are entering politics; it's _____ there will be an American female president in our lifetime.

▌WORDS IN READINGS

Read the two letters about family. Complete each one with words and expressions from the boxes.

inquire	probably	proper for me to	~~sympathetic~~	your duty to

PUSH DAD INTO ACTION?

Dear Abby:

My father hasn't had a job for two years already, and he's always telling me how little money we have. I don't understand why he doesn't get a new job. I really care about his happiness, and I try to be _____sympathetic_____, but it's hard. I have one year left in high school, and I want to go to college. I
1
_____ won't be able to go to a good school because my dad can't pay for it. I don't think
2
it would be _____ tell him what to do with his life since I'm his son and I know little
3
about the workplace, but what can I do?

Confused

Dear Confused:

Help your father by telling him that there are centers that give information about jobs. He can talk to the people there, and _____ about the kind of work he'll be able to find.
4
Also make it _____ help yourself. Start looking for scholarships*. Go visit a library.
5
Your school may also be able to help you in your search. Don't wait. Take action now, so you'll be ready for college. Good luck to you!

*A scholarship (n.) is an amount of money that is given to someone by an organization to help pay for his/her education.

(Based on information in "Dear Abby" on uxpress.com, November 14, 2005.)

a terrible blow	compose	exactly	it's a pity	miserable

MAKING MOM UNDERSTAND

Dear Amy:

I have a wonderful boyfriend. He's caring and kind, and makes me very happy. I'm twenty-four and he's twenty-eight. For both of us, this is our first serious relationship.

Naturally, it was _____ to find out how little my mother thinks of the man I love.
6
After she met him, she told me he wasn't grown up enough and that he was too quiet. She questions why I'm dating him.

I've always been close to my mother, and I've always listened to her opinion, so
_____ we can't even talk about my boyfriend without one of us getting upset.
7
What should I do? I'm _____.
8

Caught in the Middle

Dear Caught in the Middle:

Your mother may not understand how deeply her unkind words about your boyfriend hurt you.

Maybe you could _____ a letter. Write with warmth and love, but be clear when you
9
ask her to stop speaking so rudely about a person you care so much for. When you're done, keep the

letter for a couple of days. If you're still sure the letter explains _____ how you feel, then
10
send it to her.

(Based on information in "Dear Amy" in Chicago Tribune, February 8, 2006.)

WORDS IN DISCUSSION

Apply the key words to your own life. Read and discuss the questions with a partner. Try to use the key words.

1. What's the **proper** way to get a waiter's attention in a restaurant?

   EXAMPLE

   *In my country it's **proper to** lift your hand a little and wave it.*

2. Give an example of a **duty** to your family.

3. When you haven't seen a friend for a long time, what do you usually **inquire** about?

4. Do you know your **exact** height in meters? How about in feet and inches?

5. Do you think it's **probable that** people will use the Internet and no longer need libraries in the near future?

WORDS IN WRITING

Write a short answer (1–2 sentences) for each question. Try to use the key words.

1. Do you usually take a long time to **compose** a letter?

   EXAMPLE

   *If it's an important letter, I need a long time to **compose** it, especially in English.*

2. When was the last time you gave someone **sympathy**?

3. Do you think **it's a pity that** there isn't just one language in the world? Explain.

4. A friend feels **miserable**. What can you do to make him or her feel better?

5. Do you always know **exactly** what you want when you go to a store?

▌WORDS IN CONTEXT

*Use the sentences to guess what each key word means. Choose the meaning that is closest to that of the key word in **bold**.*

1. ancient
/ˈeɪnʃənt/
-adjective

- The Great Wall of China is **ancient**. It dates back to the third century B.C.
- Hippocrates was an **ancient** Greek physician. While other people still turned to magic in the fifth century B.C., he taught a natural form of medicine.

Ancient means . . .
    a. powerful and dangerous
    (b.) very old or from far back in history
    c. different or unusual

2. blame
/bleɪm/
-verb

- Don't **blame** me for your mistake. You're the one who locked the keys in the car.
- Reena **blamed** herself. She knew Tim ended their friendship because of her lies.

Blame means . . .
    a. to think someone must answer for something bad
    b. to lie about who is guilty
    c. to hurt someone's feelings

3. course
/kɔrs/
-noun

- Professor Jones is very popular. Many students try to take his **courses**.
- This semester Tom is taking a **course** on modern art. It meets once a week.

Course means . . .
    a. a textbook
    b. a teacher
    c. a class

4. entire
/ɪnˈtaɪɚ/
-adjective

- I was sick for the **entire** trip; I didn't enjoy even one day of my vacation.
- Nesrin is very tidy. She cleans the **entire** apartment every week.

Entire means . . .
    a. all of something
    b. the beginning or front part of something
    c. half of something

5. gather
/ˈgæðɚr/
-verb

- During lunchtime at school my friends and I **gather** at one table to eat and talk.
- The workers **gathered** near the director's office and waited for their paychecks.

Gather means . . .
    a. to walk slowly
    b. to come together
    c. to relax

6. motion
/ˈmoʊʃən/
-noun

- The **motion** of the rocking chair helped to put the baby to sleep.
- The up-and-down **motion** of the bus didn't make it easy to read.

Motion means . . .
    a. the way something moves
    b. the noise something makes
    c. the comfort something gives

7. practical
/ˈpræktɪkəl/
-adjective

- Wendy has worked for several years as a teacher, so she has **practical** experience.
- I like to think and talk about **practical** things, but my sister is a dreamer.

Practical means . . .   a. big or many   b. serious   c. relating to real things

8. purpose
/ˈpɚ·pəs/
-noun

- The doctor carefully explained the **purpose** of each step to the medical students.
- What's the **purpose** of washing the car? It's going to rain later today.

Purpose means . . .   a. a strong wish   b. the reason   c. instructions

9. ruin
/ˈruɪn/
-verb

- Jonathan **ruined** the party by starting a fight.
- I washed my new sweater in hot water and **ruined** it. It's much too small now.

Ruin means . . .   a. to destroy   b. to make a joke   c. to change

10. threat
/θrɛt/
-noun

- The politician received **threats** from his enemies. They promised to hurt his family if he didn't do what they wanted.
- With a gun in his hand, the robber made a **threat**. He told the bank teller to give him all the money from the drawer, or else he was going to shoot.

Threat means . . .   a. a warning   b. news   c. an invitation

▌WORDS AND DEFINITIONS

Match each key word with its definition.

1. _____ruin_____ to destroy completely

2. _____ a class on one subject

3. _____ happening or existing very far back in history; very old

4. _____ the process of moving, or the way someone or something moves

5. _____ the reason for an event, or activity, or the end result you want

6. _____ relating to real situations and events rather than ideas

7. _____ whole or complete

8. _____ a statement or warning that someone will cause trouble, pain, or sadness

9. _____ to say or think that someone should answer for a mistake or problem

10. _____ to come together and form a group

COMPREHENSION CHECK

Choose the best answer.

1. The director asked the employees to **gather** because

   (a.) she planned to make an important announcement.

   b. they were tired and wanted to go home.

   c. she believed in hard work.

2. Leon **blames** his sister because she

   a. helped him with his math homework.

   b. invited him to come to her friend's party.

   c. was in the bathroom for a long time, and then he was late for work.

3. **Ancient** books

   a. were mostly written in English.

   b. are kept in museums.

   c. have photographs to show important events in history.

4. The **motion** of the train

   a. is less expensive than going by plane.

   b. went to cities as far west as San Francisco and Portland.

   c. shakes the bridge as it rolls along.

5. If Kelly is taking four **courses**, what do we know for certain?

   a. She's studying four different subjects.

   b. She goes to four different schools.

   c. She'll have four different jobs later in life.

6. In our Italian class we learn **practical** language skills such as

   a. how to order food at a restaurant.

   b. how to write a poem.

   c. how to sing an opera.

7. The **entire** class did well on the test;

   a. half the class must retake it.

   b. the teacher became upset with everyone for not studying.

   c. the teacher is pleased with the results.

8. You can **ruin** a CD by

   a. scratching it.

   b. using your computer to record songs on it.

   c. keeping it clean and dry.

9. Which of the following is a **threat**?

   a. "Be careful. The tea is hot."

   b. "Please turn down the music. It's getting late."

   c. "If you tell anyone about this, I'll make your life miserable."

10. The **purpose** of a letter may be

   a. "Dear Sir or Madam."

   b. to introduce yourself and ask about a job opening.

   c. "Yours truly" or "Sincerely yours."

WORD FAMILIES

Now that you have studied the ten key words and their basic definitions, you are ready to learn words that belong to the same family as some of the key words. A word family includes words that look alike but have different functions (noun, verb, adjective, or adverb). Their meanings are related but different.

A. *Look at each model phrase and decide whether the word in **bold** is used as a noun, verb, adjective, or adverb.*

	NOUN	VERB	ADJECTIVE	ADVERB
1. **blame**				
• to **blame** myself		✓		
• take the **blame**	✓			
2. **entire**				
• paint the **entire** house				
• was **entirely** too friendly				
3. **gather**				
• the students **gathered**				
• a **gathering** of angry parents				
4. **motion**				
• the **motion** of the car				
• quickly **motion** for me to be quiet				
5. **purpose**				
• explain the **purpose**				
• to **purposely** hurt another				
6. **threat**				
• receive a **threat**				
• to **threaten** another person				

B. *Read the first half of each sentence and match it with the appropriate ending.*

__d__ 1. Mom surprised Dad with her new clothes and haircut; she looks

_____ 2. Still angry with me, Lily

_____ 3. Frederic thinks that my work was poor, so he's putting

_____ 4. My mean neighbor wants me to stop our dog from barking at night. He

_____ 5. The teacher knew that I wanted to ask a question, but she

_____ 6. Outside the hotel where the rock band was staying, there was

a. a large **gathering** of excited fans.

b. the **blame** on me for the low grade our group project got.

c. **threatened** to hurt it if I don't.

d. **entirely** different now.

e. **purposely** directed all her talking to Jenna and not to me.

f. **motioned** for me to wait until she finished her explanation.

SAME WORD, DIFFERENT MEANING

*Most words have more than one meaning. Study the additional meanings of **course**, **practical**, and **threat**. Then read each sentence and decide which meaning is used.*

a. **course** *n.*	a class on one subject
b. **course** *n.*	the direction of movement that someone or something takes
c. **practical** *adj.*	relating to real situations and events rather than ideas
d. **practical** *adj.*	made to be useful, or to be right for some purpose
e. **threat** *n.*	a statement or warning that someone will cause trouble, pain, or sadness
f. **threat** *n.*	someone or something that is a danger to something else

___a___ 1. This semester Henri is taking a **course** on twentieth-century Russian history.

_____ 2. My grandmother says that shoes should be **practical** not fashionable.

_____ 3. The actress saw other women in the business as a **threat** to her own career.

_____ 4. As we hiked, we followed the **course** of the river.

_____ 5. The reporter called the police because he was receiving **threats** over the phone.

_____ 6. Schools should give children **practical** knowledge that they can use in the future.

WORDS IN SENTENCES

Complete each sentence with one of the words from the box.

ancient	course	gathering	practical	~~ruin~~
blame	entirely	motioned	purposely	threatened

1. Please don't tell Pitchanee about the gift or you'll _____ruin_____ the surprise.

2. The museum worker greeted the _____ of foreign visitors.

3. These desks aren't very _____. They're too small and have no drawers.

4. Some say that _____ Polynesians arrived in Hawaii in the third century.

5. The child _____ shut his door loud enough to show his anger.

6. The little boy was standing _____ too close to the oven.

7. I always accept the full _____ for my mistakes.

8. Bad weather _____ our hike in the mountains, but luckily we finished before it snowed.

9. Beslan _____ for his dog to stop and sit.

10. The pilot did not change his _____; he knew it was best to continue to fly south.

WORDS IN COLLOCATIONS AND EXPRESSIONS

Following are common collocations (word partners) and expressions with some of the key words. Read the definitions and then complete the conversations with the correct form of the collocations and expressions.

1. **blame**
   - **blame (sb) for (sth)**   to say or think that someone should answer for a mistake or problem

2. **course**
   - **of course**   used when something is not surprising

3. **gather**
   - **gather up**   to collect or move similar things into one place

4. **motion**
   - **(be) in motion**   to be moving

5. **practical**
   - **practical experience**   experience in real situations

6. **purpose**
   - **on purpose**   not happening by accident; planned

---

1. JOB HUNTER: I think I can do a lot for your company. I'm a hard worker and a fast learner.

   EMPLOYER: I like your energy, and you have a good education, but you have no
   practical experience _____.

2. POLICE OFFICER: What happened?

   DRIVER: The other driver caused the accident. He pushed me off the road
   _____!

3. VICKY: Your parents bought a summer cottage, right?

   BOB: Yeah. _____, the place needs a lot of work, but the land is beautiful.

4. DAUGHTER: I didn't do well on the test because some students kept talking the whole time.

   MOTHER: Is that all? I don't remember you studying very hard the day before the test. Honey, I think it's not right to _____ others _____ our own mistakes.

5. CUSTOMER: I need a camera to take pictures of sports events. My son plays tennis.

   SALESPERSON: You're right that not every camera can take good action shots. I like this one. It takes clear pictures even when people are _____.

6. WORKER 1: Are you ready? I'll give you a ride home.

   WORKER 2: Thanks. That would be great. Just let me _____ my things.

Read the two articles about the environment. Complete each one with words and expressions from the boxes.

course	entire	~~gather~~	practical	purposes

GREEN BUILDINGS

As new buildings go up, people are giving more thought to the environment. In Manhattan, New York, the Bank of America Tower will _____*gather*_____ and make use of rainwater. In Guadalajara, Mexico, they're building a new soccer stadium right into a hill. This has two _____: within the hill, there will be soccer games; the outside will be used as a park. In most countries today there's a growing interest not to waste* space, materials, or energy. In short, buildings are becoming "green," or in other words, friendly to the environment.

Across the ocean, London's newest skyscraper** of forty-one floors is being called things like "Green Giant" and "Green Pickle." The man who created it, Norman Foster, took great care to make an office building that was _____ and didn't hurt Mother Nature. For example, he chose to use a lot of glass and open space, so there's less need for electric lighting. Similarly, the _____ building has a rounded shape for a very good reason: to direct wind inside so that the air conditioners aren't used as much.

Foster has plans for new "green" buildings, and so do others, from the U.S. to China. "Green-building" will hopefully continue on its _____ around the world.

Waste (v.) means to use something in a way that is not good or helpful, or to use more of it than you should.

**A skyscraper (n.) is a very tall building in a city.*

(Based on information in "Environment." National Geographic, March 2006.)

ancient	blame . . . for	in motion	ruin	threatening

THE TRUTH IS IN THE ICE

The year 2005 brought some of the worst weather ever to people everywhere. Serious storms came out of the Caribbean—a total of twenty-six—and further south, dry weather continued to _____ the Amazon. The north faced its difficulties, too, with the loss of ice up at the North Pole.

What's happening? Nature is sending messages, and scientists are trying to understand them. Deep in the _____ ice of Greenland and Antarctica lie some answers. Scientists can look at this

7

ice and see the changes in weather throughout history. Studies show that there is a gas, carbon dioxide, that's _____ our planet. This gas is 27 percent higher now than it ever was in the past. It's

8

called a "greenhouse gas" because it's making our planet very warm—much like the inside of a glass building where plants grow.

The sad truth is that we must _____ ourselves _____ putting so much

9

carbon dioxide into the air. Sadder still, we've known this truth, but we've taken too little action against it. Says William Falk, editor of *The Week* magazine, something truly terrible is already

_____. The question is can it be stopped and will we work to stop it?

10

(Based on information in William Falk, Editorial in The Week, January 6, 2006.)

▌WORDS IN DISCUSSION

Apply the key words to your own life. Read and discuss the questions with a partner. Try to use the key words.

1. Name an activity you enjoy so much that you could spend the **entire** day doing it.

> **EXAMPLE**
>
> *I love working on my computer. I could spend the **entire** day on the Internet.*

2. Have you ever **ruined** a favorite piece of clothing? Explain.
3. Name an **ancient** language.
4. What do people often **blame** the weather **for**?
5. How do you **motion** for someone to be quiet?

▌WORDS IN WRITING

Write a short answer (1–2 sentences) for each question. Try to use the key words.

1. Do you think your clothing is more **practical** or fashionable?

> **EXAMPLE**
>
> *My clothes are very **practical**. I like to be comfortable.*

2. Do you ever miss a phone call **on purpose**?
3. When was the last time you were at a family **gathering**?
4. Give an example of how people can **threaten** Mother Nature.
5. What's the most interesting **course** you've ever taken at school?

compete	divide	include	opinion	train
dismiss	field	industry	produce	treat

WORDS IN CONTEXT

Use the sentences to guess what each key word means. Choose the meaning that is closest to that of the key word in **bold**.

1. **compete**
   /kəm'pit/
   -verb

   • Athletes from all over the world **compete** at the Olympic Games.
   • Each year thousands of students **compete** to study at that university, but less than one-fourth get in.

   Compete means . . .   a. to give your attention to something   (b.) to try to be better than others   c. to ask for an invitation

2. **dismiss**
   /dɪs'mɪs/
   -verb

   • Don't **dismiss** the idea of vacations in space. It will be possible someday.
   • I grew angry when my friends **dismissed** my suggestion so quickly.

   Dismiss means . . .   a. to not explain clearly   b. to not understand   c. to not want to consider

3. **divide**
   /də'vaɪd/
   -verb

   • The teacher asked the class to **divide** into groups of four.
   • My roommate and I **divided** the room so we each had the same amount of space for our beds, desks, bookcases, and other furniture.

   Divide means . . .   a. to put into parts   b. to count   c. to agree

4. **field**
   /fild/
   -noun

   • The **field** of wheat looked like an ocean of gold under the summer sun.
   • After school I saw Kyle practicing with some friends on the soccer **field**.

   Field means . . .   a. a farm   b. an area of land   c. a large building

5. **include**
   /ɪn'klud/
   -verb

   • The price of the hotel room **included** breakfast.
   • Why won't you **include** me in your conversation? I want to say something, too.

   Include means . . .   a. to be or make a part of something   b. to invite or be invited to an event   c. to not have something

6. **industry**
   /'ɪndəstri/
   -noun

   • In the 1800s, **industry** came to the northern United States while the South continued farming.
   • The growth of **industry** brings many jobs—and not just in factories.

   Industry means . . .   a. a kind of machine   b. a group of office buildings   c. the making of things to be sold

7. opinion
/əˈpɪnyən/
-noun

- What's your **opinion** of the new company president? Do you like her?
- I don't always share my history teacher's **opinions**, but he welcomes my thoughts.

Opinion means . . .   a. an explanation   b. your ideas or beliefs   c. the truth

8. produce
/prəˈdus/
-verb

- Asian countries **produce** most of the world's rice.
- The sunny state of Florida is well-known for **producing** oranges.

Produce means . . .   a. to eat   b. to grow   c. to sell

9. train
/treɪn/
-verb

- In my first week at the restaurant, they'll **train** me to take customers' orders.
- Rochelle is **training** to be a makeup artist. She wants to work in Hollywood.

Train means . . .   a. to teach or learn a set of skills   b. to finish a job or make someone do this   c. to work hard or make someone do this

10. treat
/trit/
-verb

- Tommy **treats** some of his classmates very badly. His teachers have asked his parents to talk to him about being nicer to others.
- Penelope enjoys **treating** her dog very well. She sometimes cooks dinner for it.

Treat means . . .   a. to help others   b. to act in some way toward others   c. to think better of some people than of others

WORDS AND DEFINITIONS

Match each key word with its definition.

1. _____*field*_____ an area of land that is used for a special purpose, or that is covered in something

2. _____ the making of things to be sold, especially in factories

3. _____ to try to win something, or try to be better than someone else

4. _____ to grow something or make it naturally

5. _____ to teach someone or be taught the skills of a job or activity

6. _____ your ideas or beliefs about a subject

7. _____ to be or make someone or something a part of a group or a set

8. _____ to refuse to consider someone's idea or opinion

9. _____ to act in a way that is good, bad, nice, etc. toward others

10. _____ to put something or be put into two or more parts

Choose the best answer.

1. Paul will **train** Mary because
   a. she has more experience than he does.
   b. she just started the job and needs to learn a lot.
   c. they have the same amount of skill and experience.

2. Vianni must learn to **compete** if he wants to
   a. help others.
   b. be a strong tennis player.
   c. save money.

3. Who does NOT usually spend time on or in a **field**?
   a. a baseball team
   b. a farmer
   c. a swimmer

4. All green plants **produce**
   a. beautiful flowers.
   b. oxygen with the help of sunlight.
   c. healthy fruits or berries.

5. When I give you an **opinion**,
   a. I tell you what I think.
   b. I ask you a question.
   c. I tell you a fact.

6. This part of the city is known for **industry**;
   a. you'll see many factories here.
   b. you'll see many parks and green trees here.
   c. you'll see many colleges and universities here.

7. The teacher was able to **include** everyone in the discussion;
   a. she only let a few students speak.
   b. she asked each student a question.
   c. no one spoke, but everyone listened.

8. People should **treat** their pets
   a. in an uncaring way.
   b. with interesting names.
   c. with kindness and love.

9. My boss **dismissed** my plan;
   a. he liked it very much.
   b. he said to forget it because it was too expensive.
   c. he asked me to explain it better at the meeting next week.

10. The little girl **divided** her coins and put them
    a. into one big jar to take with her to the candy store.
    b. into two jars: one to spend and one to save.
    c. in her secret hiding place.

▌WORD FAMILIES

Now that you have studied the ten key words and their basic definitions, you are ready to learn words that belong to the same family as some of the key words. A word family includes words that look alike but have different functions (noun, verb, adjective, or adverb). Their meanings are related but different.

A. *Look at each model phrase and decide whether the word in **bold** is used as a noun, verb, adjective, or adverb.*

	NOUN	VERB	ADJECTIVE	ADVERB
1. **compete**				
• students **compete**		✓		
• very tough **competition**	✓			
2. **divide**				
• to **divide** a group of people				
• a **division** between people				
3. **industry**				
• the film **industry**				
• an **industrial** area				
4. **produce**				
• will **produce** a film				
• sell a **product**				
• **production** of cars				
5. **train**				
• can **train** filmmakers				
• to receive **training**				

B. *Read the first half of each sentence and match it with the appropriate ending.*

___c___ 1. Being number one isn't important to me, but

_____ 2. The company will open a new office

_____ 3. Children will always want toys, so toy

_____ 4. I'm not happy

_____ 5. Scot, a baker, received a lot of

_____ 6. Wool and cheese are

a. with the **division** of work. It isn't fair.

b. **training** before he opened his own shop.

c. **competition** pushes me to do my best.

d. **production** will continue well into the future.

e. in the **industrial** park across town.

f. well-known **products** of Ireland.

SAME WORD, DIFFERENT MEANING

Most words have more than one meaning. Study the additional meanings of **field**, **industry**, *and* **produce**. *Then read each sentence and decide which meaning is used.*

a.	**field** *n.*	an area of land that is used for a special purpose, or that is covered in the same plants or things
b.	**field** *n.*	all the people, companies, etc. that do an activity
c.	**industry** *n.*	the making of goods, especially in factories
d.	**industry** *n.*	a type of business or service that produces things
e.	**produce** *v.*	to grow something or make it naturally
f.	**produce** *v.*	to control the preparation of a play or movie and then show it to people

___f___ 1. American movie star Clint Eastwood acted in movies for almost twenty years before he finally **produced** a film of his own in 1982.

_____ 2. Giorgio Armani, who is famous in the fashion **industry** today, studied medicine and photography before he turned his attention to clothes.

_____ 3. The corn **fields** lay behind the farmhouse.

_____ 4. Smoke from the factories was a sign of all the **industry** in the town.

_____ 5. Emma wants to move to New York after college because that's where the best companies in her **field** have their main offices.

_____ 6. California's Napa Valley **produces** fine wines.

WORDS IN SENTENCES

Complete each sentence with one of the words from the box.

competition	division	include	opinions	training
dismissed	field	industrial	~~produce~~	treating

1. Often Hollywood directors use a popular book or play to ____*produce*____ a movie.

2. What _____ do you work in? You studied law in college, didn't you?

3. The company makes all new employees take two weeks of _____.

4. Nikki loves _____. She tries to win at everything she does.

5. I believe in _____ others with kindness; it's how I want people to behave towards me.

6. The Mason-Dixon Line, made in the 1700s, is still used to show the _____ between the North and the South in the U.S.

7. Laura's parents _____ her dreams of ballet, but she really did grow up to be a ballet dancer.

8. Many DVDs _____ other material in addition to the main film.

9. The Harrison family was happy to move away from the _____ part of the city and out into the suburbs. It was much quieter and greener there.

10. I enjoy talk shows on the radio. You get to hear many different _____.

WORDS IN COLLOCATIONS AND EXPRESSIONS

Following are common collocations (word partners) and expressions with some of the key words. Read the definitions and then complete the conversations with the correct form of the collocations and expressions.

1. **compete**	
• **compete for**	to try to win in order to get something
2. **dismiss**	
• **dismiss (sth) as (impossible, serious, crazy, etc.)**	to refuse to think about someone's opinion or idea because it seems (impossible, not practical, etc.)
3. **divide**	
• **divide (sth) between**	to give something to two people or things
• **divide (sth) into**	to put something into two or more parts
4. **opinion**	
• **in (sb) opinion**	often used to introduce your belief or idea about a subject
5. **treat**	
• **treat (sb) like (sth)**	to behave toward (sb) in a way that shows what someone thinks of (sb)

1. OLIVIA: Why do you have to be home by midnight?

   FRAN: It's one of my parents' rules. They often _____ *treat* _____ me _____ *like* _____ a child. They think I'm still eight years old and not eighteen!

2. WIFE: It's a long drive from New York to Florida.

   HUSBAND: You're right. Let's _____ the ride _____ two days. Sound good?

3. CLAIRE: Do you really think you should quit your job now? You're making good money.

   BO: I know that _____ I'm making a mistake, but trust me. Everything will be fine.

4. GLENIO: Your little brother loves talking about becoming a circus performer.

   ISAAC: I just _____ this _____ the silly idea of a child. But who knows?

5. MOTHER: Nina has learned to _____ her time _____ her studies and volleyball.

   FATHER: She's serious about both. She's really grown up over the past year.

6. TATIANA: There are so many TV programs here in the U.S.

   JOHN: Yes, and TV companies _____ viewers. Each company tries to get the highest number of people interested in their programs.

WORDS IN READINGS

Read the two articles about film. Complete each one with words and expressions from the boxes.

dismiss . . . as	divides	~~industry~~	is treated like	opinions

BOLLYWOOD

Bollywood, India's film _____industry_____ , entertains about 3.6 billion people around the world.
    1
That's a billion more than Hollywood's audience[*]. The name *Bollywood* comes from Hollywood, the

American movie capital[**] and the Indian city of Bombay, which is now called Mumbai. Many Indian

movies are made in Mumbai.

Film-goers in the West might _____ Bollywood films _____ too simple
                                            2
and complain that the stories are too long. But such _____ do not show an understanding
                                                          3
of the reasons why so many people love Indian movies: singing, dancing, and a magical world where

anything is possible.

The father-son team of Yash and Aditya Chopra know how to keep their large audience happy, and

they also bring together in film what the real world often _____: the old and new India;
                                                              4
Hindus and Muslims; those in India and those who have moved abroad. Each Bollywood movie has an

impossible dream, but as seventy-two-year-old Yash says, "You like to believe that it's possible." Shah

Rukh Khan, who has worked with the Chopras and is Bollywood's biggest star, can talk about dreams

becoming real: he's a Muslim and his family is from Pakistan, yet he _____ a god by
                                                                          5
Hindus in India. Bollywood does have its magic, for as Shah Rukh says: "It welcomes everybody with

open arms."

[*]*An audience (n.) is the people watching or listening to a concert, speech, movie, etc.*

[**]*A capital (n.) is a place that is important for a particular activity.*

(Based on information in Suketu Mehta, "Welcome to Bollywood." National Geographic, February 2005.)

competed for	field	produce
competition	includes	trained

BEIJING FILM ACADEMY

Yuan Mushi started the Beijing Film academy in the 1950s. Over the years, many have

_____ there: popular actress and director Xu Jinglei, heartthrob[*] Chen Kun, and a
    6
number of China's best filmmakers.

[*]*A heartthrob (n.) is a famous person who many young people feel romantic love for.*

Today the academy is the largest in Asia. It has a student body of over 3,300, which

_____ 150 foreign students. Some students, of course, go on to work in Chinese cinema,
 7

but about 80 percent move into the _____ of television or commercials.
 8

The academy is the best in the country, so it is not easy to enter. In 2005, nearly 6,000 people

_____ thirty openings in the acting school's program. _____ in all fields is
 9 10

tough, but so is the process of making good films. Perhaps even harder is learning to

_____ films that truly interest the students, but can still sell well. Some, like twenty-one-year-
 11

old Xiao Xiao, a student in the directing school, understand the competition that awaits them from

both other schools and foreign countries, but they say: "Right now, we are students, and we are making

the films we want to make. We don't have that many worries; we just put what we feel and think into

these films."

(Based on information from Fiona Ng, "Let a Thousand Film Students Compete." New York Times, October 2, 2005.)

WORDS IN DISCUSSION

Apply the key words to your own life. Read and discuss the questions with a partner. Try to use the key words.

1. How do you **divide** your time these days?

> **EXAMPLE**
>
> *I spend most of my time at school, but when I'm not studying, I **divide** my time **between** e-mail and TV.*

2. Name something your hometown or country **produces**.
3. What job would you like to have now or in the future? Do you need **training** for this job?
4. When was the last time you were a guest in someone's home? Did they **treat** you well? Explain.
5. Name a well-known **industrial** center. Have you ever visited this city?

WORDS IN WRITING

Write a short answer (1–2 sentences) for each question. Try to use the key words.

1. Do you enjoy **competing for** something?

> **EXAMPLE**
>
> *I like to **compete** in sports. I don't like **competition** in other situations, like at home.*

2. Has anyone ever **dismissed** an idea or suggestion of yours?
3. What **products** can always be found in your refrigerator?
4. Whose **opinion** do you trust the most?
5. You're writing to a friend you haven't seen in two years. What news would you **include** in your letter?

QUIZ 3

PART A

Choose the word that best completes each item and write it in the space provided.

1. I spent the _____*entire*_____ evening studying for today's test.
   a. practical   c. proper
   b. entire   d. probable

2. Larry _____ about Farrah's new job. She told him all about it.
   a. inquired   c. gathered
   b. composed   d. dismissed

3. You need to _____ more examples in your essay.
   a. include   c. dismiss
   b. divide   d. blow

4. Liz took a _____ on Japanese history with Professor Mizenko.
   a. field   c. course
   b. duty   d. threat

5. Batteries need to be in the _____ position for a flashlight to work.
   a. practical   c. proper
   b. ancient   d. probable

6. Gloria _____ with others to be the best. She doesn't like losing.
   a. inquires   c. divides
   b. competes   d. dismisses

7. Many _____ cities like Rome and Cairo still exist today.
   a. practical   c. proper
   b. ancient   d. probable

8. The criminal's _____ to kill again kept him in jail even longer.
   a. field   c. blame
   b. duty   d. threat

9. Fifty students _____ the school band.
   a. inquire   c. include
   b. compete   d. compose

10. After some free time on their own, the tourists _____ to continue the group tour by bus.
    a. divided   c. gathered
    b. composed   d. competed

PART B

*Read each statement and write **T** for true or **F** for false in the space provided.*

_F_ 1. A fun picnic with friends can make you feel **miserable**.

____ 2. People **train** when they need new or better skills.

____ 3. A strong autumn wind will **blow** leaves off the trees.

____ 4. Many people feel **pity** for a successful businessman.

____ 5. **Opinions** are not the same as facts.

____ 6. It's natural to be **sympathetic** when a friend loses a parent or grandparent.

____ 7. It is a parent's **duty** to teach a child how to safely cross the street.

____ 8. If I **blame** you for a mistake, I forgive you.

____ 9. If my roommate and I **divide** the housework, we share it.

____ 10. Customers want to know the **exact** price before they buy something.

PART C

Each situation shows the meaning of one of the key words. Write the appropriate key word next to the situation. Use the clues in italics.

dismiss	~~industry~~	practical	produce	ruin
field	motion	probable	purpose	treat

1. There are several *factories* in this area that *make* cars. _industry_

2. This book gives useful information *relating to real situations* that any businessman could face. _____

3. It's *likely* that the Olympic Games will continue far into the future. _____

4. In one of Claude Monet's paintings, red flowers grow beautifully in a *land* of green. _____

5. Why do you *act* so terribly *toward* Cindy? She's always been nice to you. _____

6. *The way* the ship *moved* during the storm made me feel sick to my stomach. _____

7. The teacher explained that the *reason* for giving more homework was to help us prepare for next week's test. _____

8. The terrible storm *completely destroyed* the garden. _____

9. I *refused to consider* the possibility that our team could lose. We planned to win. _____

10. *Growing* bananas and *making* sugar has helped the Jamaican economy. _____

▌WORDS IN CONTEXT

*Use the sentences to guess what each key word means. Choose the meaning that is closest to that of the key word in **bold**.*

1. **battle**
   /ˈbæt̮l/
   -noun

   - The two armies met on the field, and the **battle** began.
   - The **battle** at Gettysburg was the largest in the American Civil War.

   Battle means . . .   (a.) a fight   b. a weapon   c. a crime

2. **charm**
   /tʃarm/
   -noun

   - The old trees and colorful flowers gave the small house some **charm**.
   - The salesman used his **charm** to interest customers in different cars.

   Charm means . . .   a. something that surprises people   b. something that makes people laugh   c. something that makes people like a person or thing

3. **cheat**
   /tʃit/
   -verb

   - Dave **cheats** when he plays cards. He secretly looks at the other player's cards.
   - Gail **cheated** on the test; she copied the answers from Hector.

   Cheat means . . .   a. to share generously   b. to do something dishonest   c. to prepare for something

4. **due**
   /du/
   -adjective

   - My book report is **due** on Monday. I need to work on it this weekend.
   - The train from Brussels is **due** at 11:30 A.M. What time should we leave for the station?

   Due means . . .   a. to finish or be finished   b. to think that something will happen at a certain time   c. to be on time

5. **forbid**
   /fɚˈbɪd/
   -verb

   - Mr. and Mrs. Puntill **forbid** their son to watch TV until he finishes his homework.
   - Our boss **forbids** us to talk about company business outside the office.

   Forbid means . . .   a. to order not to do   b. to suggest doing   c. to complain about doing

6. interfere
/ˌɪntɚˈfɪr/
-verb

- I don't like to **interfere** in other people's business; I only give advice if I'm asked.
- Our parents **interfered** in our fights only if we started to hit or call each other bad names.

Interfere means . . . a. to become upset   b. to become a part of a situation   c. to make a situation worse

7. permit
/pɚˈmɪt/
-verb

- The law doesn't **permit** small children to ride in the front seat of a car.
- For safety, airlines cannot **permit** passengers to take many bags on board.

Permit means . . . a. to invite   b. to instruct   c. to allow

8. protect
/prəˈtɛkt/
-verb

- Firefighters wear special clothing to **protect** themselves from getting burned.
- Phil parks his new car in the garage to **protect** it from bad weather and theft.

Protect means . . . a. to keep safe   b. to hide from view   c. to keep warm

9. puzzle
/ˈpʌzəl/
-noun

- I put the last piece of the **puzzle** in place and looked at the picture I had made.
- Life is like a **puzzle**: we must learn how all the pieces go together.

Puzzle means . . . a. a game with lots of pieces   b. a photograph   c. toy blocks

10. rush
/rʌʃ/
-verb

- I like to finish work ahead of time. I hate to **rush** at the last minute.
- The police **rushed** into the building when they heard a gunshot.

Rush means . . . a. to run to help   b. to move or do something very quickly   c. to do one's job

▌WORDS AND DEFINITIONS

Match each key word with its definition.

1. _____forbid_____ to order someone not to do something

2. _____ to do something dishonest or act in a dishonest way in order to win or gain something

3. _____ to move or do something very quickly

4. _____ to purposely become part of a situation and take action when you are not wanted or needed

5. _____ to stop someone or something from being hurt or damaged; to keep safe

6. _____ a game or toy that has a lot of pieces that you have to put together

7. _____ a fight between two armies, especially during a longer war

8. _____ to think that something will happen or arrive at a certain time

9. _____ something special that makes people like a person or thing

10. _____ to allow something to happen, especially by a rule or law

COMPREHENSION CHECK

Choose the best answer.

1. You want to know if the essay is **due** tomorrow, so you ask your teacher:

    a. "Will you return our essays to us tomorrow?"

    b. "Do we have until tomorrow to finish our essays?"

    c. "Are we going to discuss our essays in class tomorrow?"

2. The student is going to **rush** to class because

    a. he woke up late.

    b. he's feeling sick today.

    c. he didn't do the homework.

3. Charlie has a lot of **charm**;

    a. he's lost many girlfriends because of it.

    b. many ladies fall in love with his sweet smile and clever jokes.

    c. his girlfriend complains that he's too quiet.

4. Savannah **cheated** on the test;

    a. she's the strongest student in our class.

    b. the teacher was very pleased.

    c. she later got into serious trouble with the teacher.

5. What will you NOT find in a **battle**?

    a. soldiers

    b. weapons

    c. picnic tables

6. You do not want your parents to help you with a problem, so you

    a. ask them not to **interfere**.

    b. ask them if you can **interfere**.

    c. suggest you **interfere** together.

7. Which of the following people likely enjoys doing **puzzles**?

    a. Uma likes quiet games she can do alone.

    b. Dina likes games with physical activity.

    c. Quinn likes games he can finish quickly.

8. If the teacher **permits** you to use a dictionary during the exam,

    a. you can bring one with you into the classroom.

    b. you cannot bring one with you into the classroom.

    c. you can work together with other students to complete the exam.

9. Which of the following articles of clothing do NOT **protect** us?

    a. sunglasses

    b. gloves

    c. a wristwatch

10. The famous couple **forbid** journalists to photograph their wedding;

    a. there were pictures of the celebration in every newspaper and magazine.

    b. they wanted to share their special day with close friends and family only.

    c. only a few journalists received invitations.

WORD FAMILIES

Now that you have studied the ten key words and their basic definitions, you are ready to learn words that belong to the same family as some of the key words. A word family includes words that look alike but have different functions (noun, verb, adjective, or adverb). Their meanings are related but different.

A. *Look at each model phrase and decide whether the word in **bold** is used as a noun, verb, adjective, or adverb.*

	NOUN	VERB	ADJECTIVE	ADVERB
1. **battle**				
• die in a **battle**	✓			
• to **battle** against others		✓		
2. **charm**				
• to have much **charm**				
• a **charming** house				
3. **forbid**				
• to **forbid** children to smoke				
• a **forbidden** food				
4. **permit**				
• will **permit** workers to take a vacation				
• must ask for **permission**				
• receive a **permit**				
5. **protect**				
• to **protect** your loved ones				
• find **protection**				
6. **puzzle**				
• build a **puzzle**				
• a question that **puzzles** me				

B. *Read each sentence and match the word in **bold** with the correct definition.*

___*e*___ 1. When the rain began, the campers went into their tents for **protection**.

_____ 2. In truly bad weather a pilot of a plane **battles** for control.

_____ 3. Ivanildes often says one thing and does another; her behavior **puzzles** me.

_____ 4. The hotel looked like a sweet cottage from a children's story; it was really quite **charming**.

_____ 5. I had to see the dentist the next morning, so I asked my boss for **permission** to arrive later than usual.

_____ 6. In some religions, there are foods that are **forbidden**.

_____ 7. The company wants to build a second office behind the first, but to do this it needs a **permit**.

a. to make someone confused or unable to understand something

b. not allowed because of a rule or law

c. to try very hard to do

d. the act of allowing someone to do something

e. the act of keeping someone or something safe, or what keeps someone or something safe

f. very pleasing and easy to like

g. a written statement that gives you the right to do something

SAME WORD, DIFFERENT MEANING

*Most words have more than one meaning. Study the additional meanings of **battle**, **due**, and **rush**. Then read each sentence and decide which meaning is used.*

a.	**battle** *n.*	a fight between two armies, especially during a longer war
b.	**battle** *n.*	a situation in which two people or groups compete or argue with each other
c.	**due** *adj.*	to think that something will happen or arrive at some time
d.	**due to** *adj.*	because of
e.	**rush** *v.*	to move or do something very quickly
f.	**rush** *v.*	to try to make someone do something quickly

___c___ 1. My parents went to Hawaii, but they're **due** back tomorrow.

_____ 2. The general made a bad decision and his army lost the **battle**.

_____ 3. **Due to** illness, the singer did not perform last night.

_____ 4. I **rushed** back to my house to get the book I forgot.

_____ 5. There was a **battle** for control of the country after the king died.

_____ 6. Please don't **rush** me to make this decision. I need time.

WORDS IN SENTENCES

Complete each sentence with one of the words from the box.

battled	~~cheats~~	forbidden	permission	puzzled
charming	due to	interfered	protection	rushed

1. My sister _____cheats_____ when we do housework; she always does less than me.

2. The store owner _____ to keep his business open. Much was against him.

3. My light jacket gave almost no _____ from the cold wind.

4. Elaine thought Gabe was _____. He told jokes, knew interesting facts, and treated her like a lady.

5. My mother usually gives me _____ to use her car when I want to use it.

6. Our plane arrived late _____ bad weather.

7. It was late and I was tired of shopping, so I _____ my friend out of the store.

8. Keisha's words _____ me. I didn't understand if she was angry or just tired.

9. Use of cell phones during class is _____. Teachers ask us to turn them off.

10. My older brother has _____ in my problems more than once. He feels a need to take care of me even when I don't want him to.

WORDS IN COLLOCATIONS AND EXPRESSIONS

Following are common collocations (word partners) and expressions with some of the key words. Read the definitions and then complete the conversations with the correct form of the collocations and expressions.

1. **cheat**
   - **feel cheated**   to think that you have been treated wrongly or unfairly

2. **due**
   - **be long due**   to think that something will happen and wait a long time for it to take place

3. **forbid**
   - **forbid (sb) to (do sth)**   to order someone not to do something

4. **interfere**
   - **interfere with**   to stop something from happening in the way it was planned

5. **protect**
   - **protect (sb/sth) from**   to stop someone or something from being hurt or damaged

6. **rush**
   - **(be) in a rush**   to be in a situation in which you need to hurry

1.   DRIVER: When will they ever fix this road? It seems every week there's another hole.

      PASSENGER: It's true. Repairs on this road are _____*long due*_____.

2.   EDUARDO: Hey, Neil! Got a minute before class?

      NEIL: I'm sorry. I can't talk right now. I'm _____. I'll call you later.

3.   EVAN: Hmm. There's an article in the paper about crime near the old train station.

      REGINA: My parents _____ me _____ go near that part of town. It's dangerous even in daylight.

4.   IGGY: I can't believe you paid $50 for a radio that doesn't work.

      GREG: I know. I _____.

5. MRS. TRENT: The natural wood of the piano is so beautiful. Why don't you show it off?

      MRS. DEAN: Well, we keep it covered in order to _____ it _____ dust.

6.   AL: I'm so tired. I don't sleep well at night.

      BEN: That's because you drink so much coffee during the day. Didn't you know that too much coffee can _____ your ability to sleep?

WORDS IN READINGS

Read the two articles about transportation. Complete each one with words and expressions from the boxes.

| feel cheated | long due | ~~permit (v.)~~ |
| forbidding . . . to | permit (n.) | protect |

OLD ENOUGH TO DRIVE?

A new law in Kentucky will let sixteen-year-olds start to drive, but they need sixty hours on the road with an experienced driver over the age of twenty-one. After this, teens can get an intermediate* license** that would ____permit____ them to drive between 6:00 A.M. and midnight and with only
1
one non-family member under the age of twenty. Then, after six months with no problems, they will be able to take the test for a regular license.

At the present, 16-year-olds can drive with a _____ for six months and then take a
2
test to get their regular license. Teens learning to drive right now _____ by the new law.
3
Says Kyle Martin, fifteen, "I think it's not very fair. Other people got their license when they were sixteen. We will have to wait until we are seventeen." He doesn't think that _____ teens
4
_____ drive earlier will change anything.

Lawmakers like Tom Burch of Louisville, Kentucky believe the new law is _____; he
5
lost his teenage granddaughter in a car accident. Many agree that giving young drivers more practice is a way to _____ everyone's safety on the road.
6

*Intermediate *(adj.) means done or happening between two other stages, levels, etc.*

**A license *(n.) is an official document that gives you permission to own something or do something.*

(Based on information in James Roberts, "Will Practice Make Perfect?" Central-Kentucky News-Journal online, March 8, 2006.)

| battle | charm | in a rush | interfering with | puzzle |

A NEW KIND OF RIDE ON THE STREETS OF NEW YORK

There's a new form of transportation in New York City, and many are taking an interest in it. *Cycle rickshaw, pedicab, bicycle cab, bike taxi*—its many names _____ lawmakers who aren't
7
sure how to control people's use of it.

A pedicab is really just a large tricycle*. The driver sits in front, and passengers sit in a large carriage** over the back two wheels. For those who are _____, it's a ten-minute ride or
8

*A tricycle *(n.) is a small vehicle with one wheel at the front and two wheels at the back.*

**A carriage *(n.) is a vehicle with wheels that is pulled by a horse or other means.*

less; auto-taxis cannot make the same promise. This fact suggests that the pedicab owners must face at least one _____ to stay in business.
9

The truth is that pedicab drivers have already won because New York passengers have already climbed on board. Pedicab owners and drivers explain that they aren't _____ anyone's
10
business. Horse carriages have their own _____ and always will. Auto-taxis are the most
11
common form of transportation and with 170 million rides a year; there's no sign of this changing. Pedicabs can only give city people one million rides a year.

(Based on information in Gregg Zukowski, "Regulating Rickshaws." Gotham Gazette, March 6, 2006.)

▌WORDS IN DISCUSSION

Apply the key words to your own life. Read and discuss the questions with a partner. Try to use the key words.

1. Did your parents **forbid** you **to** do anything as you were growing up?

   EXAMPLE

   *Of course. They **forbid** me **to** watch a lot of TV and eat a lot of junk food.*

2. If you take a book from a library, when is it **due** back again? Do you have any books **due** now?
3. Is there something in the English language that **puzzles** you?
4. What might a student ask **permission** from a teacher to do?
5. Sunglasses **protect** your eyes **from** the sun. Give another example of how clothing gives **protection**.

▌WORDS IN WRITING

Write a short answer (1–2 sentences) for each question. Try to use the key words.

1. Do you often **rush** to finish things?

   EXAMPLE

   *Yes. I often take a long time to start something, so then I have to **rush** to finish it.*

2. Have you ever **battled** to get something you wanted? Who or what did you **battle** against?
3. Name a place in your hometown that has a lot of **charm**.
4. Have you ever **felt cheated** because of something you bought or a service you paid for?
5. Have you ever **interfered with** a friend's plan because you thought the plan was dangerous? Do you think friends should **interfere** in such situations?

WORDS IN CONTEXT

*Use the sentences to guess what each key word means. Choose the meaning that is closest to that of the key word in **bold**.*

1. **artificial**
/ˌɑrt̬əˈfɪʃəl/
-adjective

- I watered the plant, and then learned that it was **artificial**. What a silly mistake!
- The doll's hair looks real, but when you touch it, you know it's **artificial**.

Artificial means . . .   a. dead   (b.) not natural   c. unhealthy

2. **base**
/beɪs/
-verb

- The company is **based** in London, but it has offices around the world.
- The story is **based** in Italy, but they filmed the movie in California.

Base means . . .   a. to use as your main place of activity   b. to visit often   c. to start and end in the same place

3. **obey**
/əˈbeɪ, oʊ-/
-verb

- If you do not **obey** the road laws, you can cause an accident.
- My grandfather is the head of our large family; everyone **obeys** his word.

Obey means . . .   a. to understand   b. to do what you should do   c. to carefully explain

4. **pause**
/pɔz/
-verb

- The politician **paused** to take a drink of water and then answered the question.
- Before I leave the house, I always **pause** and check to see if I have everything I need.

Pause means . . .   a. to stop doing something for a short time   b. to relax   c. to remember to do something

5. **race**
/reɪs/
-noun

- The swimmer won first place in the **race**; he even set a new world record.
- The children had a **race** to see who could run the fastest.

Race means . . .   a. a test   b. a party game   c. a competition

6. **succeed**
/səkˈsid/
-verb

- Fay is very talented and hardworking; she usually **succeeds** in everything she does.
- I did all that I could, but I didn't **succeed** in getting the job.

Succeed means . . .   a. to try hard   b. to lose something important   c. to do what you have tried to do

7. supply
/sə'plaɪ/
-noun

- We took a small **supply** of water with us on our bike ride.
- **Supplies** of clothing, food, and water were brought to the people after the flood.

Supply means . . . a. a gift   b. an amount of something   c. a cup

8. trap
/træp/
-noun

- The hunter used a **trap** to get a rabbit for his dinner.
- We took the rabbit out of the **trap** and set it free far from our garden.

Trap means . . . a. equipment to catch an animal   b. equipment to scare an animal away   c. equipment to feed an animal

9. wonder
/'wʌndɚ/
-verb

- I **wonder** about the future. Will cars be able to fly? Will computers do all the work?
- Earl said he was coming, so I **wonder** where he is. Maybe he's still at work.

Wonder means . . . a. to dream about something   b. to want to talk about something   c. to want to know the truth about something

10. worship
/'wɚʃɪp/
-verb

- A number of ancient peoples **worshiped** gods of the sun and the moon.
- Mrs. Kroyer is a very religious woman. She goes to church every day to **worship**.

Worship means . . . a. to show love for a god   b. to try to be like a god   c. to tell stories about a god

▌WORDS AND DEFINITIONS

Match each key word with its definition.

1. _____ *base* _____ to use a city, town, etc. as your main place of business or activities

2. _____ to do what you have tried to do, or to get to a high position in something such as your job

3. _____ an amount of something that can be used, or the act of giving this

4. _____ a piece of equipment for catching animals

5. _____ to show love for a god, especially by praying

6. _____ to follow a law, rule, order, etc.

7. _____ to stop speaking or doing something for a short time before starting again

8. _____ to think about something and want to know what is true about it or what is happening or will happen

9. _____ not natural, but made by people

10. _____ a competition to find out who can run, drive, swim, etc. the fastest

COMPREHENSION CHECK

Choose the best answer.

1. **Artificial** fruit
   a. can be used for decoration.
   b. grows only in warm countries.
   c. turns sour after a few days.

2. Which of the following people has **succeeded**?
   a. Martin prepared well and won the math competition.
   b. Rafe tried his best, but didn't score well on the exam.
   c. Victoria plans to go to law school.

3. Children **obey** their parents because
   a. they like to ask questions.
   b. the parents have more control as well as more experience.
   c. breaking rules is part of growing up.

4. Each of the following are usual places where people go to **worship** EXCEPT
   a. a church.
   b. a temple.
   c. a park.

5. The teacher **paused**
   a. so we could hear him better.
   b. when the class ended.
   c. and it was silent in the room for a few seconds.

6. If Lucas and Pedro are **racing** in the swimming pool,
   a. they're having a good conversation.
   b. they're trying to see who is faster.
   c. they're standing where the water isn't deep.

7. "I **wonder** how old Danae is" means
   a. I'd like to know her true age.
   b. I know her true age.
   c. I think she looks much younger than her true age.

8. Which of the following people might use a **trap**?
   a. Layla keeps her parrot in the living room.
   b. Seaton would like to have a puppy.
   c. Violetta found a mouse in her kitchen.

9. If a book is **based** in Europe,
   a. it's not sold in the United States or Australia.
   b. the author wrote it there.
   c. all the action in the story happens there.

10. If we're camping and our **supplies** are low, it means
    a. we have little food left, so we should start for home.
    b. we're feeling poorly, so we should rest.
    c. we've only started, so there's much more hiking to do.

WORD FAMILIES

Now that you have studied the ten key words and their basic definitions, you are ready to learn words that belong to the same family as some of the key words. A word family includes words that look alike but have different functions (noun, verb, adjective, or adverb). Their meanings are related but different.

A. *Look at each model phrase and decide whether the word in* **bold** *is used as a noun, verb, adjective, or adverb.*

	NOUN	VERB	ADJECTIVE	ADVERB
1. **race**				
• watch a **race**	✓			
• can **race** on our bikes		✓		
2. **succeed**				
• like to **succeed**				
• have **success**				
• a **successful** person				
3. **supply**				
• a large **supply**				
• will **supply** food for the soldiers				
4. **trap**				
• caught in a **trap**				
• must **trap** the mouse				
5. **wonder**				
• to **wonder** about the future				
• a **wonderful** idea				

B. *Read each sentence and match the word in* **bold** *with the correct definition.*

_b_ 1. The tree fell on the car and **trapped** the people inside.

___ 2. Thank you for dinner and the movie. I had a **wonderful** time.

___ 3. The children were **racing** when one of them fell. They had to start all over again.

___ 4. The dinner party was **successful**: The food was delicious, and everyone had a good time.

___ 5. Which countries does the Middle East **supply** with oil?

___ 6. I wish you much **success** in your new job.

a. the act of doing what you have tried to do or getting what you wanted

b. to make someone go into a place from which s/he cannot escape

c. having the result or effect you planned or wanted

d. to compete to see who is the fastest runner, swimmer, etc.

e. very good

f. to give people something that they need or want, especially regularly over a long time

SAME WORD, DIFFERENT MEANING

Most words have more than one meaning. Study the additional meanings of **base**, **race**, **trap**, and **wonder**. Then read each sentence and decide which meaning is used.

a.	**base** *n.*	to use a city, town, etc. as your main place of business or activities
b.	**base** *n.*	the lowest part of something, especially the part on which it stands or where it is attached to something else
c.	**race** *n.*	a competition to find out who can run, drive, swim, etc. the fastest
d.	**race** *n.*	one of the groups that humans are divided into by skin color, body type, etc.
e.	**trap** *v.*	to make someone go into a place from which s/he cannot escape
f.	**trap** *v.*	to be in an unpleasant situation from which it is difficult to escape
g.	**wonder** *v.*	to think about something and want to know what is true about it or what is happening or will happen
h.	**wonder** *n.*	a feeling of surprise and a deep liking or interest

___c___ 1. The **race** was just about to begin, and the horses and riders took their starting positions.

_____ 2. The police **trapped** the criminals in a side street right after the bank robbery.

_____ 3. People can be of different **races**, but share a similar way of living and looking at the world.

_____ 4. The dinner conversation was really boring, but I couldn't walk away without upsetting someone, so I was **trapped** for the next half hour.

_____ 5. The people watched the magic show with great **wonder**.

_____ 6. Our tour group met at the **base** of the pyramid. Not everyone wanted to climb to the top.

_____ 7. The company is **based** in Chicago, but Harry works in their New York office.

_____ 8. I **wonder** why Micheal didn't come to class today. Do you think he's sick?

WORDS IN SENTENCES

Complete each sentence with one of the words from the box.

artificial	obey	races	supply	~~wonderful~~
base	paused	successful	trapped	worship

1. You look _____wonderful_____! When did you cut your hair?

2. Most candies don't use natural fruits; the flavors are _____.

3. The _____ of the lamp was gold, and the light from above made it shine.

4. Troy _____ and thought before he answered my question.

5. It must be expensive to _____ food and water to people on a space station.

6. People can _____ through prayer, song, and dance.

7. Many _____ live in the United States.

8. Club members must _____ the rules.

9. Duty _____ Judy at home on a Friday night. She wanted to go out, but she had no choice but to stay at home and watch her younger brother and sister.

10. Nola's parents love to tell everyone how _____ she is in school.

▌WORDS IN COLLOCATIONS AND EXPRESSIONS

Following are common collocations (word partners) and expressions with some of the key words. Read the definitions and then complete the conversations with the correct form of the collocations and expressions.

1. **base**
   - **base on**
     to do something or develop something using a piece of information as the reason or starting point

2. **succeed**
   - **succeed in**
     to do what you have tried to do, or to get to a high position in something such as your job
   - **have no/some success (in)**
     to fail to do what you have tried to do, or to only do just a little of what you wanted or planned to do

3. **race**
   - **race (somewhere to do sth)**
     to go (somewhere) very quickly, or to try to do something very quickly

4. **supply**
   - **supply (sb) with (sth)**
     to give people something that they need or want, especially regularly over a long time

5. **trap**
   - **trap (sb) into**
     to use a dishonest but clever way to make someone say or do something s/he did not plan to

1. FRANCISCO: How's your job search going?

   GORDON: Not too well, but that's because I was trying to find something close to home.
   I hope to _____*have some success*_____ with companies a bit farther away.

2. TEACHER 1:   My students tried to _____ me
   _____ telling them my age.

   TEACHER 2:   How did they do that?

   TEACHER 1:   They asked me who my favorite singers were when I was a teenager.

3. WAVERLY: That was a silly movie. I think they didn't do enough research.

   PAVEL: You're right. If you want to make a historical film, you need
   to _____ the story _____ facts.

4. DAUGHTER: I can't believe I didn't win the race. Everyone thought I would.

   MOTHER: The truth is that you won't _____ everything you do, but that's what makes success so sweet.

Key Words

brave	crowd	post	replace	slip
cheer	modest	raw	slave	stir

▌WORDS IN CONTEXT

Use the sentences to guess what each key word means. Choose the meaning that is closest to that of the key word in **bold**.

1. brave
/breɪv/
-adjective

- I tried to be **brave** at the dentist's, but I was really very scared.
- The **brave** soldiers got on their horses and rode into battle.

Brave means . . .   (a.) facing difficulty with strength   b. happy and excited   c. wanting to be successful

2. cheer
/tʃɪr/
-verb

- The fans **cheered** as their team ran onto the football field.
- At the end of the concert, everyone **cheered** loudly. No one wanted the night to end.

Cheer means . . .   a. to give someone your attention   b. to shout words to show your happiness   c. to wave hello or good-bye

3. crowd
/kraʊd/
-noun

- The **crowd** on the street became excited when the queen came out to greet them.
- During the holiday season there is a **crowd** at every shopping center.

Crowd means . . .   a. a large group of people   b. the people in a city or country   c. customers or clients

4. modest
/ˈmɑdɪst/
-adjective

- Delilah is a wonderful pianist, but she's very **modest** about her talent.
- You can't be **modest** in business; you need to tell customers why your product or service is better than others.

Modest means . . .   a. embarrassed about something you did   b. afraid to hurt other people's feelings   c. unwilling to talk about what you can do or have done

5. post
/poʊst/
-verb

- At home we **post** messages for one another on the refrigerator.
- I learned about the chess club because they **posted** signs all over the school.

Post means . . .   a. to make a phone call   b. to draw a picture   c. to put up a notice

6. raw
/rɔ/
-adjective

- Sushi, a Japanese dish of **raw** fish, is popular in many other countries today.
- Vegetables can lose vitamins as you boil or fry them, so it's best to eat them **raw**.

Raw means . . .

a. not cooked   b. whole and not cut into pieces   c. cold

7. replace
/rɪˈpleɪs/
-verb

- The carpet is old. It's time to **replace** it.
- When one hockey player gets tired, another **replaces** him.

Replace means . . .

a. to start using one thing or person instead of another   b. to throw away or put away   c. to find something or someone better

8. slave
/sleɪv/
-noun

- In 1865 President Lincoln freed all **slaves** in the United States. No one could own another person ever again.
- People in that company work like **slaves**. They work very hard for almost nothing.

Slave means . . .

a. someone who treats other people unkindly   b. someone who belongs to another person and works without pay   c. someone who has a difficult job that pays a lot of money

9. slip
/slɪp/
-verb

- I **slipped** and fell on the wet floor and hurt my back.
- Don't throw that banana peel on the ground. Someone might **slip** on it.

Slip means . . .

a. to slide a short distance by accident   b. to stretch one's arm or leg   c. to make or get dirty

10. stir
/stɚ/
-verb

- You should **stir** the soup as it cooks on the stove.
- Dean **stirred** the paint in the can before he began to use it.

Stir means . . .

a. to mix a liquid with a spoon   b. to add salt to a liquid   c. to pour a liquid

WORDS AND DEFINITIONS

Match each key word with its definition.

1. _____cheer_____ to shout words to give another strength, or to show you are very pleased by something another has done

2. _____ not cooked

3. _____ to accidentally slide a short distance, or to fall by sliding this way

4. _____ unwilling to talk with open pleasure about what you can do or what you have done

5. _____ facing danger, pain, or difficult situations with strength and little fear

6. _____ someone who is owned by another person and works without pay for him/her

7. _____ to mix a liquid or food by moving a spoon around in it

8. _____ to start using one thing or person instead of another

9. _____ a large group of people in one place

10. _____ to put up a notice about something where many people can easily see it (on a wall, an information board, the Internet, etc.)

▌COMPREHENSION CHECK

Choose the best answer.

1. We **cheered**
   a. when the other team scored a point.
   b.⃝ when our team scored a point.
   c. when our team lost.

2. Which of the following statements is true?
   a. **Slaves** receive good pay.
   b. **Slaves** enjoy their work.
   c. **Slaves** are under someone else's control.

3. A **brave** person
   a. is strong enough to face difficult situations.
   b. cries if s/he feels pain.
   c. runs away from danger.

4. Many people eat **raw**
   a. tomatoes.
   b. rice.
   c. chicken.

5. Which of the following things do we NOT **stir**?
   a. coffee and cream
   b. steak
   c. paint

6. Where would you NOT find a **crowd**?
   a. in a stadium
   b. in a popular store
   c. in a car

7. Arthur **posted** a sign at school because
   a. he's an artist.
   b. he's looking for a conversation partner in Spanish.
   c. he has a secret.

8. Claudia tells you, "Don't **slip** here!" because
   a. she wants you to move more quickly.
   b. she wants you to rest.
   c. she wants you to be careful on the icy stairs.

9. Which statement is most likely said by a **modest** person?
   a. "I'm an excellent athlete. I'm stronger and faster than most everyone."
   b. "I'm terrible at sports. I can't even throw a ball straight."
   c. "I'm pretty good at sports, but that's because I've had good coaches."

10. Drew and Brianna will **replace** the picture in their living room because
   a. they do not like it anymore.
   b. everyone likes it.
   c. it was a special wedding gift.

WORD FAMILIES

Now that you have studied the ten key words and their basic definitions, you are ready to learn words that belong to the same family as some of the key words. A word family includes words that look alike but have different functions (noun, verb, adjective, or adverb). Their meanings are related but different.

A. *Look at each model phrase and decide whether the word in **bold** is used as a noun, verb, adjective, or adverb.*

	NOUN	VERB	ADJECTIVE	ADVERB
1. brave				
• a **brave** soldier			✓	
• **braved** the snowstorm		✓		
2. cheer				
• to **cheer** for your team				
• loud **cheers** from the people				
3. crowd				
• a **crowd** of teenagers				
• a **crowded** store				
4. modest				
• a **modest** person				
• have some **modesty**				
5. slave				
• work as a **slave**				
• to **slave** in a factory				
• must end all **slavery**				

B. *Read the first half of each sentence and match it with the appropriate ending.*

<u> d </u> 1. I prefer small and quiet restaurants to

_____ 2. To prepare the big holiday meal, my grandmother and mother

_____ 3. It's sad to know

_____ 4. We needed food, so my father

_____ 5. My uncle was listening to another baseball game on the radio; I could tell by

_____ 6. Janine has told everyone about winning the art contest; she has no

a. **slaved** in the kitchen from dawn to noon.

b. **modesty**.

c. **slavery** still exists in the world today.

d. noisy and **crowded** ones.

e. **braved** the strong wind and rain to get to the store.

f. the excited **cheers** I heard from his bedroom.

SAME WORD, DIFFERENT MEANING

*Most words have more than one meaning. Study the additional meanings of **modest**, **post**, **raw**, and **stir**.*
Then read each sentence and decide which meaning is used.

a.	**modest** *adj.*	unwilling to talk with open pleasure about what you can do or what you have done
b.	**modest** *adj.*	not very big in size, quantity, value, etc.
c.	**post** *v.*	to put up a notice about something where many people can easily see it (on a wall, an information board, the Internet, etc.)
d.	**post** *n.*	a strong piece of wood, metal, etc. that stands up from out of the ground.
e.	**raw** *adj.*	not cooked
f.	**raw** *adj.*	not experienced, fully trained, or completely developed
g.	**stir** *v.*	to mix a liquid or food by moving a spoon around in it
h.	**stir** *v.*	to make someone feel a strong emotion

__*g*__ 1. The girl carefully added sugar and milk, and then she **stirred** her tea.

_____ 2. I dropped the bag of rice, and my dog began to eat it **raw** right off the floor.

_____ 3. Vera has written a few books, but she's very **modest** about their success.

_____ 4. The new employee is young and smart, but his skills are a little **raw**.

_____ 5. The instructor **posted** her office hours on the information board.

_____ 6. The words and music **stirred** me to tears. It was a truly beautiful song.

_____ 7. After my brothers and I left for college, my parents moved to a **modest** two-bedroom house.

_____ 8. We made a simple table by placing a board on top of four wooden **posts**.

WORDS IN SENTENCES

Complete each sentence with one of the words from the box.

brave	crowded	~~post~~	replace	slipped
cheer	modesty	raw	slaved	stirred

1. I hit my car against a metal _____*post*_____ in the parking lot.

2. The window is old and doesn't open easily; you should _____ it.

3. In real life the actress was very shy, but she learned to _____ interviews with journalists.

4. My mother taught me that _____ and success should go together. No one likes to listen to people who only talk about themselves.

5. My co-workers gave a _____ when I sold my first car to a customer.

6. Traci _____ and almost fell; she's not used to wearing high heels.

7. The artist _____ for many hours to finish the portrait by the promised day.

8. The puppy _____ something inside me. I knew I just had to take it home with me.

9. The cafeteria is always _____ with students and teachers at lunchtime.

10. The steak was cooked on the outside, but it was still _____ on the inside.

▌WORDS IN COLLOCATIONS AND EXPRESSIONS

Following are common collocations (word partners) and expressions with some of the key words. Read the definitions and then complete the conversations with the correct form of the collocations and expressions.

1. **cheer**	
• **cheer (sb) on**	to shout words to give someone the strength to do something
• **cheer (sb) up**	to make someone feel happier, or to become happier yourself
2. **crowd**	
• **stand out from the crowd**	to be clearly better than other things or people
3. **raw**	
• **raw talent**	talent that is not fully developed
4. **slip**	
• **let (sb or sth) slip through your fingers**	to lose something or someone good, especially because you didn't try hard to keep the thing or person
5. **stir**	
• **stir up trouble**	to try to cause problems

1. COLLIN: Isn't that your girlfriend?

   STEVE: My *ex*-girlfriend. Let's walk the other way. I don't want to _____*stir up trouble*_____. The last time we spoke, we argued for an hour.

2. STAN: Cheryl's communication skills and knowledge of the business are very strong.

   ANITA: Yes. She has many skills that make her _____.

3. MAURICE: Who are the flowers for?

   IAN: My friend. She's in the hospital, and I want to _____ her _____.

4. PAULINE: I heard this coach wants only the best players on his team.

   KAY: Not really. He also looks for _____, and then he trains new players to be among the best.

5. ALEX: Ida got a job offer from a well-known company. It's a chance to make some good money.

   EVAN: Yes, I heard. I hope she won't _____ it _____ her _____.

6. JERICHO: Your brother's big race is tomorrow, right?

   MATT: Yes. My whole family will be there to _____ him _____.

▌WORDS IN READINGS

Read the two articles about music. Complete each one with words and expressions from the boxes.

| braved | ~~let . . . slip through their fingers~~ | modest | raw talent | slave |

SO YOU WANT TO BE A ROCK STAR?

You're never too old to make a dream come true. That's why some adults decide not to _____ *let* _____ the chance to be a rock star ___*slip through their fingers*___. They can spend five days in
                                                                    1
the Rock 'N' Roll Fantasy Camp in Los Angeles. Under the instruction of real stars, the students
_____ for up to sixteen hours a day, learning to turn their _____ into music
          2   3
for the stage. At the end of the camp, the students perform at a concert at the House of Blues in Hollywood.

Every year students learn from some of the best rock musicians. Each star works as the leader of one student band. The different student rock bands even spend time in a studio. One camper explained it was the experience he had wanted ever since he was a teenager. He liked the rock stars at the camp; they were _____ about their own success and ready to help others learn.
            4

In the camp's final concert in 2006, students _____ the stage with big names like
                                                            5
Roger Daltrey of the Who and Mickey Hart of the Grateful Dead. Camp producer David Fishof says the musicians enjoy their time and the students leave as changed people.

(Based on information in Mark Ellis, "Fantasy Camp Ensures that Rock Dreams Never Die." The Columbus Dispatch, February 22, 2006.)

| cheered . . . on | crowd | posted | replaced | stirred |

FROM THE FOOTBALL STADIUM TO THE OPERA HOUSE

More than one _____ has _____ Keith Miller _____. In
                      6   7
high school his football team was the state champion* for three years straight. Miller went on to play for the University of Colorado and then made it into the NFL (National Football League) as a Denver Bronco. Then his life turned in a different direction.

A champion (n.) is a person or team that has won a competition, especially in sports.

Someone had _____ a notice about auditions** for the opera "Don Giovanni." Miller
                          8
saw it, and went to the auditions. "I didn't know how to read music or speak Italian, but I did really

well, so I got the part." One part led to another and soon opera _____ football in Miller's
                                                                                    9
life. He's sung in Italy, London, Canada, and throughout the United States.

Miller had first heard opera back when he was a college student. He took a girlfriend to see

"Phantom of the Opera" and the performance _____ strong emotions much like an
                                                                10
exciting football game did—only it was better. Miller continued to play football after that first experience

with opera, but in the end he decided opera was what he wanted to do. Miller is now a student at the

Academy of Vocal Arts in Philadelphia.

**An audition (n.) is a short performance by an actor, singer, etc. that is used in order to decide if s/he should act in a play,
sing in a concert, etc.

(Based on information in Amanda Holt Miller, "Former NFL Football Player Now Catches Applause as Opera Singer." Post Independent,
March 10, 2006.)

▌WORDS IN DISCUSSION

Apply the key words to your own life. Read and discuss the questions with a partner. Try to use the key words.

1. Name something that always **cheers** you **up**.

   ### EXAMPLE

   *If I'm feeling sad, I like to listen to music. It usually **cheers** me **up**.*

2. Where do you usually **post** a message for others to see in your home?
3. Do you want to live in a **modest** home, or do you want something big and fancy?
4. What foods do you like to eat **raw**?
5. Name a reason why people **slip** and get hurt.

▌WORDS IN WRITING

Write a short answer (1–2 sentences) for each question. Try to use the key words.

1. Did you ever **stir up trouble** at home, work, or school?

   ### EXAMPLE

   *You might say I **stirred up trouble** at school once. Last year they wanted to forbid jeans and
   T-shirts, and I fought against this.*

2. Describe someone who you think **stands out from the crowd**.
3. Do you ever **slave** to do a good job?
4. Name someone you consider to be **brave**.
5. Is there anything in your home that you want to **replace**?

QUIZ 4

PART A

Choose the word that best completes each item and write it in the space provided.

1. We're taking our dog on the trip. Our hotel ____*permits*____ guests to bring pets.
   - a. permits
   - b. forbids
   - c. obeys
   - d. rushes

2. Today is a religious holiday. My family will gather to _____.
   - a. interfere
   - b. succeed
   - c. cheat
   - d. worship

3. The doctor _____ me to return to work until my back was better.
   - a. forbid
   - b. obeyed
   - c. cheated
   - d. paused

4. My roommate and I spent a quiet evening putting a _____ together.
   - a. puzzle
   - b. post
   - c. battle
   - d. race

5. Tony _____ to take a sip of water. Then he began to talk again.
   - a. slipped
   - b. obeyed
   - c. stirred
   - d. paused

6. The family had to use a _____ to catch the mice in their basement.
   - a. crowd
   - b. trap
   - c. battle
   - d. supply

7. If you want to find a roommate, you can _____ a notice at school.
   - a. rush
   - b. post
   - c. replace
   - d. supply

8. Please be careful not to _____. The snow makes the sidewalks icy.
   - a. slip
   - b. wonder
   - c. cheat
   - d. cheer

9. Isaac is a good student and studies hard; he doesn't _____ on tests.
   - a. slip
   - b. forbid
   - c. cheat
   - d. worship

10. Huseyin hasn't written to me for months. I _____ how he is.
    - a. interfere
    - b. wonder
    - c. replace
    - d. cheer

PART B

*Read each statement and write **T** for true or **F** for false in the space provided.*

_T_   1. If you woke up late and you might miss your plane, you should **rush**.

_____   2. Baked chicken is an example of **raw** meat.

_____   3. People **cheer** when they're happy or excited about something.

_____   4. There is little danger in a **battle**.

_____   5. An **artificial** plant grows big and green with the help of sunlight and water.

_____   6. To get the result that you wanted is to **succeed**.

_____   7. If your books are **due** back at the library, you have to take them there.

_____   8. It's always helpful to **interfere** in other people's problems.

_____   9. Criminals **obey** the law.

_____ 10. An umbrella's purpose is to **protect** you from the rain.

PART C

Each situation shows the meaning of one of the key words. Write the appropriate key word next to the situation. Use the clues in italics.

base	charm	modest	replace	stir
brave	crowd	race	slave	supply

1. The town had *a special quality* that made us *like it* from the moment we first arrived.   _____charm_____

2. The police made sure there was safety and order among the *large group of people* at the concert.   _____

3. Some famous actors love to talk about themselves and their work; others are *quiet about* their talent and success.   _____

4. The army needs certain *amounts of* food and water for each soldier to *use*.   _____

5. If I want to go on vacation, I need to find *another person* to work *instead* of me at the café.   _____

6. The company uses San Francisco as its *main place* of business.   _____

7. History shows that more than one country has used the practice of *owning people* and making them *work for no pay*.   _____

8. The riders held a *competition to find out* which horse was *the fastest*.   _____

9. Teemu put sugar into his coffee and *mixed it* well.   _____

10. The zookeeper showed *little fear* as he walked into the cage of the *dangerous* lion.   _____

WORDS IN CONTEXT

*Use the sentences to guess what each key word means. Choose the meaning that is closest to that of the key word in **bold**.*

1. eager
/ˈigɚ/
-adjective

- I'm **eager** to start my travels. I have my plane ticket, and my suitcases are ready.
- Cliff loves learning, so he's **eager** for classes to start again this fall.

Eager means . . .
    a. needing help
    b. having a strong wish or interest
    c. confused or needing an explanation

2. fortunate
/ˈfɔrtʃənɪt/
-adjective

- That was a terrible fall! You're **fortunate** that you didn't get hurt.
- Dale is **fortunate** to have such caring and understanding parents.

Fortune means . . .
    a. funny
    b. healthy
    c. lucky

3. freedom
/ˈfridəm/
-noun

- India won **freedom** from the political control of Great Britain in 1947.
- U.S. law gives journalists the **freedom** to report news and state opinions.

Freedom means . . .
    a. the state of not being controlled
    b. the state of not having a choice
    c. the act of fighting for control

4. horizon
/həˈraɪzən/
-noun

- The sailors watched the sun come up over the **horizon**.
- We looked ahead at the hills and saw another group of campers on the **horizon**.

Horizon means . . .
    a. a group of clouds
    b. the place where the land or ocean meets the sky
    c. the land near a body of water such as a river or sea

5. ideal
/aɪˈdiəl/
-adjective

- The couple saw the beautiful house and knew they had found the **ideal** home.
- Ms. Lowery was the **ideal** piano teacher: talented, knowledgeable, and patient.

Ideal means . . .
    a. having much strength
    b. being very comfortable or relaxed
    c. being the best possible

6. operate
/ˈapəˌreɪt/
-verb

- My aunt never cleans. She doesn't even know how to **operate** a vacuum cleaner.
- The salesman showed Gene how to **operate** the machine before he took it home.

Operate means . . .
    a. to put a machine together
    b. to make a machine work
    c. to fix a machine

7. **reserve**
   /rɪˈzɚv/
   -verb

   - The town has only two hotels. We should **reserve** a room a month ahead.
   - The restaurant looks crowded. Did you **reserve** a table?

   Reserve means . . .
   a. to choose a place, ticket, etc.
   b. to pay for a place, ticket, etc.
   c. to make plans for a place, ticket, etc. to be kept for you

8. **standard**
   /ˈstændɚd/
   -noun

   - All schools must have **standards** for students' reading, writing, and math skills.
   - The meat company must be certain that all products meet high health **standards**.

   Standard means . . .
   a. an instruction or explanation
   b. a reason for an action or thought
   c. a level of ability or goodness

9. **steady**
   /ˈstɛdi/
   -adjective

   - Dentists need a **steady** hand when they work with sharp tools in our mouths.
   - Hold the ladder **steady**. I'm going to climb higher.

   Steady means . . .
   a. not moving
   b. not opening
   c. loose

10. **wise**
    /waɪz/
    -adjective

    - Our decision to hike without a map or compass wasn't **wise**. We got lost.
    - Listen to your elders. They often share **wise** words that you can learn from.

    Wise means . . .
    a. showing experience
    b. safe
    c. loving or caring

WORDS AND DEFINITIONS

Match each key word with its definition.

1. _____horizon_____ the place where the land or ocean seems to meet the sky

2. _____ having a strong wish to do something or a strong interest in something

3. _____ to make plans for a place in a hotel, on a plane, etc. to be kept for you to use

4. _____ marked by experience and the ability to make good decisions

5. _____ the right to do whatever you want without being controlled by someone

6. _____ the level of skill or ability or the degree of goodness that is considered to be normal

7. _____ being the best that something could possibly be

8. _____ lucky

9. _____ to make a machine work

10. _____ not moving from one place, or not shaking or falling

Choose the best answer.

1. Which of the following is a good place to see what's on the **horizon**?

    a. a bedroom closet

    b. a shopping center

    (c.) an open field in the countryside

2. Claudio's legs aren't **steady** because

    a. it's his first time on a ship.

    b. he exercises to keep them strong.

    c. he's sleeping.

3. Ignacio found the **ideal** job;

    a. he might look for a new job after he pays some bills.

    b. he'll likely work at his new company for many years.

    c. he's not unhappy, but he misses his old office.

4. When you **reserve** a plane ticket,

    a. you must travel on the same day.

    b. you can travel at a later time.

    c. you can choose where to go at a later time.

5. Can you please show me how to **operate**

    a. the stereo system? I don't even know how to turn it on.

    b. a horse? I've never ridden one.

    c. this math problem? It's difficult.

6. When you travel to a new city, you're usually **eager**

    a. to see famous places.

    b. to ask for directions.

    c. to lose your wallet.

7. Restaurants must meet **standards** in order to

    a. stay in business.

    b. keep prices down.

    c. serve interesting dishes.

8. Which of the following is a **fortunate** situation?

    a. Nick was able to get a hotel room for the night.

    b. Nick had no place to spend the night.

    c. Nick spent the night sitting in a chair at the airport.

9. If a group of people want **freedom**,

    a. they prefer to let someone else make choices for them.

    b. they fear choice.

    c. they would like to have more choice in what they do.

10. If you make **wise** choices,

    a. you have few problems.

    b. you create many problems.

    c. you need to learn how to fix your problems.

WORD FAMILIES

Now that you have studied the ten key words and their basic definitions, you are ready to learn words that belong to the same family as some of the key words. A word family includes words that look alike but have different functions (noun, verb, adjective, or adverb). Their meanings are related but different.

A. *Look at each model phrase and decide whether the word in **bold** is used as a noun, verb, adjective, or adverb.*

	NOUN	VERB	ADJECTIVE	ADVERB
1. **fortunate**				
• a **fortunate** person			✓	
• **fortunately**, we're alive				✓
• your good **fortune**	✓			
2. **ideal**				
• the **ideal** time				
• **ideally**, I'd live on the beach				
3. **operate**				
• to **operate** a microwave				
• the **operations** overseas				
4. **reserve**				
• will **reserve** a plane ticket				
• must have a **reservation**				
5. **steady**				
• a **steady** hand				
• to grow **steadily**				
6. **wise**				
• a **wise** decision				
• show **wisdom**				

B. *Read each sentence and match the word in **bold** with the correct definition.*

___e___ 1. The company has grown so much; it has **operations** in five countries.

_____ 2. Grandmother has lived many years and seen many things. She's full of **wisdom**.

_____ 3. Everyone else in my family got sick, but **fortunately** I didn't.

_____ 4. Henri practices the violin every day. He's improving **steadily**.

_____ 5. Hello. We have a **reservation** for two nights. The last name is Jablonski.

_____ 6. I'm the only child but I had the **fortune** to grow up with many cousins.

_____ 7. **Ideally** no one would ever get sick.

a. lucky

b. luck

c. the ability to make good decisions, especially because of one's experience

d. done in a slow and continuous way

e. a business or company, or the work of a business

f. in a way you'd like things to be, even if it's not possible

g. plans that you make so that a place in a hotel, on a plane, etc. is kept for you to use

SAME WORD, DIFFERENT MEANING

Most words have more than one meaning. Study the additional meanings of **fortune**, **operation**, **reserve**, and **standard**. Then read each sentence and decide which meaning is used.

a.	**fortune** *n.*	luck
b.	**fortune** *n.*	a very large amount of money
c.	**operation** *n.*	a business or company, or the work of a business
d.	**operation** *n.*	the process of cutting into someone's body to fix or remove a part that is damaged
e.	**reserve** *v.*	to make plans for a place in a hotel, on a plane, etc. to be kept for you to use
f.	**reserve** *v.*	to keep something apart from other things for a later use, or to use something only for a special reason or occasion
g.	**standard** *n.*	how much skill or ability or how good someone or something must be in order to be considered normal
h.	**standard** *n.*	the ideas of what is good or normal that someone uses to compare one thing with another

__*g*__ 1. The coach's **standards** must not be so high because Eric got on the team and he can't even run for more than ten minutes.

_____ 2. Monica is a supervisor; she controls the **operations** of six stores.

_____ 3. Newspapers should make sure all articles meet **standards** of good writing.

_____ 4. Gordon **reserved** two tickets for a flight to Toronto.

_____ 5. After Grandpa's **operation**, he spent a week in the hospital.

_____ 6. The company likes to **reserve** one office on each floor for business meetings.

WORDS IN SENTENCES

Complete each sentence with one of the words from the box.

eager	freedom	ideally	reservation	steadily
fortunately	horizon	operations	standards	~~wisdom~~

1. The successful businessman wrote a book to share his _____*wisdom*_____ with others.

2. Quinn has a lot of things to take to college. _____, his father has a big car.

3. Karen got the flu, but didn't take care of herself, so her health _____ worsened.

4. Jason is very _____ to go to summer camp. It's all he talks about these days.

5. The factory is losing money. They may shut down all _____.

6. Galya kept her eyes on the _____. The bus was due to come over the hill anytime.

7. I hate Mondays. _____, no one would work or study on Mondays.

8. Good evening, and welcome to Luigi's. Do you have a(n) _____?

9. At my new company, I have the _____ to make my own schedule.

10. Our ballet instructor has very high _____, but this makes us do our very best.

WORDS IN COLLOCATIONS AND EXPRESSIONS

Following are common collocations (word partners) and expressions with some of the key words. Read the definitions and then complete the conversations with the correct form of the collocations and expressions.

1. **eager**
   - **eager to (do sth)**   to have a strong wish to (do something)

2. **fortune**
   - **fortunate to (do sth)**   to be lucky enough to (do something)
   - **spend a fortune (on sth)**   to spend a large amount of money (on something)

3. **horizon**
   - **on the horizon**   often used to talk about a possibility in the near future

4. **reserve**
   - **make a reservation (for/at)**   to make plans for a place in a hotel, on a plane, etc. to be kept for you to use

5. **standard**
   - **set high standards**   to think that others will be able to reach a high level of skill or ability and want them to do so

1.   GINNY: I feel _____*fortunate to*_____ have so many relatives in the same city.

   SEAN: Yeah. You're lucky to have family around you.

2.   PRINCIPAL: We want our students to be among the best in the country.

   PARENT: It's important to _____, but how do you help the students meet them?

3.   NANCY: I'd like to go to graduate school, but it's so expensive.

   TROY: I know. You have to _____ on education these days.

4.   BEN: Each winter we take a family skiing trip.

   HELEN: That sounds like fun. Where are you going this year?

   BEN: We decided to _____ at a hotel in Colorado.

5.   CO-WORKER 1:   Things are getting better since we got a new company president.

   CO-WORKER 2:   That's for sure. He's already filled the office with energy. I think good changes are _____.

6.   SYDNEY: Did Darren start his new job yet?

   LEE: No. His training begins on Monday. He's _____ start.

WORDS IN READINGS

Read the two articles about personal finance. Complete each one with words and expressions from the boxes.

eager to	on the horizon	operations	steadily	~~wise~~

SOON TO BE A MILLIONAIRE

There was a time right after college when Justin D'Angelo was very careful about every dollar he spent. He didn't go out to eat with friends, and he bought only what he needed. Now at age twenty–four, Justin is making $150,000 a year thanks to _____wise_____ business decisions.
₁

Justin is the owner of PoofChairs.com. One might think this young man works hard every day because he's doing so well, but he needs very little time for day-to-day _____. Computer
₂
technology lets Justin sell his big and comfortable pillow-like chairs from his desk quickly and easily.

PoofChairs.com got started while Justin was studying business at North Carolina State University. His company has grown _____. Going out to dinner with friends is no longer a worry: He
₃
now spends $500 a month on entertainment alone, and he puts $5,000 a month in the stock market*.

Justin sees more business growth _____. He's _____ start a new
₄ ₅
website called build-a-bedroom.com. With two big businesses, a home, a car, and a plan to save $5,000 a month, Justin will be a millionaire by the age of thirty-four.

The stock market (n.) is the business of buying and selling stocks (shares in a company).

(Based on information in Rob Kelley, "Web Sales Wizardry." CNN Money.com, October 20, 2005.)

fortune	freedom	ideally	reserve	standard

HOW RICH IS RICH?

Who exactly is rich? Here's what different people think about how much money it would take to call themselves rich:

- A New York banker stated his hope to have $10 to $15 million to pay for a $2 million home, his children's education, and his personal interests. He could also _____ money for his
₆
children's children.

- For another banker, money is not _____ *from* something, but freedom to *do*
₇
something. _____, she'd like $5 million to fly a plane around the world, climb the
₈
highest mountains, and sail a boat from Maine to Key West to the Caribbean.

- A North Carolina writer agrees that having at least a small _____ can bring greater
₉
choices in life. He'd like enough money so he wouldn't have to do anything but the kind of work that makes him happy.

In the end, each person has his or her own _____. Maybe it's the small business
owner who best explains what being rich is: it's having enough money so you can enjoy the simple
things and spend time with those you love.

(Based on information in Jeanne Sahadi, "The Perfect Level of 'Rich.'" CNN Money.com, June 8, 2005.)

▌WORDS IN DISCUSSION

Apply the key words to your own life. Read and discuss the questions with a partner. Try to use the key words.

1. Are you always **eager to** start the day when you wake up?

   EXAMPLE

   *Yes. I'm a morning person, so I'm usually **eager to** start my day.*

2. You're on the phone and you want to **make a reservation** at a restaurant. What do you say?
3. Is there an **ideal** time of the day to study a language?
4. Can you keep your hands **steady** enough to read or write on a bus or train?
5. How much money is a **fortune**? Do you know anyone who has a **fortune**?

▌WORDS IN WRITING

Write a short answer (1–2 sentences) for each question. Try to use the key words.

1. Do you see any changes in your life **on the horizon**? Name one.

   EXAMPLE

   *Right now I don't see any changes **on the horizon** because I have three more years of college.*

2. Name the **wisest** person you know.
3. Have you or has someone in your family had an **operation**?
4. Would you like to have more **freedom** at work or at school? Explain.
5. What is something you **set high standards** for? Explain.

WORDS IN CONTEXT

*Use the sentences to guess what each key word means. Choose the meaning that is closest to that of the key word in **bold**.*

1. **ache**
/eɪk/
-noun

• I woke up with an **ache** in my neck; I need a softer pillow.
• T. J. lifted several heavy boxes at work. Later he had **aches** in his back and legs.

Ache means . . . (a.) a continuous pain   b. no movement   c. a scratch

2. **actual**
/ˈæktʃuəl/
-adjective

• In the photograph the house looked large, but the **actual** house is quite small.
• You said the computer isn't very expensive. What's the **actual** price?

Actual means . . .   a. new   b. real   c. best

3. **blind**
/blaɪnd/
-adjective

• The man was **blind**, but he could hear very well.
• Dogs can help lead **blind** people through many daily activities outside the home.

Blind means . . .   a. unable to walk   b. unable to see   c. unable to live alone

4. **concern**
/ˈkənˈsɚn/
-noun

• There is much **concern** about the coming storm. They say it will be terrible.
• My **concern** for Barry is growing. He doesn't look healthy, and he's always tired.

Concern means . . .   a. serious talk   b. a deep understanding   c. a feeling of worry

5. **courage**
/ˈkɚɪdʒ/
-noun

• Sometimes you need a lot of **courage** to do what you think is right, especially when others are against you.
• Rafael had enough **courage** to leave the comfort of his job and start his own business.

Courage means . . .   a. the ability to be brave   b. the chance to do something difficult   c. knowledge and skill

6. **expect**
/ˈɪkˈspɛkt/
-verb

• Sarah is a strong swimmer. The coach **expects** her to win this race.
• I'm resting and taking medicine. I **expect** that I'll be feeling better in a few days.

Expect means . . .   a. to make something happen   b. to ask for something to happen   c. to think something will happen

7. mention
/ˈmɛnʃən/
-verb

- Your sister is a TV actress? How interesting! You didn't **mention** this before.
- The news report on small businesses **mentioned** our family store.

Mention means . . .   a. to question   b. to tell about in a few words   c. to share a secret

8. peace
/pis/
-noun

- After World War II, Hawaii began to enjoy **peace** and safety.
- The countries are not at war, but they must work hard to keep **peace** between them.

Peace means . . .   a. growth   b. no danger   c. no fighting

9. pretend
/prɪˈtɛnd/
-verb

- Alex **pretends** he can't hear me when I tell him it's his turn to wash the dishes.
- Megan **pretended** to be surprised, but she already knew what her birthday present was.

Pretend means . . .   a. to behave as if something is true   b. to complain about something   c. to learn how to do something

10. separate
/ˈsɛpəˌreɪt/
-adjective

- Let's make **separate** lists of what we think is needed, and then we can compare them.
- Do you think it's important to keep friendship **separate** from business?

Separate means . . .   a. not relating to each other   b. coming together to make a whole   c. similar to each other

WORDS AND DEFINITIONS

Match each key word with its definition.

1. _____*actual*_____ real, especially when compared with what is believed or planned

2. _____ to behave as if something is true when you know it is not

3. _____ a feeling of worry about something important

4. _____ a continuous dull pain

5. _____ not relating to each other in any way

6. _____ a situation or period of time in which there is no war or fighting

7. _____ to say or write about something in a few words

8. _____ the ability to be brave when you are in danger, a difficult situation, etc.

9. _____ to think that something will happen

10. _____ unable to see

Choose the best answer.

1. Two nations at **peace**
   a. send their armies into battle.
   b. are not fighting a war.
   c. have poor communication.

2. If your feet **ache**, you should
   a. wash them.
   b. scratch them.
   c. take your shoes off and rest.

3. If I **mention** my brother to you,
   a. I've told you all about him.
   b. you probably know his name and just a little bit about him.
   c. the two of you have met.

4. If Adam says the car accident and the pain in his neck are **separate** events,
   a. the pain came before the accident.
   b. the pain came after the accident.
   c. the pain is not related to the accident in any way.

5. We **expect** Nikolai to arrive this afternoon;
   a. he promised to join us for dinner tonight.
   b. he called to say he can't be here.
   c. he often changes his plans at the last minute.

6. A **blind** person CANNOT
   a. hear you call his name.
   b. speak his name out loud.
   c. see his name written on paper.

7. Lex **pretended** to be asleep;
   a. he didn't want to talk to his roommate.
   b. he had bad dreams.
   c. he set his alarm for 6 A.M.

8. Lucy told me the cat was a year old, but its **actual** age is five.
   a. She was wrong by four years.
   b. The cat is six years old.
   c. She was correct, but the cat looks much older.

9. Someone with **courage**
   a. will admit a mistake even if doing so gets him or her into trouble.
   b. will hide his or her mistakes.
   c. won't try anything difficult because he or she might fail.

10. My **concern** about my cousin has grown because
    a. she's not answering her phone, and no one has seen her for three days.
    b. she's a lot of fun to be with, and she's very smart, too.
    c. now we have the same haircut.

WORD FAMILIES

Now that you have studied the ten key words and their basic definitions, you are ready to learn words that belong to the same family as some of the key words. A word family includes words that look alike but have different functions (noun, verb, adjective, or adverb). Their meanings are related but different.

A. *Look at each model phrase and decide whether the word in **bold** is used as a noun, verb, adjective, or adverb.*

	NOUN	VERB	ADJECTIVE	ADVERB
1. ache				
• a terrible **ache**	✓			
• my arms **ache**		✓		
2. actual				
• her **actual** age				
• she **actually** wasn't sick				
3. concern				
• much **concern**				
• very **concerned** parents				
4. courage				
• have **courage**				
• be **courageous**				
5. peace				
• work towards **peace**				
• a **peaceful** home				
6. separate				
• two **separate** crimes				
• try to **separate** oil from water				

B. *Read each sentence and match the word in **bold** with the correct definition.*

<u> e </u> 1. Ray says he not a great dancer, but **actually** he's quite good. I've seen him.

_____ 2. People often perform **courageous** acts in an emergency.

_____ 3. My whole body **aches** from scrubbing the floors yesterday.

_____ 4. The countryside was very **peaceful**; it was the perfect place for Francis to relax.

_____ 5. The teachers are **concerned** about Gloria's poor performance in school lately.

_____ 6. You should **separate** dark clothes from white clothes before you wash them.

a. calm, quiet, and without problems or excitement

b. worried about something important

c. to divide something into two or more parts, or to make something do this

d. brave and not afraid

e. used when you are telling or asking someone what the truth about something is

f. to feel continuous pain

SAME WORD, DIFFERENT MEANING

*Most words have more than one meaning. Study the additional meanings of **expect**, **pretend**, and **separate**.*
Then read each sentence and decide which meaning is used.

a.	**expect** *v.*	to think that something will happen
b.	**expect** *v.*	to order that someone do something because you feel s/he must
c.	**pretend** *v.*	to behave as if something is true when you know it is not
d.	**pretend** *v.*	to think something is true or real as part of a game
e.	**separate** *adj.*	not relating to each other in any way
f.	**separate** *adj.*	physically not connected to each other or touching each other

___f___ 1. My sister and I have **separate** rooms. This is good because she snores loudly.

_____ 2. Noah **pretended** not to notice Claire's mistake; he didn't want to embarrass her.

_____ 3. We haven't seen our cousins for many years. What do you **expect** they'll be like?

_____ 4. When I was a child, I used to **pretend** my toys could talk to me.

_____ 5. Our teacher **expects** us to type all essays and reports on the computer.

_____ 6. Joan and I work in **separate** fields; she's an engineer, and I'm a journalist.

WORDS IN SENTENCES

Complete each sentence with one of the words from the box.

ache	blind	courageous	mention	pretended
actually	~~concerned~~	expects	peaceful	separate

1. Our neighbors grew _____concerned_____ when they heard all the yelling, but then they learned it was our TV.

2. In the early morning, the park was especially _____.

3. The boy waved his arms up and down and _____ to be a bird.

4. My feet _____ from dancing so much.

5. Our supervisor _____ us to work hard and do our best.

6. You didn't _____ before that you have a cat. What kind is it?

7. Do you _____ know any famous people?

8. Sadly, our dog Sam was becoming _____ in his old age.

9. In this classroom, students don't have _____ desks. They sit at tables in small groups.

10. The man was very _____. He rushed into the burning building to help the people inside.

WORDS IN COLLOCATIONS AND EXPRESSIONS

Following are common collocations (word partners) and expressions with some of the key words. Read the definitions and then complete the conversations with the correct form of the collocations and expressions.

1. **ache**
   - **headache, backache, etc.** — a continuous pain in your head, back, etc.

2. **blind**
   - **go blind** — to become blind

3. **courage**
   - **find the courage to (do sth) (have the courage to [do sth])** — to find the strength to do something difficult

4. **expect**
   - **expect (sb) to (do sth)** — to think that someone will do something, or to order that someone do something, because you feel s/he must

5. **mention**
   - **mention (sth) to (sb)** — to say or write to someone about something in a few words

6. **peace**
   - **peace and quiet** — calm, quiet, and without problems or excitement

1. CO-WORKER 1: My head is really killing me.

   CO-WORKER 2: Here. Try this. It's green tea. It helps me whenever I have a _____*headache*_____.

2. ANDRE: Where do you think Chris is?

   KEVIN: He'll probably be here later. He's helping his parents at home with some work.

   ANDRE: Oh, yeah. Didn't he _____ something about painting a fence _____ us?

3. SON: Can I borrow the car today?

   MOTHER: Yes, but I _____ you _____ be home in time for dinner. We're having guests over this evening.

4. ELIF: Did Greg ask you to the dance?

   HOLLY: Not yet. He's so shy! If he doesn't _____ ask me soon, I'm going ask him myself.

5. MOTHER: Do you hear that?

   FATHER: Hear what? With the kids at their grandmother's, there's nothing to hear.

   MOTHER: That's it. There's _____ in the house. Isn't that a change?

6. FATHER: Time to get off the computer. Give your eyes a rest.

   DAUGHTER: I'm not going to _____ from using the computer.

   FATHER: Maybe not, but you may find yourself wearing a pair of glasses in the near future.

WORDS IN READINGS

Read the two articles about literature. Complete each one with words and expressions from the boxes.

actually	concerned	expected . . . to	mention . . . to	~~pretended~~

NEW BOOK, NEW AUTHOR, NEW BEGINNINGS

Everything about *The Icarus Girl* is unusual. The story is about an eight-year-old girl who meets a Nigerian friend who looks like her but isn't real. The idea was familiar to the British author, Helen Oyeyemi, because she herself ____*pretended*____ to have a friend named "Chimmy" in childhood.
₁

Eighteen-year-old Oyeyemi had to be very clever in order to get her book sold. She decided not to _____ the book at all _____ her parents when she sent off the first twenty
₂
pages to an agent*. Her mother and father were very _____ about their daughter's school
₃
exams. They wanted her to get into Cambridge University, and they _____ her
₄
_____ study hard.

Oyeyemi faced two problems at that time: she told the agent that she had written a total of 150 pages, but _____ she only had the first twenty. How could she find time to write
₅
when her parents wanted her to give all her attention to schoolwork? Sometimes Oyeyemi pretended to study, but secretly finished the 130 pages for the agent. Luckily for Oyeyemi, two important things happened on the same day—she got a book contract** to show her parents she was serious about writing, and she got into Cambridge.

*An agent (n.) is a person or company that helps another person or company deal with business problems, finding work, etc.

**A contract (n.) is a legal written agreement between two people, companies, etc. that says what each side must do for the other.

(Based on information in "Author of the Week." The Week, July 15, 2005.)

ache	find the courage . . . to	peace
courageous	going blind	separate

NO DIRECTION HOME

No Direction Home is the first novel by Marisa Silver. The book pulls the reader into a story about the shared sadness of three children. They have all lost their fathers, but with time they learn to _____ they need _____ go on in life.
₆

There are really three _____ stories that become one. Marlene, a beautiful and clever
₇
teenager, never knew her father; he left before she was born. A deeper _____ is felt by her
₈
half-brother Will, a ten-year-old boy. Will isn't charming like Marlene, and he has no friends. What's more, he's _____. Then there is Rogelio, who at fourteen, is already working by taking care of
₉

a sick old woman—Marlene's grandmother. Both Will and Rogelio lived with their fathers for some time, but in the end, as with Marlene, their fathers left them.

The author has the talent to make the world of these children completely real, and the reader understands their families, their feelings, and their growth. By the end, Marlene and Rogelio take _____ steps to find their fathers; Will finds the strength to let go of his. What begins as a
_____10_____
sad story ends with a kind of _____ for both these children and the reader.
                                        _____11_____
(Based on information in Barbara Fisher, "Short Takes." The Boston Globe online, July 10, 2005.)

▌WORDS IN DISCUSSION

Apply the key words to your own life. Read and discuss the questions with a partner. Try to use the key words.

1. What do you usually do when you have a **headache**?

   EXAMPLE

   *I take aspirin when I have a **headache**, and then I take a nap if possible.*

2. Name something you think most people your age are **concerned** about.
3. What kind of car would you like to own? Do you know the **actual** cost of this car?
4. Name something that helps **blind** people do everyday activities.
5. Do you often **mention** your family **to** others?

▌WORDS IN WRITING

Write a short answer (1–2 sentences) for each question. Try to use the key words.

1. What do you **expect to** do with English in the future?

   EXAMPLE

   *I need English for work. With better English, I **expect to** have a better job.*

2. Do you ever **pretend** to understand something when you **actually** don't?
3. What's the most **peaceful** place you've ever visited? Do you often go there for **peace and quiet**?
4. Have you ever seen someone do something **courageous**?
5. Do you think brothers should share rooms or have **separate** ones? What about sisters?

Key Words

block	defend	grateful	patience	respect
deaf	dozen	inform	relieve	sharp

WORDS IN CONTEXT

*Use the sentences to guess what each key word means. Choose the meaning that is closest to that of the key word in **bold**.*

1. block
/blak/
-noun

- The children played on the floor with wooden **blocks** of different colors.
- The road was closed. Big **blocks** of concrete kept cars from driving on it.

Block means . . .   a. a kind of car   b. a large toy   (c.) a hard piece of material

2. deaf
/dɛf/
-adjective

- **Deaf** people don't usually use their voices to talk; they have sign language.
- My mother says listening to loud music will damage my ears and make me **deaf**.

Deaf means . . .   a. unable to hear   b. unable to talk   c. unable to think clearly

3. defend
/dɪˈfɛnd/
-verb

- In wartime people can use subway stations to **defend** themselves during attacks. The stations are often built deep enough to keep people safe.
- The man bravely **defended** his family; he put himself in danger to keep them from harm.

Defend means . . .   a. to help   b. to protect   c. to hide

4. dozen
/ˈdʌzən/
-noun

- I baked two **dozen** cookies. That's enough for the twenty-four students in my class.
- American supermarkets sell eggs by the **dozen**.

Dozen means . . .   a. a box for food   b. a group of twelve   c. a recipe

5. grateful
/ɡreɪtfəl/
-adjective

- Thanksgiving is a holiday that makes people remember they should be **grateful** for all that they have: food, a home, family, friends, health, and an education.
- When I think of all that my coach has taught me, I'm really **grateful** to him.

Grateful means . . .   a. needing more of something   b. wanting to thank someone   c. feeling excited

6. inform
/ɪnˈfɔrm/
-verb

- Teachers must **inform** parents of students' performances in school.
- You should ask your mechanic to **inform** you of the cost before he fixes your car.

Inform means . . .   a. to ask   b. to suggest   c. to tell

7. patience
/ˈpeɪʃəns/
-noun

- I don't have the **patience** to put puzzles together. I like things I can do quickly.
- You need **patience** when you are teaching a dog new skills.

Patience means . . .
  a. the ability to wait calmly
  b. free time
  c. skill with your hands

8. relieve
/rɪˈliv/
-verb

- Talking about my difficulties with others **relieved** some of my worry.
- The city plans to build another highway to **relieve** traffic during the work week.

Relieve means . . .
  a. to make a problem less serious
  b. to make a problem worse
  c. to make you forget about a problem

9. respect
/rɪˈspɛkt/
-noun

- I have a lot of **respect** for people who can talk to large groups of people.
- There's much **respect** among the townspeople for their mayor. She's well-liked.

Respect means . . .
  a. a strong interest in someone
  b. a high opinion of someone
  c. good wishes for someone

10. sharp
/ʃarp/
-adjective

- These scissors aren't **sharp**. I can't cut through the tape.
- Be careful slicing the vegetables. That knife is very **sharp**.

Sharp means . . .
  a. able to cut
  b. thin
  c. long

▌WORDS AND DEFINITIONS

Match each key word with its definition.

1. _____*deaf*_____ unable to hear

2. _____ feeling that you want to thank someone because of something kind that s/he has done

3. _____ to protect someone or something from being attacked or taken away

4. _____ a high opinion of someone because of their great knowledge or skill

5. _____ a group of twelve things

6. _____ a piece of hard material, usually in the shape of a square or rectangle

7. _____ the ability to wait calmly for a long time, or to face difficulties without becoming angry or upset

8. _____ to make a pain, problem, or bad feeling less in strength or seriousness

9. _____ to tell someone about something in a serious way or in a serious situation

10. _____ able to cut

COMPREHENSION CHECK

Choose the best answer.

1. A **block** can be made of all of the following materials *except*
   a. ice.
   b. water. *(circled)*
   c. wood.

2. Tina is **grateful** to her friend for
   a. giving her a ride to school every day.
   b. yelling at her.
   c. getting sick with the flu.

3. I'm very close with my **deaf** cousin;
   a. I write to him at least once a week.
   b. we call each other on the phone almost every week.
   c. I don't mind that he can't see me because he understands me so well.

4. If a knife is **sharp**,
   a. you should be careful not to cut yourself.
   b. it needs cleaning.
   c. you might have trouble cutting meat.

5. You can buy each of the following items by the **dozen** EXCEPT
   a. eggs.
   b. flowers.
   c. sugar.

6. Which of the following actions **relieves** pain?
   a. being outside in cold weather
   b. taking aspirin
   c. lifting heavy boxes

7. Harry **defended** himself from
   a. his kind neighbor.
   b. the dangerous attacker.
   c. the helpful salesman.

8. Reggie deeply **respects** his father;
   a. they're nothing like each other.
   b. there's a lot about him that Reggie doesn't understand.
   c. he feels lucky to be his son.

9. In which situation is the speaker **informing** another person of something?
   a. "Would you like to go to a concert with me?"
   b. "What a great movie! Let's watch it again."
   c. "If you buy a second pair of shoes today, you'll save 50 percent on both."

10. Selena had no **patience**;
    a. she waited calmly in line at the cashier's desk.
    b. she left the store angrily after only five minutes of waiting.
    c. she continued to shop for another thirty minutes.

WORD FAMILIES

Now that you have studied the ten key words and their basic definitions, you are ready to learn words that belong to the same family as some of the key words. A word family includes words that look alike but have different functions (noun, verb, adjective, or adverb). Their meanings are related but different.

A. *Look at each model phrase and decide whether the word in* **bold** *is used as a noun, verb, adjective, or adverb.*

	NOUN	VERB	ADJECTIVE	ADVERB
1. defend				
• will **defend** their homeland		✓		
• use as a **defense**	✓			
2. inform				
• to **inform** your family				
• be **informed** about the dangers				
3. patience				
• ask for **patience**				
• be more **patient**				
4. relieve				
• can **relieve** your pain				
• give some **relief**				
5. respect				
• have much **respect**				
• must **respect** your elders				
• should be **respectful**				

B. *Read the first half of each sentence and match it with the appropriate ending.*

__c__ 1. I'm sorry you had to spend the whole day helping me, but

____ 2. The town built a large concrete wall near the shore to serve as

____ 3. Evan is my supervisor, but he started from a low position like mine. That's why

____ 4. Ask questions and read a lot so that

____ 5. I like to move fast. When I walk with others, I have to tell myself

____ 6. You might not agree with other people's ideas, but it's important

a. you can make **informed** decisions.

b. I **respect** him.

c. it's such a **relief** to know that all the work is done.

d. to be more **patient** and slow down.

e. to be **respectful** of their opinions.

f. a **defense** against ocean storms.

SAME WORD, DIFFERENT MEANING

Most words have more than one meaning. Study the additional meanings of **block** *and* **patient**. *Then read each sentence and decide which meaning is used.*

a. **block** *n.*	a piece of hard material, usually in the shape of a square or rectangle
b. **block** *n.*	the distance along a city street from where one street crosses it to the next
c. **block** *v.*	to stop anything or anyone from moving through or past a place
d. **patient** *adj.*	able to wait calmly for a long time, or to face difficulties without becoming angry or upset
e. **patient** *n.*	someone who is getting medical treatment

__*a*__ 1. The base of the statue was a **block** of white marble.

____ 2. The library is only two **blocks** away from here. We can walk there.

____ 3. I'm a **patient** of Dr. Vincent.

____ 4. A big man **blocked** the door. You had to show him your ticket to get through.

____ 5. It was hard to be **patient** in the long line because I had to get home by six o'clock.

WORDS IN SENTENCES

Complete each sentence with one of the words from the box.

blocks	defense	grateful	patient	respect
~~deaf~~	dozen	informed	relief	sharp

1. _____*Deaf*_____ people can still enjoy movies because the text can be read at the bottom of the screen.

2. After a month of dry weather, the farmers were _____ for the heavy rain.

3. Sirirat lives only a few _____ away, so we sometimes study together.

4. When it gets very busy at the restaurant, the owner himself helps in the kitchen. The employees _____ him all the more for this.

5. My parents taught me to be a(n) _____ shopper. They believe it's important to learn as much as you can about products and services before you pay money for them.

6. Ice skates need to be _____. If they aren't, you're more likely to slip on the ice.

7. The small fence was no _____ against the rabbit. It continued to feast on my mother's vegetable garden.

8. The doctor left the operating room to give the _____'s family the good news.

9. Glenio bought Daphne a(n) _____ roses on her birthday.

10. The electric fan only gave some _____ from the heat. Unfortunately, it was still hot in the house.

WORDS IN COLLOCATIONS AND EXPRESSIONS

Following are common collocations (word partners) and expressions with some of the key words. Read the definitions and then complete the conversations with the correct form of the collocations and expressions.

1. **dozen**		
	• **dozens of (sth)**	a lot of something; many
2. **grateful**		
	• **grateful to (sb) for (sth)**	feeling that you want to thank someone because of something kind that s/he has done
3. **inform**		
	• **inform (sb) of (sth)**	to tell someone about something in a serious way or in a serious situation
4. **respect**		
	• **show respect to (sb)**	to not be rude to someone because you think s/he is important
5. **sharp**		
	• **a sharp pain**	a sudden and very bad pain
	• **a sharp mind**	a sharp mind is one that can think and understand things very quickly

1.   TRAINER: We need to _____ *inform* _____ the director _____ *of* _____ any travel plans with plenty of notice.

     NEW EMPLOYEE: Is two weeks enough notice?

2.   FATHER: If you ever get stopped by a police officer, remember it's best to _____ him by calling him "Officer" and answering his questions politely.

     SON: I know. But let's hope I never get stopped.

3.   CARRIE: Have you ever gone to the Italian restaurant near the theater?

     GARTH: That's my family's favorite restaurant. We've been there _____ times.

4.   BROTHER: You're home early. I thought you were at the gym.

     SISTER: I had to stop exercising when I got _____ in my side.

5.   ROOMMATE 1:   I'd really like to show Roger, Steve, and Kelli how _____ we are _____ them _____ all their help with the move into our new place.

     ROOMMATE 2:   Why don't we invite them over for a special dinner?

6.   BRIAN: Have you met the new student, Misha?

     NICK: Yes. He has _____ and a good sense of humor. He's fun to talk to.

Read the two articles about medicine. Complete each one with words and expressions from the boxes.

a sharp pain	blocking	deaf	~~defense~~	relieve

WHAT YOUR DOCTOR NEVER TOLD YOU

Knowing a few interesting pieces of information can put you in better control of your
body's _____defense_____ and performance.
1

- The next time you have a toothache, don't cry. Just put some ice on the back of your hand between
  your thumb* and index finger†. The cold has a way of _____ your body's message to
  2
  the brain that says you're in pain.

- Are you worried you might be going _____? People may just be speaking too softly.
  3
  But you could also be listening with the wrong ear. Listen to speech with your left ear; your right
  ear is better at hearing music.

- Do you ever get _____ in your side when you run? If so, breathe out each time your
  4
  left foot hits the ground. Doing so with your right foot pushes on your liver‡, which then pulls
  painfully on your diaphragm§.

- Memories find their place in your mind during sleep, so if you want to remember a speech or
  other information, try reviewing it right before you go to bed.

You don't always need medicine to _____ pain, and sometimes there's a simple,
5
natural way to make life easier. You just need to understand how your body works.

The thumb (n.) is the thickest finger on your hand.

†The index finger (n.) is the finger next to the thumb.*

‡The liver (n.) is a large organ in your body that cleans your blood.*

§The diaphragm (n.) is the muscle between your lungs and your stomach that controls your breathing.*

(Based on information in Kate Dailey, "Cool Human Body Tricks." Men's Health, November 2005.)

dozens of	inform . . . of	patients
grateful	informed	respect

MEDICINE FROM AROUND THE WORLD

There are _____ medical practices around the world. You might think that each
6
practice stays within a group of people, but that's not so. Many people today are learning not only to
_____ other medical practices, but also to try new medicines from other countries. One
7

place that's helping to educate people is London's Science Museum. Its collection called "Living Medical Traditions*" shares the medicines of Indian, Chinese, Islamic, and African peoples.

Museum workers explain how _____ they are for the chance to put this newest
                                          8
collection together because it's given them a better understanding of the older ones. It's their hope to
_____ people _____ the different medical practices, both past and present.
          9
To put the collection together, organizers interviewed both _____ and practitioners.
                                                                          10
They plan to continue their work by holding discussions about all the different kinds of medicines, from Ayurveda (Indian) to Unani Tibb (Islamic), so everyone can be better _____. The
                                                                                              11
museum doesn't place more importance on any one of the practices over the others; it wants visitors to understand that together with Western medicine these other practices create a rich world of medicine.

*A tradition (n.) is a belief or way of doing something that has existed for a long time.

(Based on information in "Amazing Medical Objects from around the World to Go on Display for the First Time Ever at the Science Museum." Press release by the Science Museum UK, February 21, 2006.)

WORDS IN DISCUSSION

Apply the key words to your own life. Read and discuss the questions with a partner. Try to use the key words.

1. Name someone you know with **a sharp mind**.

   EXAMPLE

   *My girlfriend has **a** really **sharp mind**. It's one of the things I love about her.*

2. How many city **blocks** can you walk before you get tired?
3. Who are you **grateful** to have in your life?
4. Do you know how to **defend** yourself from a physical attack?
5. Talk about a time when you weren't very **patient**.

WORDS IN WRITING

Write a short answer (1–2 sentences) for each question. Try to use the key words.

1. Name something you have **dozens of**.

   EXAMPLE

   *I have **dozens of** CDs. My friends and I sometimes make CDs for one another.*

2. Give an example of when it's important to **inform** people **of** a change in your life.
3. Your friend is afraid to fly on planes. How can you **relieve** his or her fears?
4. What are some difficulties for **deaf** people?
5. How can you **show respect to** your teachers?

QUIZ 5

PART A

Choose the word that best completes each item and write it in the space provided.

1. The ship was far away and looked small on the _____*horizon*_____.
   - a. horizon
   - b. courage
   - c. peace
   - d. dozen

2. After twenty-five years in prison, the man got out and began to enjoy _____ again.
   - a. patience
   - b. courage
   - c. concern
   - d. freedom

3. The tour leader stood on a(n) _____ of wood so that we could all see her.
   - a. ache
   - b. concern
   - c. block
   - d. peace

4. My aunt is _____, but she can find her way around with little or no help.
   - a. steady
   - b. separate
   - c. sharp
   - d. blind

5. I broke the vase and cut my finger on a _____ piece of glass.
   - a. grateful
   - b. separate
   - c. sharp
   - d. blind

6. Do you know how to _____ this machine? I'm not sure how it works.
   - a. expect
   - b. operate
   - c. defend
   - d. relieve

7. Let's talk about money for college another time. That's a _____ conversation.
   - a. steady
   - b. separate
   - c. sharp
   - d. blind

8. Since we had a long wait, we began to tell stories to _____ our boredom.
   - a. expect
   - b. operate
   - c. pretend
   - d. relieve

9. What are you doing here today? We didn't _____ you to arrive until tomorrow.
   - a. expect
   - b. mention
   - c. pretend
   - d. relieve

10. You need a _____ hand in order to sew.
    - a. steady
    - b. wise
    - c. grateful
    - d. blind

PART B

*Read each statement and write **T** for true or **F** for false in the space provided.*

__T__ 1. If you **reserve** a table at a restaurant, you shouldn't have to wait to be seated.

_____ 2. A **deaf** person has difficulty seeing or cannot see at all.

_____ 3. We feel **grateful** to people who are kind and helpful.

_____ 4. The army is not allowed to have **standards**.

_____ 5. You are **fortunate** if you lose your wallet.

_____ 6. A country that fights many wars enjoys little **peace**.

_____ 7. An **ache** in your body is a good feeling.

_____ 8. It is not **wise** to use a radio near a sink or bathtub.

_____ 9. A clear, sunny day is **ideal** weather for flying by plane.

_____ 10. It is natural for parents to feel **concern** when their children are sick.

PART C

Each situation shows the meaning of one of the key words. Write the appropriate key word next to the situation. Use the clues in italics.

actual	defend	eager	mention	pretend
courage	dozen	~~inform~~	patience	respect

1. We asked the doctors to *tell us* right away if there's any change in Uncle Zachary's health.   ___*inform*___

2. It was clear that the students had a *strong interest* in science and a *strong wish* to learn as much as possible.   _____

3. The plates and bowls come in a *set of twelve*. That should be plenty for family gatherings.   _____

4. Chulsoo *wrote just a few words* about his new job; most of his letter was about his family and friends.   _____

5. The *real* experience of seeing the Great Wall of China was even better than I *believed* it could be.   _____

6. I knew Ruth's secret, but I *behaved* as if I didn't know the *truth*.   _____

7. There's no need to get upset. Let's be *calm* and *wait* a little longer, and I'm sure they'll find our suitcases.   _____

8. The situation became *dangerous*, but Ali had to be *brave*.   _____

9. I have a *high opinion* of people who are not afraid to say they made a mistake.   _____

10. Soldiers are trained to *protect* their country and the people living in it.   _____

Key Words

bunch	loan	postpone	rough	sincere
condition	official	praise	shelter	wage

WORDS IN CONTEXT

Use the sentences to guess what each key word means. Choose the meaning that is closest to that of the key word in **bold**.

1. **bunch**
   /bʌntʃ/
   -noun

   • I took a **bunch** of carrots and put it in my shopping cart.
   • There was a **bunch** of letters in the mailbox when I came home from my trip.

   Bunch means . . .   (a.) a group of things   b. a large box of things   c. a small gift

2. **condition**
   /kənˈdɪʃən/
   -noun

   • My brother bought a used car that's eight years old, but it's in great **condition**.
   • After the war, people lived in poor **conditions**: no heat, little food, and ruined buildings.

   Condition means . . .   a. a period of time   b. a state of being   c. a temperature

3. **loan**
   /loʊn/
   -noun

   • Trudy received a generous **loan** to help pay for law school.
   • Tess and Keith need some money to fix their roof, so they are trying to get a **loan** from their bank.

   Loan means . . .   a. money you get as a gift   b. money you borrow   c. money you work for

4. **official**
   /əˈfɪʃəl/
   -adjective

   • A passport is an **official** document that shows which country you're from.
   • We all know that William will be the new director, but we have to wait for the **official** decision before we congratulate him on his new position.

   Official means . . .   a. coming from those in power   b. correct or true   c. done or made over a long period of time

5. **postpone**
   /poʊstˈpoʊn/
   -verb

   • If the snow gets any worse, we'll have to **postpone** the party until the storm is over.
   • The director fell ill yesterday, so she **postponed** the meeting until next week.

   Postpone means . . .   a. to move an event to a later time   b. to keep an event at the same time   c. to organize an event

6. **praise**
   /preiz/
   -verb

   • I was a little embarrassed when the teacher **praised** me for the essay I wrote.
   • My sister **praises** my little nephew for small things like tying his shoes.

   Praise means . . .   a. to yell at someone   b. to give a hug   c. to say someone has done well

7. rough
/rʌf/
-adjective

- The fisherman's hands were **rough** from many years of hard work.
- I used the tree to sit and rest; I didn't care that it was **rough** against my back.

Rough means . . .   a. sharp and not safe   b. cold and not comfortable   c. not smooth or soft

8. shelter
/'ʃɛltɚ/
-noun

- Do not run to the trees for **shelter** during a rainstorm. Lightning hits tall objects.
- The church served as a **shelter** after the flood. Many families lived there for days.

Shelter means . . .   a. a place to visit   b. a safe place   c. a free place to live

9. sincere
/sɪn'sɪr/
-adjective

- I truly needed your help today. You have my **sincere** thanks.
- Rita said the meal was delicious, but I don't think she was being **sincere**. She only ate a few bites of the food on her plate.

Sincere means . . .   a. careful   b. honest and true   c. excited

10. wage
/weɪdʒ/
-noun

- I enjoyed my summer job, but the hourly **wage** was low.
- In a city like New York a **wage** of seven dollars an hour is not much to live on.

Wage means . . .   a. the number of hours you work each day   b. the money you pay to live somewhere   c. the money you receive for your work

WORDS AND DEFINITIONS

Match each key word with its definition.

1. _____praise_____ to say good things about someone, especially in the presence of others

2. _____ the amount of money you receive for work you do, usually for each hour

3. _____ to change an event to a later time or date

4. _____ a group or number of similar people or things, or a large amount of something

5. _____ a given agreement or something done by someone in power

6. _____ honest and true, or based on what you really feel or believe

7. _____ a place that protects you from danger or the weather

8. _____ the state that something or someone is in

9. _____ an amount of money that you borrow from a bank

10. _____ having an uneven feel, not smooth or soft

Choose the best answer.

1. The mother **praised** her child for
   a. running into the home with dirty shoes.
   b. getting good grades in school.
   c. opening the door.

2. The professor **postponed** the lecture;
   a. it was one hour longer than usual.
   b. she gave us additional homework to do instead.
   c. we're meeting later in the week instead.

3. Which of the following items is **rough**?
   a. a silk scarf
   b. a concrete sidewalk
   c. a cotton tablecloth

4. It's normal for a buyer to ask about the physical **condition** of all the following items EXCEPT
   a. a house.
   b. a car.
   c. a plane ticket.

5. If I have a **bunch** of nuts,
   a. I don't have enough to share with you.
   b. I have enough to share with you.
   c. I have no more because I ate them all.

6. The **official** language of a country is
   a. what is spoken in every home.
   b. what all tourists must learn.
   c. what politicians, teachers, and businessmen must use.

7. When a bank **loans** you money,
   a. they keep it safe for you.
   b. you must pay it back.
   c. you can quit your job forever.

8. Donna's kind words were **sincere**;
   a. I could tell by the sweet smile on her face.
   b. she often lies.
   c. she had a hard time talking to me.

9. Gideon receives a high **wage**
   a. his long hours make him very tired.
   b. so he's able to rent an apartment by himself.
   c. because he studies very hard.

10. Which of the following people need **shelter**?
    a. a family relaxing on the beach
    b. children living on the streets
    c. college students looking for part-time work

▍WORD FAMILIES

Now that you have studied the ten key words and their basic definitions, you are ready to learn words that belong to the same family as some of the key words. A word family includes words that look alike but have different functions (noun, verb, adjective, or adverb). Their meanings are related but different.

A. *Look at each model phrase and decide whether the word in **bold** is used as a noun, verb, adjective, or adverb.*

	NOUN	VERB	ADJECTIVE	ADVERB
1. loan				
• ask for a **loan**	✓			
• to **loan** money to your friend		✓		
2. official				
• an **official** document				
• ask the **official**				
• **officially** done				
3. praise				
• loudly **praised** the student's performance				
• to receive a lot of **praise**				
4. shelter				
• found **shelter**				
• can **shelter** us from the rain				
5. sincere				
• a **sincere** thank-you				
• to speak **sincerely**				

B. *Read the first half of each sentence and match it with the appropriate ending.*

<u> d </u> 1. The parade was well organized thanks to

_____ 2. Rani forgot her wallet at home, so I

_____ 3. The politician wasn't thinking of public opinion; he

_____ 4. The director was very pleased to read

_____ 5. Martin Luther King, Jr. Day

_____ 6. The mother bird

a. all the **praise** for his movie in the newspapers.

b. **officially** became a U.S. holiday in 1983.

c. **sheltered** her eggs from the cold rain.

d. the **officials**. They kept everything under control.

e. **sincerely** wanted to help the people.

f. **loaned** her five dollars for lunch.

SAME WORD, DIFFERENT MEANING

Most words have more than one meaning. Study the additional meanings of **condition**, **rough**, *and* **wage**. *Then read each sentence and decide which meaning is used.*

a.	**condition** *n.*	the state that something or someone is in
b.	**condition** *n.*	a person or animal's state of health (used especially when the person or animal is under a doctor's care)
c.	**rough** *adj.*	having an uneven feel; not smooth or soft
d.	**rough** *adj.*	using physical strength or action that might hurt others
e.	**wage** *singular n.*	the amount of money you receive for work that you do, usually for each hour of work
f.	**wages** *plural n.*	the money you get each day, week, or month for the work you do, usually paid by the hour

__*b*__ 1. At the hospital, the doctor talked to us about Grandmother's **condition**.

_____ 2. When the girl fell, she hurt her knees on the **rough** sidewalk.

_____ 3. Because I walked in the mud, my shoes were no longer in great **condition**.

_____ 4. The restaurant workers complained about their low **wage** and long hours.

_____ 5. The police officer himself had to be a little **rough** in order to stop the fight.

_____ 6. I receive my **wages** by check every other week.

WORDS IN SENTENCES

Complete each sentence with one of the words from the box.

bunch	loan	postpone	rough	sincerely
condition	officially	~~praise~~	shelter	wage

1. The artist received a lot of _____*praise*_____ for his newest paintings.

2. The cat's poor _____ made me think that it had no home.

3. We had no umbrella, but my dad tried to _____ me with a newspaper.

4. I _____ money to friends when they really need it; they always pay me back.

5. The new dentist was a little _____. I'm almost scared to go back to her.

6. You need a job that pays an hourly _____ of nine dollars or more if you want to pay your rent.

7. Nelson had no time for lunch; he grabbed a(n) _____ of crackers and ran out the door.

8. I don't feel ready for the exam; maybe I'll get lucky and the teacher will _____ it.

9. Did you know that the captain of a ship can _____ marry people?

10. I _____ hope Lisa will be happy with her new husband.

WORDS IN COLLOCATIONS AND EXPRESSIONS

Following are common collocations (word partners) and expressions with some of the key words. Read the definitions and then complete the conversations with the correct form of the collocations and expressions.

1. **bunch**
   - **a whole bunch of (sth)** — a large amount of something

2. **condition**
   - **in good condition** — in a good state
   - **in no condition to (do sth)** — not in a healthy enough state to do a certain activity

3. **loan**
   - **loan (sth) to (sb) (loan sb sth)** — to lend someone something, especially money

4. **rough**
   - **rough conditions** — a situation in which one faces difficulties and discomfort

5. **shelter**
   - **take shelter** — to find a place that protects you from danger or the weather

---

1. ROB: I know this apartment is old, but your hardwood floors are _____*in good condition*_____.

   MARCUS: Thanks. When I removed the old carpet, I was happily surprised.

2. DORA: You camped in the woods for one whole week?

   RICH: It's true we lived in _____, but I loved being so close to nature.

3. YURI: You've been going to your sister's house a lot lately. Is she okay?

   TANNER: Merryl hurt her back last week. She's _____ do housework, so I help her when I can.

4. SON: If you know a tornado* is coming, you should _____ in your basement.

   FATHER: Where did you learn that? That's right, but luckily we don't have tornadoes here.

5. LAUREN: My sister cleaned out her closet and found _____ clothes that were too small.

   LYNN: So that's where you got all the new clothes from. She has good taste. You're lucky.

6. SHANNA: Can you _____ fifty dollars _____ me? I get paid next week, so it's not for long.

   PAM: Well, if it's just until next week, that's all right. I don't have much extra cash now.

---

*A tornado (n.) is a very strong wind storm that can cause a lot of damage.

WORDS IN READINGS

Read the two articles about being in service to others. Complete each one with words and expressions from the boxes.

loans	official	~~postpone~~	sincerely	wage

A TIME TO THINK AND A TIME TO HELP

Where will I live? What do I really want to do? These are the kinds of questions that many in their early twenties are not ready to answer. One way to _____postpone_____ these big decisions is to enter a

1
program called Teach for America. When young adults agree to teach in poor schools for a period of two years, they not only have time to think about their future, they also have a chance to make a difference in the lives of many schoolchildren in need of an education.

These young people do not have the _____ teaching papers schools usually ask for,

2
but they are all strong students themselves, most have experience with children, and each of them
_____ wants to help his or her country. While they work in the program, they receive the

3
same _____ as other beginning teachers. Then after the two-year period, they get $9,450,

4
which they can use to help pay their education _____ or use for additional schooling.

5

Many who finish the program go on to become doctors, lawyers, and architects. But more than half of these young adults choose to continue working in education, thanks to their experience with Teach for America.

(Based on information in Tamar Lewin, "Options Open, Top Graduates Line Up to Teach the Poor." New York Times, October 2, 2005.)

a whole bunch of	conditions	praises	rough conditions	shelters

LESSONS ABOUT THE WORLD OUTSIDE SCHOOL

Ten Canadian students from Fort McMurray are learning about the world in a very special way. They use their free time to work in _____ different organizations that help others, from

6
soup kitchens that prepare meals for those who are hungry to _____ for women and

7
children who need a safe place to stay. They all belong to a club at Father Patrick Mercredi High School, and their hope is to give other teenagers a deeper understanding of the problems in their town, in their country, and in the world today.

One of the club leaders, Racette Griffin, _____ her group of teens: "They've learned a

8
lot, and they were always sensitive* to the needs of others."

Sensitive (adj.) is to be able to understand the feelings, problems, etc. of other people.

Their next plan is to travel to Mexico to visit an orphanage*. The teens will live and work in _____ that are completely new for them: sleeping on the floor, not having a private bathroom, and living without air conditioning in the summer heat.

For Kathryn Dimla and her classmates, _____ are part of the experience. Of the people in the other places the club has gone to, Kathryn says, "They are normal people, just with a little less."

*An orphanage (n.) is a place for children whose parents are dead or unable to care for them.

(Based on information in Paula Ogonoski, "Students Reach Out to Help Others." Fort McMurray Today online, March 8, 2006.)

▌WORDS IN DISCUSSION

Apply the key words to your own life. Read and discuss the questions with a partner. Try to use the key words.

1. Do you have a **bunch** of clothes that are all the same color?

   EXAMPLE

   *I do. I have a **bunch** of things in black: shoes, shirts, pants . . .*

2. How do you know if someone is speaking **sincerely**?
3. Can you name the **official** holidays of your country?
4. Name something that's **rough** to the touch.
5. Can you name a job with a low **wage**? How about a high **wage**?

▌WORDS IN WRITING

Write a short answer (1–2 sentences) for each question. Try to use the key words.

1. Do you **loan** money **to** friends?

   EXAMPLE

   *My friends and I don't **loan** money **to** one another, but we often take turns paying when we go out.*

2. When should teachers **praise** students?
3. Have you ever **postponed** a trip? What's a good reason for doing this?
4. How can you keep a pair of new shoes **in good condition**?
5. If you are far from home, where can you **take shelter** during a storm?

Key Words

balance	guide	honor	loyal	position
deal	hesitate	local	matter	support

WORDS IN CONTEXT

*Use the sentences to guess what each key word means. Choose the meaning that is closest to that of the key word in **bold**.*

1. **balance**
   /ˈbæləns/
   -noun

   • Li carefully held her **balance** on the top step of the ladder as she painted the ceiling.

   • Monkeys have good **balance**; they use it to climb trees.

   Balance means . . .
   a. a strong and useful piece of equipment
   b. a state in which you hold your breath
   c. a state in which you are not shaking or falling

2. **deal**
   /dil/
   -noun

   • The two businessmen will discuss a **deal** to create a new company.

   • The band signed a **deal** to perform three nights a week at the night club.

   Deal means . . .
   a. a law or rule
   b. an agreement
   c. a suggestion

3. **guide**
   /gaɪd/
   -noun

   • The **guide** led the tour group around the city.

   • The park is huge, and it's easy to get lost; inexperienced hikers should have a **guide**.

   Guide means . . .
   a. someone who sells tickets for travel and tourism
   b. someone who shows you the way
   c. someone who invites guests

4. **hesitate**
   /ˈhɛzəˌteɪt/
   -verb

   • Elaine needed a moment to consider her answer, so she **hesitated** before speaking.

   • Devin is very wealthy; he never **hesitates** to buy something he really likes.

   Hesitate means . . .
   a. to pause
   b. to worry
   c. to ask for help

5. **honor**
   /ˈanɚ/
   -noun

   • The whole family gathered in **honor** of the grandmother's seventy-fifth birthday.

   • At the funeral, soldiers shot twenty-one times from their guns to show **honor** for the dead general.

   Honor means . . .
   a. sadness
   b. celebration
   c. respect

6. **local**
   /ˈloʊkəl/
   -adjective

   • Boston newspapers report national news as well as **local** news.

   • My **local** library doesn't have the book I need, but the library in a neighboring town can send it to me.

   Local means . . .
   a. having to do with one area
   b. having to do with the whole country
   c. having to do with the present time

7. **loyal**
/lɔɪəl/
-adjective

- Dogs are called man's best friend because they're considered to be **loyal** animals.
- The **loyal** soldiers fought to their death to protect their king and their country.

Loyal means . . .   a. being strong enough to fight   b. never changing your good feelings for someone or something   c. happy and friendly to all

8. **matter**
/mætɚ/
-noun

- Lying at a job interview is a serious **matter**. Dishonesty always causes problems.
- Gigi is unsure about going to college. She will discuss the **matter** with her teachers.

Matter means . . .   a. a difficult subject or situation   b. a bad decision or action   c. a serious crime

9. **position**
/pəˈzɪʃən/
-noun

- The ballerina held her **position** as her partner lifted her into the air.
- It was a long bus ride, and Myrna's whole body hurt after sitting in the same **position** the whole time.

Position means . . .   a. the way you stand or sit   b. a long and serious look   c. comfortable shoes

10. **support**
/səˈpɔrt/
-verb

- Do you **support** the idea of keeping people in prison for life, or are you against it?
- The Vice President told the newspaper that he **supported** the President's decision, but privately he disagreed.

Support means . . .   a. to suggest   b. to question   c. to say that you agree

WORDS AND DEFINITIONS

Match each key word with its definition.

1. _____deal_____ an agreement especially in business or politics

2. _____ never changing your good feelings for a person, a set of beliefs, or a country

3. _____ having to do with a place or area, especially the place you live in

4. _____ a subject or situation that you have to think about or face, often one that causes problems

5. _____ to pause before doing or saying something because you are uncertain

6. _____ someone whose job it is to show you the way to a place

7. _____ the way someone stands or sits, or the direction in which an object is pointing

8. _____ to say that you agree with an idea, group, or person and want him, her, or it to succeed

9. _____ a state in which even use of body weight helps you stay in one place without shaking or falling

10. _____ the respect that someone or something receives from other people

COMPREHENSION CHECK

Choose the best answer.

1. Terry works as a **guide** at the university;
   a. she often helps professors correct tests and essays.
   b. her students enjoy her classes very much.
   c. she gives campus tours about two times a week.

2. If a gymnast loses her **balance** during a performance, she
   a. will win the competition.
   b. can fall and hurt herself.
   c. should find a new coach.

3. When you make a bad decision that causes a problem, a **loyal** friend
   a. tells you to fix the problem on your own.
   b. doesn't remind you of your mistake but helps you fix it.
   c. embarrasses you by telling others about your bad decision.

4. Which of the following is NOT an example of people making a **deal**
   a. A politician and a crime leader decide to help one another gain power.
   b. A salesperson and a customer agree on a price.
   c. A literature teacher recommends a book to her students.

5. Which of the following people will NOT likely **hesitate**?
   a. Cynthia is confident of her answer to the teacher's question.
   b. Hyungsub must go on stage to perform, but he's very nervous.
   c. Gwen is afraid that telling the truth will hurt Ben's feelings.

6. Which of the following is NOT a **matter** that family members usually argue over?
   a. how to spend money
   b. who gets to choose a TV program
   c. what the weather will be like tomorrow

7. Ned works in a **local** factory, so he
   a. often chooses to walk instead of taking the bus.
   b. spends much time driving there and back every day.
   c. doesn't get paid very well.

8. If the employees **support** the director's new plan, they will
   a. complain about all the problems the plan can create.
   b. work together with him to make it happen.
   c. ask the director to explain it again in simpler words.

9. Which of the following situations is NOT an example of showing **honor**?
   a. A family asks the grandfather to sit at the head of the table.
   b. A waiter smiles as he says hello and introduces himself.
   c. Townspeople greet their returning soldiers with a parade.

10. People usually do all of the following activities in a sitting **position** EXCEPT
    a. play the piano.
    b. write a long letter.
    c. paint a room.

WORD FAMILIES

Now that you have studied the ten key words and their basic definitions, you are ready to learn words that belong to the same family as some of the key words. A word family includes words that look alike but have different functions (noun, verb, adjective, or adverb). Their meanings are related but different.

A. *Look at each model phrase and decide whether the word in **bold** is used as a noun, verb, adjective, or adverb.*

	NOUN	VERB	ADJECTIVE	ADVERB
1. **balance**				
• have good **balance**	✓			
• try to **balance** two things		✓		
2. **guide**				
• to work as a **guide**				
• will **guide** us around campus				
3. **hesitate**				
• often **hesitate** to spend so much				
• understand your **hesitation**				
4. **loyal**				
• a **loyal** friend				
• respect your **loyalty**				
5. **matter**				
• a difficult **matter**				
• what **matters** to me				
6. **support**				
• cannot **support** your idea				
• to need their **support**				

B. *Read each sentence and match the word in **bold** with the correct definition.*

_e_ 1. I was lost until the librarian **guided** me to the right bookshelf.

____ 2. The company expects **loyalty** from its workers. People spend many years working here.

____ 3. The waitress skillfully **balanced** all the drinks on her tray.

____ 4. I don't understand your **hesitation** to take the job. It's perfect for you!

____ 5. Public television needs financial **support** from viewers.

____ 6. Does it **matter** if we eat dinner a little later tonight? Will it ruin any plans?

a. the action of pausing because you are uncertain

b. to be important, or to cause a change or have an influence on what happens

c. to get in a steady position without falling to one side or the other or to put something in this position

d. the things people do to help something succeed, or the act of helping it succeed

e. to take and show someone around a place that you know very well

f. unchanging feelings for someone or something you like or care for

SAME WORD, DIFFERENT MEANING

*Most words have more than one meaning. Study the additional meanings of **balance**, **guide**, **position**, and **support**. Then read each sentence and decide which meaning is used.*

a.	**balance** *n.*	a state in which even use of body weight helps you stay steady and not fall
b.	**balance** *n.*	a state in which different things are given equal importance
c.	**guide** *v.*	to take someone around a place that you know very well and show it to him or her
d.	**guide** *v.*	to strongly influence someone
e.	**position** *n.*	the way someone stands or sits, or the direction in which an object is pointing
f.	**position** *n.*	a job, or the level of your job within a company
g.	**support** *v.*	to say that you agree with an idea, group, person, etc. and want him, her, or it to succeed
h.	**support** *v.*	to give enough money for someone to live

__a__ 1. When I got off the roller coaster, I had trouble keeping my **balance**.

_____ 2. The basketball coach **guided** his players to become a stronger team.

_____ 3. Surprisingly, most of the students **support** the idea of wearing uniforms.

_____ 4. Martina has found a **balance** between career and family.

_____ 5. Our Belgian hosts **guided** us around Brussels and showed us their favorite places.

_____ 6. Eva found it difficult to hold the same **position** while the artist drew her picture.

_____ 7. After the divorce, Edward continued to **support** his ex-wife and children.

_____ 8. Hello. I'm calling to see if the **position** for a secretary is still open.

WORDS IN SENTENCES

Complete each sentence with one of the words from the box.

balanced	guided	honor	loyalty	position
deals	hesitation	~~local~~	matters	support

1. This area is popular for skiing, so _____*local*_____ businesses make most of their money during the winter season.

2. Cliff _____ the large box on one shoulder and walked up the stairs.

3. Money is important, but is that all that _____?

4. We raise flags in _____ of the soldiers who fought and died for our country.

5. When the actor received his award, he thanked his family for their _____.

6. The dishonest police officer was making money from _____ with criminals.

7. The salesperson saw Eric's _____ to buy the car and lowered the price.

8. Tami's been in the same _____ for four years at work. She isn't happy.

9. The flight attendant _____ the blind passenger to his seat.

10. Leo thought about quitting the soccer team, but _____ to his teammates stopped him from doing it.

WORDS IN COLLOCATIONS AND EXPRESSIONS

Following are common collocations (word partners) and expressions with some of the key words. Read the definitions and then complete the conversations with the correct form of the collocations and expressions.

1. **balance**
   - **lose your balance** — to be unable to keep from falling or shaking
   - **balance (one thing) with (another)** — to give equal importance to two or more things

2. **deal**
   - **deal with** — to not lose confidence or to not become too upset in a difficult situation

3. **matter**
   - **make matters worse** — to make a situation more difficult
   - **(to be) a matter of money, respect, etc.** — a decision or situation that concerns money, respect, or something else

4. **position**
   - **not in a position to (do sth)** — to not have the power or money to do something

1. WORKER 1: I hate when the boss yells at us. I can't ____*deal with*____ it.

    WORKER 2: Don't let it upset you too much.

2. PATIENT: Did I hurt my back seriously?

    DOCTOR: You'll be fine in about a month. Be sure to rest and be careful on the stairs. If you _____ and fall again, the result could be much more serious.

3. TRAVIS: Did you explain to Heather that Stephanie is your cousin?

    BRENT: No. It's _____ trust. Heather should know me well enough to trust me.

4. GRETCHEN: Why don't we tell the teacher why I let you copy the homework from me?

    LONI: No, you'll just _____. Let's not make her any angrier.

5. PLAYER 1: How do you like playing on our team?

    PLAYER 2: We have some really good players. I don't always agree with what the coach tells us to do, but since I'm still kind of new, I'm _____ suggest changes.

6. STUDENT 1: How do you find time to exercise? I feel like I'm always studying.

    STUDENT 2: You need to _____ your studies _____ some kind of activity to relax. I spend a lot of time studying, too, but staying healthy is also important.

WORDS IN READINGS

Read the two articles about careers. Complete each one with words and expressions from the boxes.

deal with	~~guided~~	honor	local	support (*n.*)	support (*v.*)

FIRST JOBS, FIRST LESSONS

Lessons learned from first jobs have _____*guided*_____ more than one person to success. Their
___1___
stories teach us that everyday places can become life's classroom.

Clint Black is a famous country singer. Making a career in the music world hasn't been easy, but
he's learned not to quit even when there's not a lot of _____. He believes his first job at
___2___
fourteen taught him how to be strong. He worked after school trying to get new customers for a
_____ newspaper. After knocking on people's doors, he heard "no" many times, but he
___3___
learned to keep going.

Louis Caldera studied at the U.S. Military Academy and Harvard University before becoming the
Secretary of the Army. When he was ten, he began to help his mother and father as they cleaned a
shopping center parking lot—at three o'clock in the morning. With school, homework, and a job, he
learned to _____ having a lot to do and little time to do it. He also learned that there's
___4___
_____ in all jobs; we should respect people who work to _____ themselves
___5___   ___6___
and their families.

In every successful person's past there's at least one good lesson that helped them get where they
are today.

(Based on information in Daniel Levine, "My First Job." Reader's Digest online, 2001.)

balance	hesitate	loyal	matters	positions

KEEPING WORKERS HAPPY

It's easy to see differences between older and younger people today in the workplace. Those in their
fifties are usually very _____ to one company because they've worked there for years.
___7___
They started in low _____ and worked their way up to higher ones. But those in their
___8___
twenties move around more easily, looking for what makes them happy.

What _____ to today's younger worker? It's not money or power. 77 percent wouldn't
___9___
_____ to move to a new company for the chance to do more interesting work. 51 percent
___10___
would quit if they could work from home for another company. 61 percent would leave their present
job for another that let them make their own schedule.

Are there companies that give younger workers what they want? Yes. For example, Whole Foods Markets understands that younger workers like to feel equal, so everyone works on teams and takes turns being the leader. The Michigan company Plante & Moran understands the need for _____ in one's life, so they teach new parents how to spend less time in the office and more time at home.

In short, companies today keep workers with the right conditions, not loyalty.

(Based on information in Anne Fisher, "What Do Gen Xers Want." CNN Money online, January 17, 2006.)

▌WORDS IN DISCUSSION

Apply the key words to your own life. Read and discuss the questions with a partner. Try to use the key words.

1. Who gives you the most **support**?

   EXAMPLE

   *My father's really great, and he gives me a lot of **support**. He often gives me more confidence in myself.*

2. How often do you eat in a standing **position**?
3. Do you know any city well enough to **guide** a group of tourists?
4. Can you recommend a **local** restaurant?
5. Do people make **deals** with salespeople in your country, or does everything have a fixed price?

▌WORDS IN WRITING

Write a short answer (1–2 sentences) for each question. Try to use the key words.

1. Do you have to **balance** your studies **with** something else? Explain.

   EXAMPLE

   *I'm on the basketball team, so I have to **balance** sports **with** school.*

2. Is family **loyalty** important to you? Give an example of family **loyalty**.
3. Was there ever a time when telling the truth **made matters worse**?
4. Do you sometimes **hesitate** to speak in English?
5. Name someone you have shown **honor** to.

▍WORDS IN CONTEXT

*Use the sentences to guess what each key word means. Choose the meaning that is closest to that of the key word in **bold**.*

1. arrest
/əˈrɛst/
-verb

- The police **arrested** the angry sports fans who fought in the street after the game.
- They'll **arrest** the woman because she tried to steal clothes from the store.

Arrest means . . .   (a.) to catch a guilty person   b. to punish a guilty person   c. to forgive a guilty person

2. beat
/bit/
-verb

- Our school has the best basketball team in the state. No other team can **beat** us.
- Ralph **beat** everyone at cards. He didn't lose a single game.

Beat means . . .   a. to win   b. to teach someone a skill   c. to lie to someone

3. beg
/bɛg/
-verb

- The children **begged** their father for another bedtime story; they didn't want to sleep.
- Mrs. Evans **begged** her son not to get married because she believed the young woman only wanted his money and could never make him happy.

Beg means . . .   a. to try not to do something   b. to warn someone   c. to ask for something

4. envy
/ˈɛnvi/
-noun

- Shelly felt **envy** toward her older sister, who was dating a popular boy at school.
- Carl tried to hide his **envy** for all the nice things his rich friend had.

Envy means . . .   a. a feeling of not wanting help from others   b. a feeling of wanting to have what someone else has   c. a feeling of wanting to hurt or upset someone

5. evil
/ˈivəl/
-adjective

- The **evil** men stole children and sold them as slaves.
- The terrible witch used her **evil** magic to hurt the beautiful princess.

Evil means . . .   a. being ugly   b. being bad   c. being weak

6. **guard**
/gard/
-noun

- **Guards** at a bank must have guns; if there is a robbery, they can try to stop it.
- The **guard** took the lawyer through the jail to meet the prisoner.

Guard means . . .   a. someone who protects people and things   b. someone who kills others   c. someone who breaks the law

7. **point**
/pɔɪnt/
-noun

- The teacher asked Ty to state his **point** more quickly, so others could share their ideas.
- We discussed the writer's **point** and agreed she supported her opinion with examples.

Point means . . .   a. a plan   b. a question   c. an idea

8. **poison**
/ˈpɔɪzən/
-noun

- We had to use **poison** to kill the rats in our basement.
- In the play, Romeo was heartbroken without Juliet. He drank the **poison** and died.

Poison means . . .   a. something that hides you   b. something that can kill you   c. something that protects you

9. **rot**
/rat/
-verb

- You need to brush your teeth, or they will turn black as they **rot**.
- Some apples that fell to the ground lay there for days. Soon they began to **rot**.

Rot means . . .   a. to slowly be destroyed   b. to get dirty   c. to get old

10. **sore**
/sɔr/
-adjective

- We danced to every song at the party last night. Today my feet are **sore**.
- Leena broke her leg in childhood. It still gets **sore** during cold, rainy weather.

Sore means . . .   a. broken   b. painful   c. very large

▮ WORDS AND DEFINITIONS

Match each key word with its definition.

1. _____*beat*_____ to win over someone in a game or competition, or to do better than someone or something

2. _____ to catch someone and take him or her away because he or she is believed to be guilty of a crime

3. _____ a single fact, idea, or opinion in an argument or discussion

4. _____ being mean on purpose

5. _____ to slowly be destroyed by a natural chemical process, or to make something do this

6. _____ to ask for something you think is very important and want or need to have right away

7. _____ painful as a result of being hurt, having an infection (a disease or sickness in your body), or doing too much exercise

8. _____ something that can kill you or make you sick if you eat it, breathe it, etc.

9. _____ someone whose job is to protect people, places, or objects

10. _____ the feeling of wanting to have what someone else has

COMPREHENSION CHECK

Choose the best answer.

1. If I **envy** you your new leather jacket,
   a. I ask you to lend it to me.
   b. I want to have one just like it.
   c. I think it doesn't look nice on you.

2. Julie **beat** John;
   a. he wasn't happy about losing.
   b. she wasn't happy about losing.
   c. they played equally well.

3. The food was beginning to **rot**;
   a. the delicious smells made me hungry.
   b. we had to put it all back in the oven to get warm again.
   c. we had to throw it all away.

4. If Jack is **begging** you to visit him, he
   a. wants you to come right away.
   b. would like you to come when you get the chance.
   c. thinks it would be better to postpone your visit.

5. You can easily find a **guard** at each of the following places EXCEPT
   a. a museum.
   b. the palace of a king or queen.
   c. a bus stop.

6. Your arm might feel **sore** for any of the following reasons EXCEPT
   a. you cut it on broken glass.
   b. you played a long, hard game of tennis.
   c. you took a hot shower.

7. What will most likely happen if you breathe in **poison**?
   a. You'll get sick, and you may die.
   b. You'll sneeze loudly.
   c. You'll like the smell.

8. The teacher didn't understand the **point** of my paragraph;
   a. he asked me to explain my main idea.
   b. he asked me to type and not write by hand in the future.
   c. he asked me to add an example to strengthen my opinion.

9. Which of the following actions is **evil**?
   a. talking with your mouth full of food
   b. studying hard for a test
   c. telling lies to hurt someone

10. You can be **arrested** for
    a. walking too slowly.
    b. drinking alcohol and driving.
    c. standing on the bus.

▎WORD FAMILIES

Now that you have studied the ten key words and their basic definitions, you are ready to learn words that belong to the same family as some of the key words. A word family includes words that look alike but have different functions (noun, verb, adjective, or adverb). Their meanings are related but different.

A. *Look at each model phrase and decide whether the word in **bold** is used as a noun, verb, adjective, or adverb.*

	NOUN	VERB	ADJECTIVE	ADVERB
1. envy				
• look with **envy**	✓			
• never **envy** other people		✓		
• be **envious** of others			✓	
2. evil				
• an **evil** witch				
• fight against **evil**				
3. guard				
• the king's **guards**				
• to **guard** the gold				
4. poison				
• to drink the **poison**				
• a **poisonous** snake				
5. rot				
• will **rot** slowly				
• a **rotten** apple				

B. *Read the first half of each sentence and match it with the appropriate ending.*

_*d*_ 1. The castle was in danger, but the king's men

____ 2. The mother wanted to protect her children from

____ 3. There was an unpleasant smell coming from

____ 4. I admit that when my friend got the job I wanted I felt

____ 5. Ron has a way with people; I

____ 6. Some plants are

a. **poisonous**; they should be kept away from pets and small children.

b. **envy** him his ability to make friends.

c. **envious**. Even so I wished her well.

d. **guarded** it well.

e. all the **evil** in the world.

f. the **rotten** food; we needed to throw it away.

SAME WORD, DIFFERENT MEANING

Most words have more than one meaning. Study the additional meanings of **beat**, **beg**, and **point**. Then read each sentence and decide which meaning is used.

a.	**beat** v.	to win over someone in a game, competition, etc., or to do better than someone or something
b.	**beat** v.	to hit someone many times with something
c.	**beg** v.	to ask for something you think is very important and want or need to have right away
d.	**beg** v.	to ask someone for food, money, etc. because you are very poor
e.	**point** n.	a single fact, idea, or opinion in an argument or discussion
f.	**point** n.	the purpose of doing something
g.	**point** v.	to show someone something by holding your finger out toward it

__c__ 1. Molly **begged** Luke to understand and forgive her.

_____ 2. I saw no **point** to the exercise, so I decided not to do it.

_____ 3. Peng **beat** the competition easily; he was the strongest swimmer in every race.

_____ 4. In literature class, we discussed several **points** of the play.

_____ 5. The homeless woman stood in the subway and **begged** for money.

_____ 6. There were three different kinds of black boots, so I **pointed** to the pair I wanted the salesperson to bring.

_____ 7. The man was arrested for **beating** his wife.

WORDS IN SENTENCES

Complete each sentence with one of the words from the box.

arrested	begged	evil	point	rotten
beat	~~envy~~	guard	poisonous	sore

1. I _____envy_____ you your calm nature. Before a test, I get so nervous that I shake.

2. In most situations it isn't polite to _____ at other people.

3. The _____ egg cracked open and a strong smell filled the room.

4. After the dentist pulled my tooth, my mouth was _____ for a couple of days.

5. It's a crime to _____ your pet. If you see someone hurt an animal, report it to the police.

6. Carbon monoxide is a(n) _____ gas that cars put into the air we breathe.

7. The police _____ Mr. Wilson and questioned him about the murder.

8. Amanda and Abby bought a big dog to _____ their home.

9. Many films and books are about the fight between good and _____.

10. Dressed in old, dirty clothes, the hungry children _____ for food.

WORDS IN COLLOCATIONS AND EXPRESSIONS

Following are common collocations (word partners) and expressions with some of the key words. Read the definitions and then complete the conversations with the correct form of the collocations and expressions.

1. **arrest**
   - **arrest (sb) for (sth)** — to catch someone and take him/her away because s/he is believed to be guilty of a crime

2. **beat**
   - **beat (sb) to (sth)** — to get or do something before someone else is able to

3. **envy**
   - **be the envy of** — to be something that other people want

4. **point**
   - **point (sth) out** — to tell someone something that s/he does not already know or has not yet noticed
   - **make a point of (doing sth)** — to do something because you want to and you should

5. **sore**
   - **a sore point/spot** — something that is likely to make you upset or angry if others talk about it

1. DON: Dorothy's new red sports car is _____ *the envy of* _____ the neighborhood.

   GALINA: And I'm one of the people who'd love to have such a car!

2. BOSS: You've made a good suggestion, but I have to _____ that your plan would cost the company a lot of money.

   EMPLOYEE: Yes, but in time, the company will make it all back and then some.

3. TED: I don't think it's terrible for a homeless person to steal food.

   JEREMY: Well, it's easy to understand the person's reason, but the police still have the right

   to _____ anyone _____ trying

   to steal.

4. DANIELLA: Why didn't you ask Norma to the dance?

   CARLSON: I wanted to, but Chris _____ me

   _____ it. She already said yes to him.

5. MOTHER: Did you talk to Joan's teacher?

   FATHER: Yes, and to Joan, too. She knows she did poorly on the last exam, but she said

   she'll _____ studying more regularly from now on.

6. HUSBAND: Why do you think Mrs. Robinson got so upset when I asked about Doug's wedding?

   WIFE: His future wife was married three times before, so the subject is

   _____ with his mother.

WORDS IN READINGS

Read the three articles about readers' opinions. Complete each one with words and expressions from the boxes.

WHAT'S RIGHT OR WRONG

arrested	guard	rot

Question 1:

The rules state that students at my college cannot take food or drink out of the cafeteria. But if I run out with a sandwich because I'm late, is it wrong?

Reader's Opinion:

At my school, they had a(n) _____ at the exit to stop students from taking food. I remember
        1
how I nearly got "_____" for trying to take an orange and some water to a friend who
                2
wasn't feeling well. It was stupid. I had paid for the college meal plan. Would they rather see that

orange _____ or just be thrown away? A little more understanding was needed.
        3

(Based on information in "Reader's Opinion: You're the Ethicist." New York Times online, February 28, 2001.)

begged	envy	make a point of	poison

Question 2:

Can a good person do wrong things and still be good?

Reader's Opinion:

On the one hand, we all need to be a little bad; it's part of how we come to understand and live with the

rules that are made for us. On the other hand, as I get older, I find myself turning away from the bad

things my parents always _____ me not to do. And it's funny, because I'm not trying to
                4
_____ being good and following the rules; those bad things—like staying out all night,
    5
smoking, or eating a lot of candy—just make me tired or even sick. I _____ those young
                                                            6
people who party all night without feeling like there's _____ in their bodies the next day!
                                                7

(Based on information in "Reader's Opinion: You're the Ethicist." New York Times online, November 26, 2005.)

beats	evil	a sore point

Question 3:

Would it be wrong during a business meeting with foreigners to use an interpreter* even if you

understand their language quite well? Would it be even more wrong not to share this fact?

*An interpreter (n.) is someone who changes the spoken words of one language into another.

Reader's Opinion:

Using language in a disrespectful way is _____ with me. My family now lives in Japan,
                                                            8

and when we arrived, I taught my kids an important rule: Remember that people may understand

your language even if they can't speak it well. You should never use your own language as an excuse

to speak poorly of others or to share secrets. Language is not meant to be used as a(n)

_____ tool. Some international businessmen don't seem to understand this. Too bad if
              9

someone _____ them in a business deal because they thought no one understood them
                    10

and their secrets while they spoke in their own language at the meeting.

(Based on information in "Reader's Opinion: You're the Ethicist." New York Times online, November 26, 2005.)

▌WORDS IN DISCUSSION

Apply the key words to your own life. Read and discuss the questions with a partner. Try to use the key words.

1. Do you **envy** any of your friends?

   ### EXAMPLE

   *I **envy** my friend An-Mei. She has a pretty singing voice, and I sing quite badly.*

2. Is it polite in your country to **point** at things or people?

3. Are there any **poisonous** snakes where you live?

4. Name a well-known **evil** person from a film or book.

5. Is there any **rotten** food in your refrigerator at home?

▌WORDS IN WRITING

Write a short answer (1–2 sentences) for each question. Try to use the key words.

1. Is there a game you can **beat** most others at?

   ### EXAMPLE

   *I learned to play checkers as a small child. I can **beat** most of my friends.*

2. Did you ever **beg** your parents for something? Explain.

3. Your close friend has been **arrested** for the crime of shoplifting (stealing products from a store). Do you believe s/he's guilty?

4. If your feet are **sore** from walking too much, what can you do?

5. Do you **guard** secrets carefully or do you easily share them?

QUIZ 6

PART A

Choose the word that best completes each item and write it in the space provided.

1. A _____*bunch*_____ of flowers can give color and beauty to a room.
   - a. guide
   - b. shelter
   - c. bunch
   - d. guard

2. The dancer lost his _____ and fell.
   - a. guide
   - b. balance
   - c. matter
   - d. guard

3. Banks, schools, and most stores are closed on _____ holidays.
   - a. sore
   - b. loyal
   - c. sincere
   - d. official

4. A member of the audience shared an interesting _____, and the lecturer decided to discuss it further.
   - a. guide
   - b. balance
   - c. point
   - d. honor

5. The wood of the old boat was slowly _____; it sat in the water unused for so long.
   - a. rotting
   - b. beating
   - c. postponing
   - d. praising

6. Yoko has been a good and _____ friend of mine for many years.
   - a. sore
   - b. loyal
   - c. rough
   - d. official

7. My feet became _____ from walking outside without shoes in the summer.
   - a. evil
   - b. local
   - c. rough
   - d. sincere

8. Sam must decide what to study in college. He's given the _____ much thought.
   - a. guard
   - b. matter
   - c. position
   - d. honor

9. In some countries, students show _____ to their teachers by standing to greet them.
   - a. shelter
   - b. matter
   - c. point
   - d. honor

10. The criminal's act of harming young children was _____.
    - a. evil
    - b. loyal
    - c. sore
    - d. official

PART B

*Read each statement and write **T** for true or **F** for false in the space provided.*

_F_ 1. When you feel **envy**, you are truly happy with all that you have in life.

_____ 2. People want to know the **condition** of a house before they buy it.

_____ 3. A person without a home needs **shelter**, especially in the winter.

_____ 4. People **hesitate** when they are not certain what to say or do.

_____ 5. If the professor **postpones** a lesson, it means we'll never hear that lesson.

_____ 6. A **sincere** person often lies to others.

_____ 7. It can be difficult to stand up and walk if your legs are **sore**.

_____ 8. If I **support** your opinion, I disagree with you.

_____ 9. A **local** job requires you to travel a great distance.

_____ 10. When you receive a **loan**, you'll have to return the money in the future.

PART C

Each situation shows the meaning of one of the key words. Write the appropriate key word next to the situation. Use the clues in italics.

arrest	beg	guard	poison	praise
beat	deal	guide	position	wage

1. Mr. and Mrs. Dealey were pleased to hear the teachers *say* so many *good words* about their son. _____praise_____

2. The other woman played much *better*; she *won* the tennis match very quickly. _____

3. Owen's *job* is to *protect* the priceless artwork in the museum. _____

4. It's not unusual for people to complain about *the amount of money they receive for the work they do.* _____

5. I don't like the idea of *making business agreements* with friends. _____

6. They *took the criminal away* in the police car. _____

7. Virawat's *job* is to *show people their way* around the museum and give information about the different works of art. _____

8. The *bite* of some snakes can *cause death.* _____

9. The artist showed me *the way to sit* and where to look, and then he began to draw my picture. _____

10. Flavia wanted to go camping with her friends, and she *asked* her parents to give their permission for the trip *right away.* _____

Key Words

class	fresh	liquid	opportunity	quality
exchange	interrupt	mild	permanent	trick

WORDS IN CONTEXT

Use the sentences to guess what each key word means. Choose the meaning that is closest to that of the key word in **bold***.*

1. **class**
   /klæs/
   -noun

   • Money, jobs, and education place people in the lower, middle, or upper **class**.

   • Our mayor is not from a rich family. He grew up in the working **class**.

   Class means . . .   a. a political party   (b.) a similar group of people   c. a club

2. **exchange**
   /ɪksˈtʃeɪndʒ/
   -verb

   • These jeans are too small. Can I **exchange** them for a bigger pair?

   • Cassie is **exchanging** English conversation practice for Italian lessons with Lucia.

   Exchange means . . .   a. to give in return for something   b. to pay for something   c. to borrow something

3. **fresh**
   /frɛʃ/
   -adjective

   • The maid brings **fresh** towels to our hotel room every morning.

   • Nick made sure the water in the dog's bowl was **fresh** before he left for school.

   Fresh means . . .   a. additional or new   b. unusual or special   c. warm

4. **interrupt**
   /ˌɪntəˈrʌpt/
   -verb

   • Lisa **interrupts** others in class when she's too excited to wait for her turn to speak.

   • Bailey **interrupted** us to ask who we were talking about.

   Interrupt means . . .   a. to question someone   b. to yell at someone in anger or excitement   c. to stop someone from speaking

5. **liquid**
   /ˈlɪkwɪd/
   -noun

   • Above 32°F (0°C), ice melts and becomes a **liquid**.

   • Bottles are used to hold **liquids** such as water, shampoo, and medicine.

   Liquid means . . .   a. something that you breathe   b. something that can flow or be poured   c. something that is hard and doesn't move

6. **mild**
   /maɪld/
   -adjective

   • The crime wasn't serious, so the punishment was **mild**.

   • The singer had only a **mild** cough, but she decided it was best not to perform.

   Mild means . . .   a. very strong   b. not too serious   c. painful

7. opportunity
/ˌɑpɚˈtunəṭi/
-noun

- My father didn't grow up with a computer, so he didn't have the **opportunity** to learn how to use one until he started working.
- Summer break gives me the **opportunity** to spend more time with my friends.

Opportunity means . . .   a. a time to work   b. a time to relax   c. a chance to do something

8. permanent
/ˈpɚmənənt/
-adjective

- Nestor travels a lot, so he uses his parents' address as his **permanent** one.
- The change will be **permanent**, so please be certain that you want to do this.

Permanent means . . .   a. for a long time   b. for a short time   c. for the present time

9. quality
/ˈkwaləṭi/
-noun

- Your honesty is a **quality** I appreciate.
- Nurses need to have the **qualities** of responsibility and caring.

Quality means . . .   a. one of your skills   b. your job   c. parts of your personality

10. trick
/trɪk/
-noun

- Salespeople often say they can give you a special price only today. It's a **trick** to make you buy their product or service.
- Robby uses clever **tricks** to get both parents to say yes to his requests.

Trick means . . .   a. a dishonest way to get what you want   b. a bad habit   c. a talent for playing jokes

▌WORDS AND DEFINITIONS

Match each key word with its definition.

1. ____*fresh*____ said of something that is added to what was there before to put it in good condition, or something that is newer than what was there before

2. _____ to give something to someone who gives you something else in return

3. _____ something you do to make someone believe something that is not true

4. _____ not too bad or serious

5. _____ continuing to exist for a long time or forever

6. _____ the good parts of someone's personality

7. _____ a group of people in society with a similar amount of money and education

8. _____ an occasion when it is possible for you to do something

9. _____ to stop someone from speaking by suddenly saying or doing something, or to start speaking before another person is finished

10. _____ something that is not hard or a gas, but that can flow or be poured

Choose the best answer.

1. At a hotel, you may ask for
   a. a **fresh** view.
   (b.) **fresh** sheets.
   c. a **fresh** bill.

2. Which of the following people likely has **mild** pain?
   a. Lyle fell down the stairs and broke his ankle.
   b. Banner hurt her back in a serious car accident.
   c. Zack lightly hit his knee against the chair.

3. Which of the following items is NOT a **liquid**?
   a. juice
   b. oil
   c. glass

4. Which of the following are Yozo's **qualities**?
   a. tall, dark hair, and wears glasses
   b. skiing, traveling, and cooking
   c. honest, funny, and helpful

5. Craig **interrupted** the teacher
   a. to ask a question.
   b. to show respect.
   c. to listen more carefully.

6. Kiwoong **exchanged** a jacket at a store
   a. to see if it looked good on him.
   b. because he couldn't pay for it today.
   c. when he saw that it had a hole in the sleeve.

7. Nancy never finished high school and works as a waitress. Which of the following people belongs to the same **class** as Nancy?
   a. Bob went to medical school and is now a well-known doctor.
   b. Theresa is a law student and comes from a rich family.
   c. Sydney quit college and took a job as a mail carrier.

8. Vacations give an **opportunity** to do all of the following activities EXCEPT
   a. relax.
   b. travel.
   c. work.

9. Pete might use a **trick** in order to
   a. show he's sorry.
   b. work hard.
   c. get money from his brother.

10. Arcadio made a **permanent** move from New York to California. That means
    a. California is his new home.
    b. New York will always be his home.
    c. he often travels between the two states.

WORD FAMILIES

Now that you have studied the ten key words and their basic definitions, you are ready to learn words that belong to the same family as some of the key words. A word family includes words that look alike but have different functions (noun, verb, adjective, or adverb). Their meanings are related but different.

A. *Look at each model phrase and decide whether the word in **bold** is used as a noun, verb, adjective, or adverb.*

	NOUN	VERB	ADJECTIVE	ADVERB
1. exchange				
• try to **exchange** a shirt		✓		
• to make an **exchange**	✓			
2. fresh				
• some **fresh** coffee				
• will **freshen** the air				
3. interrupt				
• often **interrupts** me				
• create an **interruption**				
4. liquid				
• pour a **liquid**				
• use **liquid** soap				
5. mild				
• to have **mild** pain				
• to be **mildly** upset				
6. trick				
• a mean **trick**				
• can **trick** the public				
• a **tricky** question				

B. *Read each sentence and match the word in **bold** with the correct definition.*

__c__ 1. Mint chewing gum **freshens** your breath.

____ 2. Pedro arrived at the meeting ten minutes late. He apologized for the **interruption**.

____ 3. I help my parents around the house, and they let me use the family car; it's a fair **exchange**.

____ 4. My younger sister can't swallow pills, only **liquid** medicine.

____ 5. When I first met Mrs. Crawford, Nina **tricked** me and made me think she was Nina's older sister and not her mother!

____ 6. I continued to watch the TV show, but I was only **mildly** interested.

____ 7. My classmate Hong-Ning complains that grammar is a **tricky** subject.

a. not hard and able to flow or be poured

b. to make someone believe something that is not true to get what you want

c. to make something clean and new

d. the act of stopping an event or activity for a short time by suddenly saying or doing something

e. a little; somewhat

f. difficult to deal with, especially because the situation is difficult to understand

g. the act of giving something to someone who gives you something else in return

SAME WORD, DIFFERENT MEANING

Most words have more than one meaning. Study the additional meanings of **fresh**, **interrupt**, and **quality**.
Then read each sentence and decide which meaning is used.

a. **fresh** *adj.*	said of something that is added to what was there before to put it in good condition, or something that is newer than what was there before
b. **fresh** *adj.*	looking, feeling, smelling, or tasting clean, cool, and nice
c. **interrupt** *v.*	to stop someone from speaking by suddenly saying or doing something, or to start speaking before another person is finished
d. **interrupt** *v.*	to stop a process or activity for a short time
e. **quality** *n.*	the good parts of someone's personality
f. **quality** *n.*	the degree to which something is good or bad

__e__ 1. What **qualities** do you look for in an employee?

_____ 2. The sudden start of rain **interrupted** our volleyball game.

_____ 3. The office worker put **fresh** paper in the copy machine.

_____ 4. Komaki buys clothes of fine **quality**.

_____ 5. Please let me explain and try not to **interrupt** until I'm finished.

_____ 6. The spring air from the windows gave the room a **fresh** smell.

WORDS IN SENTENCES

Complete each sentence with one of the words from the box.

| class | freshen | ~~liquid~~ | opportunity | quality |
| exchange | interruptions | mildly | permanent | tricky |

1. The dentist told me to eat a(n) _____liquid_____ diet for a week because of my sore mouth.

2. Families in the upper _____ can easily pay for private schools.

3. I'm taking a trip to Hollywood. I hope I have the _____ to see some film stars.

4. Before the game began, there was a quick _____ of handshakes between the two players.

5. We turn off our cell phones in class because our teacher doesn't like any _____.

6. Be careful not to get any paint on the floor. The paint is _____.

7. Because we have a dog and two cats, my mother is always trying to _____ the air in our home.

8. I was _____ surprised when Paul told a joke because he's usually serious.

9. The better the _____, the higher the price.

10. How do you open this bottle? Why do they make lids so _____?

WORDS IN COLLOCATIONS AND EXPRESSIONS

Following are common collocations (word partners) and expressions with some of the key words. Read the definitions and then complete the conversations with the correct form of the collocations and expressions.

1. **exchange**
   - **in exchange for** — to be done or given in return for another action or object

2. **fresh**
   - **fresh air** — air from outside, especially away from a city where the air is cleaner
   - **freshen up** — to wash your hands and face in order to feel comfortable

3. **mild**
   - **to put it mildly** — said when you are saying something unpleasant in the most polite way you can

4. **opportunity**
   - **give (sb) an/the opportunity to (do sth)** — to make it possible for someone to do something

5. **trick**
   - **trick (sb) into (doing sth)** — to make someone believe something untrue in order to get them to do something

1. LORI: People spend too much time watching TV. They should get out and see the world.

   FRED: I disagree. Television can _____*give*_____ people _____*the opportunity to*_____ learn about places all over the world. I don't think I'll ever go to all the countries I've seen on TV programs.

2. FRAN: My mother used to _____ us _____ eating our vegetables.

   NELA: Mine, too. She told us that green foods would make us lucky in life.

3. DENISE: Grandma often talks about getting a small apartment in the city.

   RICH: Yes, she misses city life. But Grandpa says he'll never move back to the city because there's no _____ there.

4. ELI: Do you and your brother get along?

   OLIVER: _____, we don't agree on a lot of things.

5. CARLOS: How does your brother get to work without a car? Does he take the bus?

   PAULINE: No, he cuts our neighbor's grass _____ a ride to work.

6. DAUGHTER: Can we stop in the restroom before we get our bags?

   MOTHER: Yes. I also wanted to _____ before the plane landed, too, but the line to the restroom was long.

WORDS IN READINGS

Read the two articles about lifestyles. Complete each one with words and expressions from the boxes.

~~fresh~~	liquid	quality	to put it mildly	tricked . . . into

WHEN DRINKING WATER BECOMES A LIFESTYLE*

Can you tell the difference between tap water† and bottled water? Not many people can. So why does an American drink about twenty-four gallons of bottled water each year? If it's not _____*fresh*_____
                                              1

tasting water people want, then maybe it's the _____ of the water that they're paying for.
          2

But both The Archives of Family Medicine and the University of Geneva agree that tap water is just as good as bottled water.

The reason countries like the United States spend billions of dollars on a bottled _____
          3

that they could get for free in their own homes is marketing‡. Companies selling bottled water have

_____ people _____ thinking it's best to drink water from a bottle. Most of
          4

us also think of it as fashionable. In other words, drinking bottled water has become a lifestyle.

_____, it's unwise for rich countries to spend money on bottled water. It costs more
          5

than gasoline, and the empty bottles create extra trash. The money people spend on bottled water could help bring clean tap water into homes in poor countries. More than a billion people today are in need of safe drinking water; remember that the next time you are thinking of buying a bottle of water.

*A lifestyle *(n.)* is the way that someone lives.

†Tap water *(n.)* is water that comes out of a faucet (the part of a sink you turn on and off to get water).

‡Marketing *(n.)* is the activity of deciding how to tell people about a product in order to get them to buy it.

(Based on information in Tom Standage, "Bad to the Last Drop." *New York Times* online, August 1, 2005.)

class	exchange . . . for	interruption	opportunities	permanent

HOME IS ANYWHERE

There are families that move every few years from one city to the next, or even to a new country.

Who are these people and why do they _____ one life _____ another so
          6

often? After all, each move is a(n) _____.
          7

These families are the "relos" of America: the parents choose to relocate for new job

_____; the kids move around with them. They are part of the upper middle
          8

_____, and their numbers are growing along with companies that keep opening new
          9

offices. They may be electronic engineers, accountants, bankers, managers, or salespeople, among other jobs, and they make no less than $100,000 a year. With each move, they hope to help their careers and give more to their families.

Many choose only to see the good things their families get from relocating. But others complain of the difficulties. As a relo family, you have no hometown, and there is no chance for _____ ties to anything.
10

All relos are in search of a lifestyle in which companies pay more, and with each move the houses get bigger, the schools are better, the neighborhoods are safer, and the cars get nicer and nicer. It's the new American dream.

(Based on information in Peter Kilborn, "The Five-Bedroom, Six-Figure Rootless Life." New York Times online, June 1, 2005.)

WORDS IN DISCUSSION

Apply the key words to your own life. Read and discuss the questions with a partner. Try to use the key words.

1. Have you ever **exchanged** an unwanted gift at a store?

   EXAMPLE

   *I bought shoes last month that looked nice, but weren't comfortable. I decided to **exchange** them for another pair.*

2. Name two things in your refrigerator that are **liquids**.
3. Have you ever changed your **permanent** address?
4. What do you do when someone **interrupts** you?
5. Do you usually take medication for **mild** pain?

WORDS IN WRITING

Write a short answer (1–2 sentences) for each question. Try to use the key words.

1. What do the holidays **give you the opportunity to** do?

   EXAMPLE

   *Holidays **give me the opportunity** to eat good food with friends and family.*

2. Name a place you visit that has **fresh air**.
3. What **quality** do you like most in your best friend?
4. Did you ever **trick** your parents **into** giving you something you wanted?
5. Which **class** of people is the biggest in your country?

Key Words

accept	determine	express	frequent	increase
appear	examine	formal	hook	limit

WORDS IN CONTEXT

*Use the sentences to guess what each key word means. Choose the meaning that is closest to that of the key word in **bold**.*

1. accept
/ək'sɛptəbəl/
-*verb*

- Will you please **accept** my help? I'm happy to loan you the money.
- Parents teach children not to **accept** candy from strangers.

Accept means . . . a. to say thank you for something   b. to want something   c. to take something

2. appear
/ə'pɪr/
-*verb*

- Rainbows **appear** when there is both sun and rain at the same time.
- Dark circles **appeared** under Nadeem's eyes after two nights of no sleep.

Appear means . . . a. to grow   b. to begin to be seen   c. to go away

3. determine
/dɪ,tɚmən/
-*verb*

- The doctors are trying to **determine** what causes Ray to have stomachaches.
- Scientists have **determined** that the Earth is about 4.5 billion years old.

Determine means . . . a. to teach   b. to find out   c. to guess

4. examine
/ɪg'zæmɪn/
-*verb*

- A dentist **examines** your teeth to make sure they are healthy and clean.
- The art collector **examined** the painting to make sure it was the original.

Examine means . . . a. to study something carefully   b. to ask about something   c. to take care of something

5. express
/ɪk'sprɛs/
-*verb*

- People **express** their anger in different ways. Some yell; others throw things.
- Jenna **expressed** how sorry she was for not being able to come to my party.

Express means . . . a. to show your feelings   b. to control your feelings   c. to hide your feelings

6. formal
/'fɔrməl/
-*adjective*

- In a business letter, you should use a **formal** greeting such as *Dear Sir or Madam*.
- Weddings are **formal** occasions, so guests should dress nicely.

Formal means . . . a. official or serious   b. happy or pleasant   c. careful

7. frequent
/ˈfrikwənt/
-adjective

- My headaches have become more **frequent**, so I need to see a doctor.
- Tom got tired of answering his little nephew's **frequent** questions.

Frequent means . . .   a. happening often   b. happening rarely   c. becoming weaker

8. hook
/hʊk/
-noun

- There is a row of **hooks** on the wall where students can hang their coats.
- Dad keeps his bathrobe on the **hook** behind the bathroom door.

Hook means . . .   a. an object for hanging things   b. a way of hanging things   c. a closet for hanging long clothes

9. increase
/ɪnˈkris/
-verb

- They're moving to a bigger office because the number of workers has **increased**.
- On this exam, the computer **increases** the difficulty if you answer questions correctly.

Increase means . . .   a. to be or keep the same   b. to become or make larger   c. to become or make smaller

10. limit
/ˈlɪmɪt/
-noun

- Each family has a **limit** on spending money; some must save more than others.
- There is a **limit** on the amount of time I have for daytime calls on my cell phone.

Limit means . . .   a. the amount that you need   b. the amount that you want   c. the amount that is allowed

▌ WORDS AND DEFINITIONS

Match each key word with its definition.

1. _____hook_____ a curved object that you hang things on

2. _____ to find out the facts about something

3. _____ to look at something carefully in order to make a decision or find out something

4. _____ following the official or social rules for serious situations

5. _____ to use words or actions in order to let people know what you are thinking or feeling

6. _____ to begin to be seen

7. _____ the greatest amount, number, etc. that is allowed or is possible

8. _____ to become or make larger in number, amount, or degree

9. _____ happening very often

10. _____ to take something that someone offers you

Choose the best answer.

1. If the police **determined** the way a robber entered a home, they
   a. want to know how the criminal entered.
   b. cannot understand how the criminal entered.
   c. know how the criminal entered.

2. Hal and Tonia take **frequent** trips because
   a. Tonia is afraid of flying on planes.
   b. they love to travel.
   c. Hal works long hours six days a week.

3. Maureen **accepted** my apology for being late; she
   a. is a very understanding person.
   b. told me I should have a good reason.
   c. is very angry with me.

4. The police detective **examined** the weapon;
   a. he wanted to keep it in a secret place.
   b. he was looking for fingerprints.
   c. he showed it to others.

5. People often place each of the following items on a **hook** EXCEPT
   a. a towel.
   b. a pair of socks.
   c. a jacket.

6. Which of the following things **appear** in the sky only at night?
   a. a rainbow
   b. clouds
   c. the moon

7. Which of the following situations is an example of a **limit**?
   a. Our cat sleeps all day.
   b. Oliver buys music CDs every chance he gets.
   c. Valerie lets her children watch only two hours of TV a day.

8. Which of the following events is NOT **formal**?
   a. a visit to the zoo
   b. a funeral
   c. a job interview

9. You can **express** your thanks for a great gift in all of the following ways EXCEPT
   a. by writing a thank-you note.
   b. by hiding your happiness.
   c. by doing something nice in return.

10. The temperature in New York City **increases**
    a. during the summer months.
    b. in December.
    c. when the wind blows.

WORD FAMILIES

Now that you have studied the ten key words and their basic definitions, you are ready to learn words that belong to the same family as some of the key words. A word family includes words that look alike but have different functions (noun, verb, adjective, or adverb). Their meanings are related but different.

A. *Look at each model phrase and decide whether the word in* **bold** *is used as a noun, verb, adjective, or adverb.*

	NOUN	VERB	ADJECTIVE	ADVERB
1. accept				
• please **accept** my invitation		✓		
• **acceptable** work			✓	
2. appear				
• will **appear** in our city				
• care about your **appearance**				
• to **disappear** from the neighborhood				
3. express				
• cannot **express** my happiness				
• the **expression** on your face				
4. formal				
• a **formal** dress				
• an **informal** meeting				
5. increase				
• to **increase** the temperature				
• must **decrease** the prices				
6. limit				
• know the **limits**				
• to **limit** the time				

B. *Read each sentence and match the word in* **bold** *with the correct definition.*

___*f*___ 1. Road laws **limit** the speed we drive for our own safety.

_____ 2. Vitaly wore an **expression** of surprise after learning that he won the contest.

_____ 3. The partners met for an **informal** lunch and discussed everything but business.

_____ 4. The teacher said that my handwritten essay was not **acceptable**. I must type it.

_____ 5. Taylor knows that he must rewrite his essay and **decrease** the number of spelling mistakes.

_____ 6. With his suit and briefcase, Yu-Sin's **appearance** was very professional.

_____ 7. I can't find my glasses. Where did they **disappear** to?

a. relaxed and friendly

b. a look on someone's face that shows what s/he is thinking.

c. to become less in size, number, or amount, or to make something do this

d. to become impossible to see or find

e. good enough for a certain purpose

f. to stop an amount, number, etc. from increasing beyond a certain point

g. the way someone or something looks or seems to other people

SAME WORD, DIFFERENT MEANING

*Most words have more than one meaning. Study the additional meanings of **accept**, **appear**, and **expression**. Then read each sentence and decide which meaning is used.*

a. **accept** *v.*	to take something that someone is willing to give you
b. **accept** *v.*	to let someone join an organization or university
c. **appear** *v.*	to begin to be seen
d. **appear** *v.*	to seem
e. **expression** *n.*	a look on someone's face that shows what s/he is thinking or feeling
f. **expression** *n.*	a word or phrase that has a certain meaning

___f___ 1. *The good old days* is an **expression** we use to talk about a pleasant time in the distant past, usually a time from our youth.

_____ 2. A small bird **appeared** at my window.

_____ 3. Ajay got his test back; from the **expression** on his face I can tell he passed.

_____ 4. The actress cried happy tears as she **accepted** the prize.

_____ 5. Nisha **appears** to be worried, but she says that everything is all right.

_____ 6. Colleen got **accepted** to the graduate school of her choice.

WORDS IN SENTENCES

Complete each sentence with one of the words from the box.

acceptable	determine	examined	~~frequent~~	informal
decreased	disappear	expression	hook	limit

1. As my uncle's health grew worse, he had to make more ___frequent___ trips to the doctor's office.

2. Did the medical tests _____ what caused the illness?

3. We're very _____ in the office. We don't use any titles, just first names.

4. Oversleeping is not a(n) _____ excuse for missing class.

5. The scientist _____ the results of the test before writing her report.

6. I placed my hat on the _____.

7. We should all _____ the amount of salt, sugar, and fatty foods in our diet.

8. *Every now and then* is a(n) _____ that means *occasionally*.

9. How could the money _____? Clearly, someone stole it.

10. When the factory closed, people lost jobs and business activity _____.

WORDS IN COLLOCATIONS AND EXPRESSIONS

Following are common collocations (word partners) and expressions with some of the key words. Read the definitions and then complete the conversations with the correct form of the collocations and expressions.

1. **accept**
   - **accept (sth) from (sb)** — to take something that someone offers you

2. **express**
   - **express an interest in (sth)** — to say that you are interested in something
   - **express yourself** — to use words or actions in order to let people know what you are thinking or feeling

3. **hook**
   - **be hooked on (sth)** — to like something a lot, almost to the point where you cannot live without it

4. **limit**
   - **be limited to** — to exist or happen only in a certain place, time, or group
   - **speed limit** — the greatest speed allowed by law on a certain road

1. PATIENT: I still feel so weak. How will I be able to do things around the house?

   DOCTOR: It's normal to be weak after an operation. You'll need to _____*accept*_____ help _____*from*_____ others for a few weeks. You'll be back on your feet soon enough.

2. MONICA: Wow! Your bedroom is so cool. I love the painted stars on the ceiling.

   ELLIE: Thanks. My parents let me decorate the room however I wanted. It was a lot of fun to _____ myself through colors, pictures, and drawings.

3. CO-WORKER 1: Who do you think our new supervisor will be?

   CO-WORKER 2: I know that Florencia wrote a letter to the director to _____ her _____ the position. So I think he'll consider her.

4. STUDENT: Can I ask you a question about the ancient Egyptian rulers?

   TEACHER: Sure. I'll try to answer it, but my knowledge is really _____ modern history, starting from about the 1300s onward.

5. MOTHER 1: My son spends so much time on the computer.

   MOTHER 2: Mine, too. I try to limit him, though. Thankfully, my daughter isn't _____ computer games like my son is.

6. POLICE OFFICER: Ma'am, do you know the _____ on this highway?

   DRIVER: Uh . . . sixty-five?

   POLICE OFFICER: That's correct, ma'am. You were going eighty miles per hour.

WORDS IN READINGS

Read the two articles about science and technology. Complete each one with words and expressions from the boxes.

~~accepts~~	appear	express yourself	hooked on	limited to

WHO LIVES IN CYWORLD?

In South Korea you can buy a couch in a place called Cyworld for only six *dotori*. That's less than a U.S. dollar. Cyworld _____*accepts*_____ only *dotori*, which is digital* money, because it's not a store; it's an Internet service.

Getting into Cyworld is free, and once you do, you can create an amazing home page. Just ask the 15 million people who use the service. In fact, 90 percent of them say they are _____ it. That's because Cyworld is more than just a place to show your photos and tell about your interests. Your home page is much like a room in your own home that lets you _____ by decorating it. Play your kind of music. Sit down on your digital couch and chat with a friend—both of you _____ on the home page in digital form.

For many, Cyworld is not _____ the computer screen. For some, Cyworld has opened doors to career changes. For others, the service has helped their personal lives. Kim Joon, a thirty-one-year-old software engineer, met his wife through a Cyworld club, and they were able to try family life in Cyworld first before getting married.

SK Telecom, the creator of this Internet service, is already looking at other countries to repeat its success. Is the rest of the world ready to live in Cyworld?

*Digital (adj.) is a system in which information is represented in the form of changing electrical signals.

(Based on information from Moon Ihlwan, "E-Society: My World Is Cyworld." Business Week, September 26, 2005.)

determine	formal	increase
examining	frequent	informal

CAN A COMPUTER UNDERSTAND OUR EMOTIONS?

Software* called Emotive Alert could help us know what our callers were feeling at the time they recorded their messages. The software can _____ a caller's emotion by _____ the way the person spoke: how loud or soft, how high or low, and how fast or slow. The system then tells the listener such information as how important the message is and if the message is _____ or _____. It can also read the emotions of the speaker: happy, sad, excited, or calm.

*Software (n.) is a set of programs that you put into a computer when you want it to do a particular job.

But tests show that Emotive Alert is not always correct. This is because the system studies *how* a person is speaking and not *what* a person is saying. The answer to this problem may be in making a software that can be programmed to read the emotions of one's most _____ callers by learning their normal speech patterns.

                                                                    10

Is this just the beginning of voice-reading software? Just think: In the car, a computer can help calm down an upset driver. Also, during computer games, if the computer knows that the player is losing interest, it can _____ the difficulty. It seems Emotive Alert is part of a future that

                                        11

is coming quickly.

(Based on information in Celeste Liever, "Voicemail software recognises callers' emotions." New Scientist online, January 11, 2005.)

▌ WORDS IN DISCUSSION

Apply the key words to your own life. Read and discuss the questions with a partner. Try to use the key words.

1. Name something you're **hooked on.**

   EXAMPLE

   *Last year a friend invited me to a concert. Since then, I've been **hooked on** jazz.*

2. When was the last time you went to a **formal** event?
3. When was the last time a dentist **examined** your teeth?
4. Name a place you make **frequent** visits to.
5. Do you **limit** the amount of time you watch TV or use the computer?

▌ WORDS IN WRITING

Write a short answer (1–2 sentences) for each question. Try to use the key words.

1. What subject would you like to **increase** your knowledge about.

   EXAMPLE

   *I would like to **increase** my knowledge about cars. I think it's helpful to know how to fix them.*

2. Name a situation in which you worry about your **appearance**. Explain.
3. Name a university in your country that is difficult to get **accepted** to. Would you like to study at this school?
4. Do you understand the **expression** *happy as a clam*? When can you use it?
5. Can you easily **determine** a person's age by looking at him or her? Give an example.

CHAPTER 21

Key Words

border	former	immediate	necessary	spread
century	hire	native	split	suit

WORDS IN CONTEXT

Use the sentences to guess what each key word means. Choose the meaning that is closest to that of the key word in **bold**.

1. **border**
   /ˈbɔrdɚ/
   -noun

   • Poland and Ukraine share a **border**.
   • The guards checked our passports when we crossed the **border**.

   Border means . . . (a.) a line between two countries   b. a political system   c. a country's capital

2. **century**
   /ˈsɛntʃəri/
   -noun

   • The United States is a young country; it's less than three **centuries** old.
   • The twentieth **century** brought great developments in science and technology.

   Century means . . .   a. a lifetime   b. a 100-year period   c. a 1,000-year period

3. **former**
   /ˈfɔrmɚ/
   -adjective

   • I miss my **former** school. I'm in a new school, and nothing is familiar.
   • **Former** presidents of the U.S. still have opportunities to be active in politics.

   Former means . . .   a. before now   b. present   c. future

4. **hire**
   /haɪɚ/
   -verb

   • Our secretary plans to quit working here, so we need to **hire** a new one.
   • Mrs. Furlow **hired** Lori to babysit her children this summer.

   Hire means . . .   a. to make someone do work for you   b. to ask someone to stop working   c. to pay someone to work for you

5. **immediate**
   /ɪˈmidiɪt/
   -adjective

   • The driver was badly hurt in the accident and needed **immediate** medical help.
   • A VIP, or very important person, gets **immediate** service at any restaurant.

   Immediate means . . .   a. without a wait   b. special   c. very polite

6. **native**
   /ˈneɪt̬ɪv/
   -adjective

   • You said your parents live in Madrid. Is Spain your **native** country?
   • World travel is very popular, but most people live and die in their **native** land.

   Native means . . .   a. where you visit   b. where you were born   c. where you work or study

7. necessary
/'nɛsə,sɛri/
-adjective

- Dad's taking a nap, and he said not to wake him if it's not **necessary**.
- If Suzanne borrows your dress, it'll be **necessary** to shorten it. She's a little shorter.

Necessary means . . .   a. helpful   b. needed   c. wise

8. split
/splɪt/
-verb

- The teacher asked the class to **split** into small groups of three or four.
- A lunch break **splits** a long workday into two shorter periods.

Split means . . .   a. to divide   b. to plan   c. to choose

9. spread
/sprɛd/
-verb

- Mother **spread** a tablecloth over the table and then placed the flowers in the center.
- The volleyball team **spread** out on their side of the net and got ready to play.

Spread means . . .   a. to lie or lay down   b. to make something straight or stand straight   c. to cover a big area

10. suit
/sut/
-verb

- The house is perfect; it **suits** all of our needs.
- The karate instructor is very good, but the class schedule doesn't **suit** me.

Suit means . . .   a. to be interesting   b. to be helpful   c. to be right for you

▎WORDS AND DEFINITIONS

Match each key word with its definition.

1. _____hire_____ to pay someone to work for you

2. _____ something that existed or was true before, but not now

3. _____ to open something so that it covers a big area, or to place a number of things over a big area

4. _____ happening or done at once with no wait

5. _____ the official line that separates two countries or states

6. _____ to divide or make something divide into two or more groups, parts, etc.

7. _____ needed in order for you to do something or have something

8. _____ to be acceptable or right for you

9. _____ belonging to the place where you were born

10. _____ one of the 100-year periods counted forward or backward from the year of Christ's birth

COMPREHENSION CHECK

Choose the best answer.

1. If France is my **native** country, then
   a. I speak French.
   b. I don't understand French.
   c. I plan to study French.

2. The fog **spread**;
   a. our plane flew through sunny skies.
   b. our plane could finally land safely.
   c. our plane couldn't land safely.

3. The teacher **split** us in order to
   a. have small group discussions.
   b. have a whole class discussion.
   c. speak to us one at a time.

4. If Fabiana has lived for a **century**,
   a. she is one hundred years old.
   b. she is fifty years old.
   c. she is ten years old.

5. What do you need to cross another country's **border?**
   a. a tour guide
   b. a map
   c. a passport

6. Ten o'clock tomorrow morning **suits** me.
   a. Can we meet earlier?
   b. I'll see you then.
   c. Let's choose another day.

7. An **immediate** change
   a. happens over several weeks.
   b. happens now.
   c. happens later.

8. The boss will **hire** an employee
   a. to replace one who left.
   b. who doesn't perform well.
   c. to spend less of the company's money.

9. My **former** address
   a. is where I lived before.
   b. is where I live now.
   c. is where I'm moving to.

10. It's **necessary** to buy a ticket for all of the following activities EXCEPT
    a. to fly on a passenger plane.
    b. to go to a play at a theater.
    c. to take a taxi ride.

▌WORD FAMILIES

Now that you have studied the ten key words and their basic definitions, you are ready to learn words that belong to the same family as some of the key words. A word family includes words that look alike but have different functions (noun, verb, adjective, or adverb). Their meanings are related but different.

A. *Look at each model phrase and decide whether the word in **bold** is used as a noun, verb, adjective, or adverb.*

	NOUN	VERB	ADJECTIVE	ADVERB
1. **border**				
• share a **border**	✓			
• Texas **borders** Mexico		✓		
2. **immediate**				
• take **immediate** action				
• to come **immediately**				
3. **native**				
• my **native** country				
• met the **natives**				
4. **necessary**				
• a **necessary** action				
• to change **necessarily**				
• do **unnecessary** work				
5. **suit**				
• **suits** me fine				
• a **suitable** time				

B. *Read the first half of each sentence and match it with the appropriate ending.*

__c__ 1. With one poor test score you won't

____ 2. Alberto is

____ 3. Do you know which countries

____ 4. If someone invites me to dinner and I don't want to go, what is

____ 5. If you already sent a thank-you note, then a phone call is

____ 6. Can you send the letter

a. **immediately**?

b. **border** Germany?

c. **necessarily** fail the course.

d. a **suitable** answer?

e. a **native** of northern Italy.

f. **unnecessary**.

SAME WORD, DIFFERENT MEANING

Most words have more than one meaning. Study the additional meanings of **split**, **spread**, and **suit**. Then read each sentence and decide which meaning is used.

a.	**split** v.	to divide or make something divide into two or more groups, parts, etc.
b.	**split** v.	to divide something among two or more people in equal parts
c.	**spread** v.	to open something so that it covers a big area, or to place a number of things over a big area
d.	**spread** v.	to make something widely known, or to become widely known
e.	**suit** v.	to be acceptable or right for you
f.	**suit** v.	to make someone look good physically

___e___ 1. Let's meet on Tuesday at 7 P.M. Does that **suit** you?

_____ 2. News of the prince's engagement **spread** quickly throughout the country.

_____ 3. The question of slavery **split** the United States into the North and the South.

_____ 4. Trista, you look so pretty today! That color really **suits** you.

_____ 5. The boys **spread** their toy soldiers on the floor and began a game of war.

_____ 6. This is a big sandwich. Do you want to **split** it with me?

WORDS IN SENTENCES

Complete each sentence with one of the words from the box.

border	former	immediately	split	suits
century	~~hired~~	native	spread	unnecessary

1. Mother _____hired_____ a woman to clean our house once a week for sixty dollars.

2. Many cooks add salt when they boil pasta, but it's _____.

3. E-mail is an easy way to _____ news among your friends and family.

4. When Grandfather died, my father and aunts _____ the family money equally.

5. The hairdresser told me that short hair _____ me better.

6. Besides Alaska, which U.S. states _____ Canada?

7. Mr. Simpson asked you to call him _____. He said it's very important.

8. John F. Kennedy was a(n) _____ of Boston, Massachusetts.

9. In which _____ was William Shakespeare born? The 1500s, right?

10. I finished high school almost five years ago, but I'm still in touch with my _____ teachers and classmates.

WORDS IN COLLOCATIONS AND EXPRESSIONS

Following are common collocations (word partners) and expressions with some of the key words. Read the definitions and then complete the conversations with the correct form of the collocations and expressions.

1. **hire**
   - **get/be hired**   to receive employment
2. **native**
   - **native language**   the language you first learned to speak
   - **native speaker**   someone who learned the language in question as a baby
3. **necessary**
   - **not necessarily**   seeming likely, but not for certain
4. **split**
   - **split up**   to end a marriage or relationship
5. **spread**
   - **spread (yourself) too thin**   to accept too many duties so you are always too busy

1. RASHIM: Your English is really good. You understand the grammar very well.

    DANILO: Thanks. But I'd like to have more conversation practice with a
               _____*native speaker*_____. There are still a lot of words and expressions
               I don't understand.

2. EDGAR: I hope it doesn't rain on our trip. Bad weather can ruin a vacation.

    JUNE: _____. A good hotel offers a lot to do inside.

3. VICKY: You _____.

    JEROME: I know I do, but I can't seem to say no when people ask me to do things.

4. CARRIE: What's your _____? I thought it was English.

    DORI: No, it's Tagalog. I grew up in the Philippines.

5. MONA: Do you plan to keep busy this summer? Do you have a job?

    DALE: Yes. I _____ at the movie theater last week.

6. MATTEO: How long were the Beatles together?

    SHANE: They _____ after about ten years. I think it happened
               in 1970.

WORDS IN READINGS

Read the two articles about world travel. Complete each one with words and expressions from the boxes.

border	~~century~~	former	necessary	split

RIDE THROUGH HISTORY

Soon bikers and hikers will travel through history. The European Union (EU) has plans to turn 4,250 miles into the Iron Curtain Trail*. For nearly half a _____*century*_____, the Iron Curtain
1
_____ Europe in two: communism† in the East, and capitalism‡ in the West. The trail
2
will make sure that people never forget this important period in Europe's past.

Many people are helping to make this ride through history possible. Mikhail Gorbachev,
_____ president of the Soviet Union, was the person to suggest making the trail in the
3
first place. MEP§ Michael Cramer of Germany liked the idea and pushed to make it happen. He
believes that knowing and understanding the past is _____ for life in the future.
4

The Iron Curtain Trail is to be the longest of its kind, starting from the Arctic Ocean and ending at the Black Sea. Tourists can visit many countries along the way. One can walk or ride down the old
_____ between eastern and western Germany as well as the border between the former
5
Yugoslavia and Hungary.

It's Cramer's hope that the trail will not only keep a part of history alive, but also celebrate the EU itself.

*A trail (n.) is a path across open country or through the forest.

†Communism (n.) is a political system in which the government controls all the production of food and goods.

‡Capitalism (n.) is an economic and political system in which most businesses do not belong to the government.

§MEP (title) means Member of European Parliament.

(Based on information in Anthony Browne, "Iron Curtain Turns into Tourist Trap." The Times [UK] online, September 28, 2005.)

hired	immediately	native	natives	spreading	suit

A TOUR JUST FOR YOU

For sixty British pounds an hour (that's about $109 U.S.) you can have a ride in a Karma Kab. You're sure to enjoy the decorations inside—the sari* material, disco balls, and plastic flowers—but that's not the reason these taxis cost so much. When a Karma Kab driver is _____,
6
he doesn't just give you a ride around London; you get special entrance to the kind of life only
_____ of the city usually know. "If the people are cool," says owner and driver Tobias
7
Moss, "I can get them into any place that they normally couldn't get in."

*A sari (n.) is a type of loose clothing worn by many Indian and Bangladeshi women and some Pakistani women.

Moss helped create what is being called a "lifestyle tour." He and his drivers give visitors tours to _____ their interests. Once inside a Karma Kab, you _____ have a
        8   9
connection to the same food, shops, and fun that true Londoners know. Some of his customers include stars like filmmaker Oliver Stone and actress Scarlett Johansson.

Lifestyle tours are _____ throughout European cities. For around twenty euros, an
            10
Amsterdam company offers a shopping tour, a visit with Dutch artists, or a home-cooked meal. Visitors feel less like tourists and more like friends to their _____ guides. Without a lifestyle tour,
            11
you may visit all the usual places, but you won't get a deeper understanding of the country and people.

(Based on information in Gisela Williams, "Locals Who Will Open Doors and Minds." New York Times online, February 12, 2006.)

WORDS IN DISCUSSION

Apply the key words to your own life. Read and discuss the questions with a partner. Try to use the key words.

1. You have a time machine. Which **century** do you want to visit?

   EXAMPLE

   *I want to see the distant future. I want to visit the twenty-fifth **century**.*

2. Which countries **border** your own?

3. Name a **former** leader of your country. Was s/he a good leader?

4. Name something your parents or another family member did for you that was **unnecessary** but very nice.

5. You **got hired** to create a new student lounge in your school. What will it look like?

WORDS IN WRITING

Write a short answer (1–2 sentences) for each question. Try to use the key words.

1. Name a food that you usually **split** because it's too much for one person to eat.

   EXAMPLE

   *I love pizza, but I can't eat a whole pizza by myself, so I **split** it with my roommates.*

2. You have the power to make an **immediate** change in your hometown. What will you change?

3. In your opinion, what color(s) **suits** you? Do you often wear this color?

4. Do you **spread yourself thin**? Is it easy for you to say no to requests?

5. Name something you love about your **native** country.

QUIZ 7

PART A

Choose the word that best completes each item and write it in the space provided.

1. The waitress added _____*fresh*_____ coffee to my cup.
   - a. mild
   - b. fresh
   - c. frequent
   - d. necessary

2. Luke _____ the blanket over the sheets.
   - a. spread
   - b. examined
   - c. expressed
   - d. hired

3. I had a terrible headache this morning, but now the pain is only _____.
   - a. mild
   - b. fresh
   - c. formal
   - d. necessary

4. Being helpful is a good _____ in a co-worker.
   - a. border
   - b. class
   - c. hook
   - d. quality

5. On a clear night, hundreds of stars _____ in the sky.
   - a. split
   - b. determine
   - c. express
   - d. appear

6. Doctors _____ patients to better understand the condition of their health.
   - a. increase
   - b. examine
   - c. determine
   - d. hire

7. Scientists can _____ the truth through experiments.
   - a. split
   - b. determine
   - c. exchange
   - d. appear

8. The teacher always gives us the _____ to ask questions during the lesson.
   - a. border
   - b. century
   - c. hook
   - d. opportunity

9. The company plans to _____ a dozen new people to handle the additional work.
   - a. spread
   - b. determine
   - c. exchange
   - d. hire

10. Travelers need to show their passports when they cross the _____.
    - a. border
    - b. class
    - c. hook
    - d. liquid

PART B

*Read each statement and write **T** for true or **F** for false in the space provided.*

<u> F </u> 1. A successful banker and a homeless person belong to the same **class**.

_____ 2. If it's **necessary** to complete a form, you must do it.

_____ 3. An **immediate** change happens right away.

_____ 4. **Tricks** are a part of every good friendship.

_____ 5. When a person says yes, he or she is **accepting** your invitation.

_____ 6. A game of cards with your friends is an example of a **formal** event.

_____ 7. A rainstorm is **permanent**.

_____ 8. Soup is a **liquid**.

_____ 9. If Ben receives and makes **frequent** phone calls, he talks a lot on the phone.

_____ 10. **Hooks** are used to put away plates, bowls, and glasses.

PART C

Each situation shows the meaning of one of the key words. Write the appropriate key word next to the situation. Use the clues in italics.

century	express	increase	limit	split
exchange	former	interrupt	~~native~~	suit

1. Carla was *born in* Argentina. It's always been her home.   ____*native*____

2. Some say the Beatles were the most important rock group of the past *one hundred years*.   _____

3. Do you think I can *give* this DVD back to the store and buy *something else*?   _____

4. The *number* of customers *became higher* during the holiday season.   _____

5. You can't try on so many clothes at one time. Five items is *the most allowed* in this store.   _____

6. We shopped for a new couch, but we couldn't find one that was *right* for us.   _____

7. Kim *stopped* her brother *from speaking* about her bad grade in math class before their parents could get upset.   _____

8. The director *before this one* was very good; I learned a lot about the business from him.   _____

9. The army *divided into two groups*. One came from the north; the other came from the south.   _____

10. In ballet, dancers use *movement* instead of *words* to *let people* in the audience *know what they are thinking or feeling*.   _____

▌WORDS IN CONTEXT

*Use the sentences to guess what each key word means. Choose the meaning that is closest to that of the key word in **bold**.*

1. apply
/əˈplaɪ/
-verb

- Do you know which colleges you want to **apply** to?
- Quinn wants to work at that company. He's already **applied** for a job there.

Apply means . . . (a.) to make a request for   b. to learn about   c. to visit

2. bargain
/ˈbɑrgən/
-noun

- The saleswoman gave me a good **bargain** on the stereo. I paid seventy-five dollars less for the stereo than the posted price.
- Luciana saves money by finding **bargains** in every store she goes to.

Bargain means . . .   a. something you get for free   b. something bought at a low price   c. something of good quality

3. confess
/kənˈfɛs/
-verb

- When the police questioned the woman, she **confessed** to the murder.
- Harry knew it was best to **confess** that he knew who stole the money.

Confess means . . .   a. to admit   b. to lie about   c. to understand

4. disappoint
/ˌdɪsəˈpɔɪnt/
-verb

- I try hard in class because I don't want to **disappoint** my teachers.
- Beth's decision not to come on the trip with us **disappointed** me.

Disappoint means . . .   a. to confuse you   b. to surprise you   c. to make you unhappy

5. gradual
/ˈgrædʒuəl/
-adjective

- As summer came closer, there was a **gradual** increase in the temperature.
- The change in Don and Felice's relationship was **gradual**. They started as friends, and over the first year the friendship deepened into a great love.

Gradual means . . .   a. changing slowly   b. starting suddenly   c. happening quickly

6. host
/hoʊst/
-noun

- We rang the doorbell, and the **host** welcomed us into his home.
- The **host** of the party introduced me to the other guests.

Host means . . .   a. a person who is invited to a party   b. a person who organizes a party   c. a person who is hired to serve food and drinks

7. literature
/ˈlɪt̬ərətʃə/
-noun

- Shakespeare's plays add to the richness of English **literature**.
- Glen is studying **literature** at his university; he's always loved to read.

Literature means . . . a. entertainment   b. books and plays   c. the study of language

8. private
/ˈpraɪvɪt/
-adjective

- The restaurant has a special room for **private** parties.
- Paul and Janna have beautiful paintings in their **private** collection.

Private means . . .   a. for school or learning b. not for everyone   c. for large groups

9. regret
/rɪgrɛt/
-verb

- I **regret** not spending more time with my grandfather while he was alive.
- Josie lived to **regret** that she didn't marry Fernando in her youth.

Regret means . . .   a. to feel angry   b. to feel sorry   c. to feel tired

10. shame
/ʃeɪm/
-noun

- After Molly lied to her parents, she was filled with **shame**.
- I treated Ross badly; later I felt great **shame**.

Shame means . . .   a. the feeling of being   b. the feeling of   c. the feeling of guilt
without hope   confusion

WORDS AND DEFINITIONS

Match each key word with its definition.

1. _____host_____ the person at a party who invited guests and organized the party

2. _____ happening, developing, or changing slowly over a long time

3. _____ the feeling of being guilty or embarrassed that you have after doing something that is wrong

4. _____ books, plays, and other written works that are considered very good and that people have liked for a long time

5. _____ to feel sorry about something you have done and wish you had not done it

6. _____ to make a formal, especially written, request for a job, place at a college, etc.

7. _____ something bought for less than its usual price

8. _____ to admit that you have done something wrong or against the law

9. _____ only for use by one person or group, not for everyone

10. _____ to make someone unhappy because something he or she hoped for does not happen or is not as good as he or she expected

Choose the best answer.

1. **Literature** includes each of the following EXCEPT
   a. plays.
   b. poems.
   c. songs.

2. Which of the following situations shows a **gradual** change?
   a. Marcia takes off her boots and puts on slippers.
   b. A sunflower grows taller and bigger.
   c. A cat jumps down from the sofa and walks into the kitchen.

3. Kerry feels **shame** for
   a. being honest to her mother.
   b. keeping her promise to her mother.
   c. stealing money from her mother's wallet.

4. The TV was a **bargain**;
   a. we saved over $100.
   b. we paid $100 more than we wanted to.
   c. it doesn't work.

5. The student **regrets**
   a. not failing the test.
   b. not making many mistakes on the test.
   c. not studying for the test.

6. Which of the following statements would a **host** make?
   a. "Could I bring something? Maybe dessert?"
   b. "Thank you for coming."
   c. "Dinner was delicious."

7. You do NOT **apply** for
   a. a loan.
   b. a job.
   c. a doctor.

8. If a room is **private**,
   a. not everyone can enter.
   b. anyone can enter.
   c. you must pay to enter.

9. The man **confessed** to the crime;
   a. the police must now prove he is guilty.
   b. he will go to jail.
   c. he is able to describe what the robbers looked like.

10. The book **disappointed** me;
    a. don't waste your time reading it.
    b. I'm surprised I enjoyed it.
    c. you'll love it, too.

WORD FAMILIES

Now that you have studied the ten key words and their basic definitions, you are ready to learn words that belong to the same family as some of the key words. A word family includes words that look alike but have different functions (noun, verb, adjective, or adverb). Their meanings are related but different.

A. *Look at each model phrase and decide whether the word in **bold** is used as a noun, verb, adjective, or adverb.*

	NOUN	VERB	ADJECTIVE	ADVERB
1. **apply**				
• to **apply** to college		✓		
• send in an **application**	✓			
2. **disappoint**				
• sorry to **disappoint** you				
• great **disappointment**				
• feel deeply **disappointed**				
3. **host**				
• a kind **host**				
• will **host** a party				
4. **private**				
• a **private** room				
• to need some **privacy**				
5. **regret**				
• to **regret** your decision				
• my many **regrets**				
6. **shame**				
• feel great **shame**				
• to be **ashamed** of yourself				

B. *Read each sentence and match the word in **bold** with the correct definition.*

___d___ 1. My one **regret** is not learning to play an instrument.

_____ 2. The public showed **disappointment** in the film; they expected a lot more.

_____ 3. I completed the job **application** and returned it to the secretary.

_____ 4. Noossaba enjoys **hosting** dinner parties. She's a great cook.

_____ 5. The students are **disappointed** that the school dance will not be held.

_____ 6. David allowed himself to cry only in the **privacy** of his own room.

_____ 7. Louisa felt **ashamed** of her family's house because it was so small and old.

a. the state of being able to be alone and not seen or heard by other people

b. a feeling of sadness because something is not as good as you expected or has not happened

c. to be the person who invited guests and organized a party

d. sadness that you feel about something because you wish it had not happened or that you had not done it

e. feeling embarrassed or guilty about something

f. unhappy because something did not happen, or because something or someone is not as good as s/he expected

g. a formal, usually written, request for a job, place at a college, etc.

SAME WORD, DIFFERENT MEANING

Most words have more than one meaning. Study the additional meanings of **confess**, **literature**, and **private**. Then read each sentence and decide which meaning is used.

a.	**confess** *v.*	to admit that you have done something wrong or against the law
b.	**confess** *v.*	to admit that you feel embarrassed or surprised about something
c.	**literature** *n.*	books, plays, etc. that are considered very good and that people have liked for a long time
d.	**literature** *n.*	printed information written by a company or organization to sell you something or give you advice
e.	**private** *adj.*	only for use by one person or group, not for everyone
f.	**private** *adj.*	not relating to, owned by, or paid for by the government*

*A government (n.) is the group of people who control a country, state, etc.

___e___ 1. My father has a **private** phone line in our home for business calls.

_____ 2. The businessman **confessed** to setting fire to his unsuccessful restaurant.

_____ 3. The salesman handed me some **literature** about his company's services.

_____ 4. The Angeles family sends their three children to **private** schools.

_____ 5. My roommate **confessed** that she didn't know how to cook anything.

_____ 6. Kevin has studied French **literature**.

WORDS IN SENTENCES

Complete each sentence with one of the words from the box.

applications	bargain	disappointment	host	privacy
ashamed	confessed	gradual	literature	~~regrets~~

1. Grandpa says, "Live life fully and without fear, or you'll die with many ___*regrets*___."

2. Vincent _____ that he had never been in love.

3. I often take long walks when I need some _____.

4. I plan to _____ a party for my sister, who's getting married.

5. If you are a careful shopper, you can always find a good _____.

6. High school seniors are busy in the fall with college _____.

7. Do you have some _____ about your different cell phone plans?

8. When Sabrina learned how poor her roommate's family was, she was _____ of her earlier complaints about not having enough money for fun things.

9. I like to make my parents happy; I hate to cause them any _____.

10. Business hasn't been growing in our city. Not surprisingly, there's been a _____ decrease in the population as people move away to find new jobs.

WORDS IN COLLOCATIONS AND EXPRESSIONS

Following are common collocations (word partners) and expressions with some of the key words. Read the definitions and then complete the conversations with the correct form of the collocations and expressions.

1. **apply**	
• **application form**	the document used to make a formal, especially written, request for a job, place at a college, etc.
2. **confess**	
• **confess that**	to admit something that you feel embarrassed or surprised about
3. **private**	
• **in private**	without other people listening or watching
4. **regret**	
• **have no regrets (about sth)**	to not be sorry at all about doing something
• **regret that/regret (doing sth)**	to feel sorry about something you have done and wish you had not done it
5. **shame**	
• **it's a shame (that/to do sth)**	used in order to say that a situation is disappointing

1. FUMIHIKO: I studied English in high school. Did you study a foreign language?

   JANE: Yes, Latin. It's not very useful, is it? Sometimes I _____*regret that*_____ I didn't choose another language.

2. SECRETARY: Here's a(n) _____.

   MINJUNG: May I please have a pen to complete it?

3. HILDA: I discussed my problems with my boss _____.

   LUCIA: Did he agree to give you some time off?

4. DINA: _____ that your cousin couldn't visit you this summer. I've heard so much about her. I think it would be fun to spend time with her.

   FRANCINE: Maybe later in the year she'll come. I'm sorry she couldn't visit, too.

5. KURT: Do you miss your family back home?

   GUSTAVO: I do, but I _____ about going away to college. The instructors here are great, and student life is fun.

6.   BART: How's the American literature class going?

       CARLA: Good, but there are still so many authors I don't know. When the teacher started talking about Edgar Allan Poe, I had to _____ I'd never read any of his work.

▌WORDS IN READINGS

Read the two articles about education. Complete each one with words and expressions from the boxes.

confess that	disappointment	hosts
~~disappointed~~	gradually	it's a shame

WE WANT TO STUDY GERMAN

I am presently in my second year of German at Lexington High School, and I have decided to write this letter to say how ___*disappointed*___ I would be if language classes at our school are canceled. In
order to save money, the school may _____ take German away from the students over the
next few years.

I must _____ I cannot understand why our school places so little importance on the German program. I strongly believe that knowledge of a foreign language is a big plus. Unlike some other subjects, a foreign language can be put to use in the real world right after high school. My
_____ is also directed at our town and our country. It is not surprising that America has poor foreign relations when people cannot find a way to keep foreign language programs in our schools.

Finally, I also think _____ to take away a subject that brings so much enjoyment to the students. Every year Lexington High School _____ a German festival. This event is special to everyone who attends. Students have fun and learn at the same time. Surely there must be a way to give us the chance to learn something we love and something we need—a foreign language.

(Based on information in Sara Harari, "Letter: Don't Cut German Program." Lexington Minuteman online, March 2, 2006.)

applying	bargain	literature	has no regrets	private

CHOOSING A COLLEGE ACROSS THE OCEAN

The Callahan-Flintofts, an American family, have agreed to send their daughter to Trinity College in Dublin, Ireland's oldest and best school. Why didn't they choose a school in the United States? Because top U.S. universities and colleges are much more expensive. At $25,000 a year for all costs, Trinity College is a(n) _____.

More and more American students are _____ to foreign colleges as far away as
8
Scotland and Australia. Money is not the only reason students decide to study outside the country.
Joshua Eldeman of Wisconsin also studied at Trinity, and he explains that being in another country
was an education in itself. He _____ about giving up an American college experience. In
9
its place, he deepened his understanding of the world.

Others, like Eliav Shtull-Trauring of New York, prefer a European education to an American one.
First of all, Eliav didn't like all the _____ sent out by American schools. He called it
10
"glitzy"—trying too hard to show how great the school buildings and activities were, instead of placing
importance on students' studies.

The foreign colleges themselves get something out of this situation, too. Since most are not
_____ schools and only get money from the government, they are happy to make use of
11
the money Americans are willing to pay.

(Based on information in Leslie Berger, "Far, Far and Away." New York Times, January 8, 2006.)

▌WORDS IN DICUSSION

Apply the key words to your own life. Read and discuss the questions with a partner. Try to use the key words.

1. What is a good gift to bring the **host** of a dinner party?

   ### EXAMPLE

   *I think in most countries, it's nice to bring your **host** flowers or some kind of dessert.*

2. What kind of information do you give on a college **application**?

3. When people speak English too fast or with too many new words, do you **confess that** you don't understand?

4. Do you like to shop for **bargains**?

5. You feel **ashamed** because you hurt a friend's feelings. What do you do?

▌WORDS IN WRITING

Write a short answer (1–2 sentences) for each question. Try to use the key words.

1. Did you ever take a trip that led to **disappointment**?

   ### EXAMPLE

   *I felt **disappointed** when I went to Disney World last year. There were long lines, and it was too hot in Orlando.*

2. Have you read **literature** from other countries? Did you read the works in the authors' native language(s)? If not, what works of **literature** do you like to read?

3. Do you **regret that** you didn't start studying English any earlier?

4. Name a skill that you have which came to you **gradually** and with a lot of practice.

5. Are you a person who needs much **privacy**?

WORDS IN CONTEXT

Use the sentences to guess what each key word means. Choose the meaning that is closest to that of the key word in **bold***.*

1. **companion**
   /kəmˈpænən/
   -noun

   - I didn't have any brothers and sisters, so my dog was my one true **companion** in childhood.
   - The two men became good **companions** during their long trip.

   Companion means . . .   a. a guide   b. a protector   c. a friend

2. **curious**
   /ˈkyʊriəs/
   -adjective

   - I've always been **curious**, so it's my habit to ask many questions.
   - The **curious** child wanted a closer look at each animal at the zoo.

   Curious means . . .   a. rude   b. wanting to know   c. talkative

3. **desire**
   /dɪˈzaɪɚ/
   -noun

   - Mrs. Dixon has a strong **desire** to spend time with all her grandchildren.
   - During the interview I explained my **desire** for a job that allows me to travel and use my language skills.

   Desire means . . .   a. a habit   b. a wish   c. a regret

4. **heal**
   /hil/
   -verb

   - Daphne hurt her ankle when she fell. It took a few weeks for it to **heal**.
   - If you want that cut to **heal**, you should keep it clean.

   Heal means . . .   a. to become healthy   b. to become clean   c. to become strong

5. **manner**
   /ˈmænɚ/
   -noun

   - The waiters and cooks work together in a very organized **manner**.
   - Thelma threw her books and bag on the bed in a very careless **manner**.

   Manner means . . .   a. way   b. voice   c. thought

6. **observe**
   /əbˈzɚv/
   -verb

   - The math teacher **observed** the students' work on the board and helped as needed.
   - Daryl loves to **observe** the changes in the stars from season to season.

   Observe means . . .   a. to help   b. to watch   c. to correct

7. **prevent**
/prɪvent/
-verb

- To **prevent** a fire, don't leave dish towels or napkins near the stove.
- You should wear a seatbelt to **prevent** getting seriously hurt in an accident.

Prevent means . . .
   a. to stop from happening
   b. to make happen
   c. to do something carefully

8. **pure**
/pyʊr/
-adjective

- I buy only **pure** apple juice. I don't like juices with added sugar and coloring.
- The necklace must be **pure** gold because it's very expensive.

Pure means . . .
   a. not real
   b. not cheap
   c. not mixed

9. **remind**
/rɪ'maɪnd/
-verb

- I forgot the name of our neighbor; my wife had to **remind** me.
- Please **remind** me to buy some bread or else we won't have any for dinner.

Remind means . . .
   a. to make you remember
   b. to ask someone to do something
   c. to share a secret

10. **suffer**
/'sʌfɚ/
-verb

- The family was thankful that the grandfather didn't **suffer** much before his death.
- The bus ride was awful; we **suffered** the summer heat without any air conditioning.

Suffer means . . .
   a. to become unhealthy
   b. to become angry
   c. to experience something bad

▍WORDS AND DEFINITIONS

Match each key word with its definition.

1. ____*curious*____ wanting to know or learn about something

2. _____ to become healthy again (said of a hurt or broken part of the body)

3. _____ to make someone remember something they should know but forgot, or to make someone remember something s/he must do

4. _____ to stop something from happening, or to stop someone from doing something

5. _____ a strong hope or wish

6. _____ to experience something bad, such as pain or sickness

7. _____ not mixed with anything else

8. _____ someone whom you spend a lot of time with, especially a friend

9. _____ to watch someone or something carefully

10. _____ the way in which something is done or happens

COMPREHENSION CHECK

Choose the best answer.

1. Each of the following situations can cause you to **suffer** EXCEPT
   a. having a headache.
   b. making a new friend.
   c. losing your job.

2. Which of the following people must have a careful **manner**?
   a. a farmer putting on an old pair of boots
   b. a boy playing in the rain
   c. a doctor performing a heart operation

3. I must **remind** my roommate to put dirty dishes in the sink because
   a. she's very good at remembering to do this.
   b. we have a new dishwasher.
   c. she often forgets to do this.

4. All of the following can **heal** EXCEPT
   a. gray hair.
   b. a broken finger.
   c. sunburn.

5. Fumiye **prevented** an accident by
   a. blowing out a candle before leaving the house.
   b. leaving a lit candle in an empty room.
   c. putting a lit candle near the curtains.

6. Who does NOT **observe** other people as part of their job?
   a. a doctor
   b. a reporter
   c. an architect

7. **Companions**
   a. spend a lot of time together.
   b. envy each other.
   c. compete with each other.

8. Which of the following people is NOT **curious**?
   a. Rich is taking a nap on the living room couch.
   b. Polly's looking in her neighbor's window.
   c. Stefan's staying after class to ask his teacher more questions.

9. Brigita has a **desire** to travel around the world; she is
   a. close to her family and never wants to go far away from them.
   b. afraid to travel by air or sea.
   c. learning English and Spanish to make her travels easier.

10. Which of the following items is **pure**?
    a. sugar
    b. concrete
    c. iced tea

▌WORD FAMILIES

Now that you have studied the ten key words and their basic definitions, you are ready to learn words that belong to the same family as some of the key words. A word family includes words that look alike but have different functions (noun, verb, adjective, or adverb). Their meanings are related but different.

A. *Look at each model phrase and decide whether the word in **bold** is used as a noun, verb, adjective, or adverb.*

	NOUN	VERB	ADJECTIVE	ADVERB
1. companion				
• a good **companion**	✓			
• to look for **companionship**	✓			
2. curious				
• a **curious** child				
• a deep **curiosity**				
3. observe				
• closely **observed** his behavior				
• the **observer's** report				
• share my **observations**				
4. remind				
• can **remind** someone				
• a **reminder** about the meeting				
5. suffer				
• to **suffer** greatly				
• stop their **suffering**				

B. *Read each sentence and match the word in **bold** with the correct definition.*

__d__ 1. Our science teacher developed our **curiosity** about the world around us.

_____ 2. Cort's **observation** about Roy's performance was fair.

_____ 3. Margot says that her cat gives all the **companionship** she needs.

_____ 4. The medicine would stop the patient's **suffering**, but it couldn't cure him.

_____ 5. The nature **observer** took notes about each bird and animal she saw.

_____ 6. I put **reminders** on my calendar and look at it each morning to remember what I must do.

a. someone whose job it is to watch a situation, system, business, etc.

b. a friendly relationship

c. the act or process of carefully watching someone or something, or one of the facts you learn from doing this

d. the wish to know something or to learn about something

e. something that makes you notice or remember something

f. the state of experiencing pain, sickness, or other great difficulty

SAME WORD, DIFFERENT MEANING

Most words have more than one meaning. Study the additional meanings of **manner**, **pure**, and **remind**. Then read each sentence and decide which meaning is used.

a. **manner** *n.*	the way in which something is done or happens
b. **manners** *pl. n.*	polite ways of acting in the company of other people
c. **pure** *adj.*	not mixed with anything else
d. **pure** *adj.*	complete or total (often said of a person's emotions to show how strongly something is felt)
e. **remind** *v.*	to make someone remember something
f. **remind** *v.*	to make someone remember someone or something from past times, or to make someone think of and compare a person or thing to another that is similar

_c_ 1. We bought a jar of **pure** honey.

_____ 2. You **remind** me of my cousin; he has a great sense of humor, too.

_____ 3. The **manner** in which this bakery makes bread hasn't changed in one hundred years.

_____ 4. Winning the game after months of hard practice gave the athlete **pure** joy.

_____ 5. Mother made sure my brothers and I had excellent table **manners**.

_____ 6. Why do I always have to **remind** you to turn off the lights?

WORDS IN SENTENCES

Complete each sentence with one of the words from the box.

companionship	desire	manners	prevent	reminder
curiosity	healed	observation	pure	~~suffering~~

1. Medicines like aspirin have helped to end much ____suffering____.

2. The boy's scratched knees _____ quickly.

3. Thongchai shared his _____ with the supervisor and made a suggestion to improve the business.

4. The book raised my _____ about life on other planets.

5. Someone had posted a(n) _____ in the office to recycle paper.

6. My parents have a(n) _____ to see me finish college.

7. Spencer is such a gentleman. It's hard to find a man with good _____ these days.

8. Tamara felt _____ envy when she saw Kelly's beautiful home and happy family.

9. Uncle Cal missed Aunt Jo's _____; her death left him very lonely.

10. Making safety a habit can _____ accidents in the home.

WORDS IN COLLOCATIONS AND EXPRESSIONS

Following are common collocations (word partners) and expressions with some of the key words. Read the definitions and then complete the conversations with the correct form of the collocations and expressions.

1. **curious**
   - **curious about (sth)/to do (sth)** — wanting to know or learn about something
   - **out of curiosity** — asking out of the desire to learn or know about something

2. **desire**
   - **desire for (sth)/to do (sth)** — a strong hope or wish for something or to do something
   - **your heart's desire** — your greatest hope or wish

3. **observe**
   - **make an observation** — to say what you have noticed

4. **prevent**
   - **prevent (sb) from (doing sth)** — to stop someone from doing something

1. WIFE: You want us to take scuba diving lessons?! Whatever gave you that idea?

   HUSBAND: I've always had the _____ *desire to* _____ see life near the ocean floor. It'll be fun.

2. SUPERVISOR: If you'll allow me to _____, I noticed that everyone in the office is dressed rather casually today. Why is that?

   WORKER: Sir, don't you recall? Fridays are a casual dress day.

3. SON: Why do I have to wear a hat and a scarf? It's not that cold outside.

   MOTHER: It's winter, and it's snowing. I'm just trying to _____ you _____ getting sick.

4. CHAD: Your parents met at a disco club? _____, how old are they?

   LISA: They're both 56 . . . and just so you know, their love for disco ended in the 1970s!

5. ROSARIO: I never want to get married.

   TINA: I do. I guess because my own childhood was kind of lonely, it's been my _____ to have a large family of my own one day.

6. CHAYENNE: Why do you want to become a doctor?

   QUINN: I've always been _____ how the human body works, but it's more than that. I also feel the need to help others, and by healing them, I can do that.

WORDS IN READINGS

Read the two articles about psychology. Complete each one with words and expressions from the boxes.

curious	heal	prevent . . . from	remind	~~suffering~~

THE NEED TO WATCH BAD NEWS

It's not easy to turn away from bad news on television. Reporters show us pictures of people who are ___*suffering*___, and we watch. In fact, the more terrible the situation, the more time we
1
usually spend in front of the TV. What are the reasons for watching such stories over and over again?

Are we simply _____? No, it's much more than that.
2

First of all, we watch because of our need for safety. Psychologists explain that when we watch horrors on TV news, we are really paying attention to how the people in those situations act; we learn from others' experience just like we can learn from our own. If we ever face a similar situation in the future, we are better prepared. We may even be able to _____ the same dangers
3
_____ happening to us.

Also, for some, there is a need to watch and then joke about the terrible events. Is this humor wrong? Bill Ellis, Ph.D., of Pennsylvania State University explains that joking is a way to

_____. A joke can create needed distance between you and the horror. It can also
4
_____ us that life goes on, and we must, too.
5

(Based on information in Richard Conniff, "Addicted to Bad News?" Men's Health, December 2005.)

companion	desire	manner	observed	observers	pure

THE PET DOG: A MIRROR OF ITS OWNER

We've all likely _____ that pet dogs and their owners often look alike, but why is this
6
so? Psychologist Nicholas Christenfeld explains that when people choose a dog, especially one of a

_____ breed*, they do so in a careful _____. "You look for dogs who are
7   8
like you," says Christenfeld.

These findings come from a study in which _____ were able to match dogs and their
9
owners by looking at photographs. Matches were correct 64 percent of the time when the dogs were of a pure breed.

Even more interesting, the likeness between pet dogs and their owner may go beyond the

_____ to find a natural _____. Because pets need attention just like a child,
10   11
it's possible that some people think of them as children. In other words, a dog that looks like its owner can create the need to care for it, just like one's own child would.

A breed (n.) is a type of animal.

So do people choose a pet dog by looks alone? Not always. The same study suggests that personality, in addition to looks, plays a part in the decision. By understanding a dog's nature, we can likely understand the personality of its owner.

(Based on information in "Who's Your Doggy?" National Geographic, May 2005.)

▌WORDS IN DISCUSSION

Apply the key words to your own life. Read and discuss the questions with a partner. Try to use the key words.

1. Do you believe good **manners** are important?

   ### EXAMPLE

   *Yes. My parents taught me good **manners**, and I'm glad they did.*

2. When was the last time you **suffered** from a headache? Did you take medicine?
3. **Make an observation** about the city you live in or the people of this city.
4. Does anyone you know **remind** you of someone famous?
5. Did you ever burn yourself? How long did it take to **heal**?

▌WORDS IN WRITING

Write a short answer (1–2 sentences) for each question. Try to use the key words.

1. Name something you eat that gives you **pure** joy.

   ### EXAMPLE

   *My grandmother makes a delicious chocolate cake that gives me **pure** joy.*

2. Did you ever have a pet that gave you **companionship**? If not, what animals do you think make good **companions**?
3. What is a subject you are very **curious about**?
4. Did you ever have the **desire to** be famous?
5. Did your parents or a close friend ever **prevent** you **from** doing something? Are you thankful?

Key Words

adopt	committee	possess	realize	solve
advantage	depend	property	responsible	tax

▌WORDS IN CONTEXT

*Use the sentences to guess what each key word means. Choose the meaning that is closest to that of the key word in **bold**.*

1. adopt
/əˈdapt/
-verb

- The Taylors weren't able to have children of their own, so they **adopted** a son.
- Danielle was **adopted** at the age of two; she has no memory of her birth mother.

Adopt means . . .
- **(a.)** to make a child part of your family
- b. to give birth to a child
- c. to take a child away from his or her family

2. advantage
/ədˈvæntɪdʒ/
-noun

- The basketball game wasn't fair; the older boys had the **advantage** of being taller.
- Bruno's knowledge of computers gave him an **advantage**; he got the job right away.

Advantage means . . .
- a. something that you are born with
- b. something that hurts others
- c. something that helps you

3. committee
/kəˈmɪt̬i/
-noun

- Bo is on the **committee** of students and teachers that is organizing the spring picnic.
- The president formed a **committee** to do more research; he chose me as the head.

Committee means . . .
- a. a group of people chosen to do something
- b. a political party
- c. a student club

4. depend
/dɪˈpɛnd/
-verb

- Our cat doesn't go outside to hunt; it **depends** on us for food.
- After Rogerio lost his job, he had to **depend** on his parents for money.

Depend means . . .
- a. to need someone's help
- b. to want someone's help
- c. to not accept someone's help

5. possess
/pəˈzɛs/
-verb

- Helen of Troy **possessed** great beauty.
- The family **possessed** almost nothing when they first arrived in the country.

Possess means . . .
- a. to desire
- b. to steal
- c. to have

6. property
/ˈprɑpɚ ṭi/
-noun

- The plants and paintings in my office are my personal **property**. The company only gave me a lamp, bookcase, chair, and desk.
- My roommate doesn't share much; she tells me clearly what is her **property**.

Property means . . .   a. what someone buys for you   b. what you own   c. what you borrow

7. realize
/ˈrɪə,laɪz/
-verb

- We didn't **realize** how big New York City was until we took a cab Uptown.
- The professor gave us the list of books for our class, and I began to **realize** the amount of reading I'd have to do.

Realize means . . .   a. to ask about something   b. to finally understand something   c. to complain about something

8. responsible
/rɪˈspɑnsəˈbɪləṭi/
-adjective

- The two drivers argued over who was **responsible** for the accident.
- The supervisor wanted to know who was **responsible** for breaking the photocopier.

Responsible means . . .   a. saying that someone else is wrong   b. answering for something bad   c. hiding something bad you did

9. solve
/salv/
-verb

- How can we **solve** the problem of homeless pets?
- At the meeting we discussed ways to **solve** the company's financial problems.

Solve means . . .   a. to fix a problem   b. to discuss a problem   c. to make a problem worse

10. tax
/tæks/
-noun

- Joey earns more at his new job, but that also means he'll pay higher **taxes**.
- The price of the TV is $1,995. With **tax** it will be over $2,000.

Tax means . . .   a. money that you pay a store   b. money that you earn   c. money that you pay the government*

WORDS AND DEFINITIONS

Match each key word with its definition.

1. ___advantage___ something that helps you be better or more successful than others

2. _____ something that someone owns

3. _____ to need the help, support, or existence of someone or something

4. _____ a group of people chosen to do a job or make decisions

5. _____ to find an answer to a problem or a way of dealing with a difficult situation

6. _____ to know or understand the importance of something that you did not know before

7. _____ answering for a mistake, accident, or problem

8. _____ the money you must pay the government

9. _____ to own or have something

10. _____ to have someone else's child become a part of your family

COMPREHENSION CHECK

Choose the best answer.

1. Which of the following is an example of private **property**?
   a. your singing voice
   b. your bicycle
   c. your telephone number

2. The boss put together a **committee**;
   a. we all enjoyed the office party.
   b. no one has taken the time to read it yet.
   c. their job is to reorganize the office space.

3. Which of the following Italian language students has an **advantage**?
   a. Jim can cook Italian dishes.
   b. Paolina plans to visit Italy next summer.
   c. Maria hears her grandparents speak Italian at home.

4. If you **solve** a problem, you
   a. discuss it with others.
   b. make it worse.
   c. find a way to fix it.

5. I didn't **realize** your native language wasn't English;
   a. it really surprised me when I heard your family speak Chinese.
   b. I'm glad you told me when we met.
   c. I've always known that your family speaks Chinese at home.

6. Which of the following people do NOT **depend** on animals?
   a. Marcus has pet goldfish that he feeds every day.
   b. Mrs. O'Malley lives alone and has two big dogs to protect her.
   c. The Smith family sells eggs and milk from the animals on their farm.

7. You NEVER pay **tax** when you
   a. buy things in a store.
   b. have a job and receive wages.
   c. receive money as a gift.

8. Curtis was **responsible** for breaking the window;
   a. he saw who broke it.
   b. he paid to get it fixed.
   c. he was very careful not to hit it with his baseball.

9. When someone **adopts** a son or daughter,
   a. the child gains a new family.
   b. the child becomes homeless.
   c. the child spends time in two different families.

10. Hongsun **possesses** a great amount of money; in other words,
    a. she lost all her money.
    b. it's her dream to be rich one day.
    c. she doesn't have to worry about money.

WORD FAMILIES

Now that you have studied the ten key words and their basic definitions, you are ready to learn words that belong to the same family as some of the key words. A word family includes words that look alike but have different functions (noun, verb, adjective, or adverb). Their meanings are related but different.

A. *Look at each model phrase and decide whether the word in* **bold** *is used as a noun, verb, adjective, or adverb.*

	NOUN	VERB	ADJECTIVE	ADVERB
1. advantage				
• have an **advantage**	✓			
• be at a **disadvantage**	✓			
2. depend				
• to **depend** on your parents				
• a **dependable** employee				
• be **dependent** on your performance				
3. possess				
• must **possess** these skills				
• a **possessive** husband				
4. responsible				
• be **responsible** for the damage				
• accept **responsibility** for your actions				
5. solve				
• can **solve** a problem				
• found a **solution**				

B. *Read the first half of each sentence and match it with the appropriate ending.*

_e_ 1. If readers lose a library book, they must take

____ 2. Complaining won't help. Let's try to find

____ 3. The professor said that my grade is

____ 4. As a college graduate, not having any work experience was

____ 5. You can trust Allen to help when you need it. He's

____ 6. Zhanna doesn't like her boyfriend to have any female friends; she's

a. **dependent** on my performance on the final exam.

b. a **solution** to the problem.

c. so **possessive**.

d. a **disadvantage**.

e. **responsibility**.

f. a **dependable** person and a good worker.

SAME WORD, DIFFERENT MEANING

Most words have more than one meaning. Study the additional meanings of **adopt, property, responsible,** and **responsibility.** Then read each sentence and decide which meaning is used.

a.	**adopt** v.	to have someone else's child become a part of your family
b.	**adopt** v.	to begin to have or use an idea, plan, or way of doing something
c.	**property** n.	something that someone owns
d.	**property** n.	land, buildings, or both together
e.	**responsible** adj.	answering for a mistake, accident, or problem
f.	**responsible** adj.	having good sense and able to be trusted
g.	**responsibility** n.	a duty to answer for something bad you did
h.	**responsibility** n.	something you must do because it's your duty or a part of your job

__c__ 1. All the computers and the information on it are the company's **property**.

_____ 2. Son, are you **responsible** for breaking Mr. Dean's window with your baseball?

_____ 3. Valerie and Don plan to **adopt** a child from another country.

_____ 4. The Johnsons feel their daughter is **responsible** enough to drive the family car.

_____ 5. The company **adopted** a new casual dress policy.

_____ 6. My **responsibilities** as cashier are to take orders and accept payments.

_____ 7. My parents bought some **property** in the country. They'll build a cottage there.

_____ 8. When something goes wrong, my co-workers and I share **responsibility** for any mistakes.

WORDS IN SENTENCES

Complete each sentence with one of the words from the box.

adopted	~~dependable~~	possessive	realize	solution
committee	disadvantage	property	responsible	taxes

1. This company needs _____dependable_____ workers.

2. Neither of us likes to cook, so the best _____ is to eat in restaurants often.

3. I'd like to know more about the job. What will I be _____ for?

4. Grandma is _____ during her visits; she asks us to spend all our time with her.

5. Our club _____ the idea of helping to clean up the city parks.

6. The workers complained about how much of their money goes to _____.

7. The students rode their bikes over the grass and ruined school _____.

8. Hasan is in the hospital? I didn't _____ he was sick.

9. The student _____ did a fine job of organizing the fall dance.

10. Not knowing all the students' names was a(n) _____ for the new teacher.

WORDS IN COLLOCATIONS AND EXPRESSIONS

Following are common collocations (word partners) and expressions with some of the key words. Read the definitions and then complete the conversations with the correct form of the collocations and expressions.

1. **advantage**	
• **give (sb) an advantage over (another)**	to give you something that helps you be better or more successful than others
• **put (sb) at a disadvantage**	to place you in a position in which you cannot be better or more successful than others
• **(use sth) to your advantage**	to be useful or helpful to you
2. **depend**	
• **it/that depends (on sth)**	used in order to say that because you do not know what will happen yet, you cannot decide
3. **realize**	
• **realize your dream**	to get something that you have been hoping for or working for
4. **tax**	
• **property tax**	money you must pay to the government based on the land and/or buildings you own

1. STUDENT: Do we have to read the next chapter before Monday's class?

   PROFESSOR: It's not necessary, but it's _____ *to your advantage* _____ if you do.

2. FRED: Are you busy tonight?

   MARCELO: _____ on Megan; I asked her out to dinner tonight, but she still hasn't said yes.

3. BRAD: Do your parents own two homes?

   GUS: Yes. They spend most of the year in Florida, but they still have to pay _____ on their apartment in Boston.

4. JUSTIN: Do you think I should talk a lot about my old job during the interview?

   RENEE: You should let them know you have experience in a similar position. That can always _____ you _____ others applying for the same job.

5. DAUGHTER: I want to be a pilot like Aunt Cynthia. I think that's a fun job.

   MOTHER: I'm sure it can be fun, but I know it took hard work and many years for Cynthia to _____ her _____ of becoming a pilot.

6. DAVID: The fight was over too quickly.

   FABIO: The smaller wrestler's weight _____ him _____. He didn't have much chance of winning.

WORDS IN READINGS

Read the two articles about politics. Complete each one with words and expressions from the boxes.

committees	responsibilities	solve
~~realize their dreams~~	responsible	use this to our advantage

WHEN A TEENAGER RULES OVER A CITY

Some take a lifetime to _realize their dreams_ ; Michael Sessions did it by the age of eighteen. He's
                              1
now the mayor* of Hillsdale, Michigan, a city 100 miles southwest of Detroit. Because he's still in high

school, Michael will make his _____ to the city his after-school job.
                                      2

The teenager has already begun to make a difference. He wanted to call attention to Hillsdale, so

he's agreed to many TV and newspaper interviews. "If we can _____, we could bring in
                                                                      3
business, bring jobs to folks**, [and] bring in other folks to live in our [city]."

Michael's own father, Scott, lost his job at a car factory, and before he found new work, life was

difficult for the whole family. "We didn't eat some nights," says the teen. He feels _____
                                                                                            4
for the 6.2 percent of the people who are jobless in his city, and he wants to help them just as he

would his own family.

Michael will be the mayor for four years, running meetings and taking part in all

_____. Although Michael is so young, the people of Hillsdale have decided to give him a
    5
chance to help _____ their problems and make the city a better place to live.
                      6

*A mayor *(n.)* is someone who is chosen to lead the government of a town or city.*

**Folks *(plural n.)* are people.*

*(Based on information in "High School Mayor Sworn In," CBS News online, November 22, 2005; "18-Year-Old Mayor Sworn In," WTOL
News online, February 7, 2006; William Hamilton, "When the War Room Is the Family Room." New York Times online, December 15, 2005.)*

adopt	dependent	possess	property taxes

PROGRAMMED FOR POLITICS?

Do children _____ the political beliefs of their parents once they become adults? This
                  7
question isn't easy to answer. Political scientists have always thought the experiences we have growing

up shape our political views, but a new report states that such views are in our blood. That is to say, we

_____ something at birth that makes us generally open to change (liberal) or closed to
    8
change (conservative).

These findings came from a study of the political beliefs of more than 8,000 sets of twins*. Three

political scientists used twenty-eight questions about difficult subjects like religion in schools, the

*A twin *(n.)* is one of two children who are born at the same time to the same mother.*

environment, and _____9_____. The twins showed similar feelings on each subject, but these were only general political views. The scientists explained that political behavior is only partly _____10_____ on nature. Being liberal or conservative is decided at birth, but as we get older, our experiences push us towards different political views. For example, people may be against raising school taxes once their own kids finish school.

In any case, it's becoming clearer that people really fall into two groups, conservative or liberal, and nature decides where we belong on the day that we're born.

(Based on information in Carey Benedict, "Some Politics May Be Etched in the Genes." New York Times online, June 21, 2005.)

❚ WORDS IN DISCUSSION

Apply the key words to your own life. Read and discuss the questions with a partner. Try to use the key words.

1. Are you comfortable letting others use your personal **property**?

   EXAMPLE

   *Of course, it's nice to share, but I'm not always comfortable letting others use my personal **property**. It's easy for me to share only with a very close friend.*

2. Name one of your **responsibilities** at home (such as feeding the dog).
3. Have you ever worked on a **committee**?
4. How much sales **tax** do you pay when you buy groceries, clothes, or appliances?
5. Name something you **possess** that you would hate to lose or see damaged.

❚ WORDS IN WRITING

Write a short answer (1–2 sentences) for each question. Try to use the key words.

1. You lost your wallet, and you don't even have money for a bus ride home. Is there an easy **solution** to this problem?

   EXAMPLE

   *The easiest **solution** is to ask someone for money. Another solution is to walk home if it's not far.*

2. You say hello to someone, and then you **realize** you called him/her by the wrong name. What do you do?
3. How might good-looking people **use** their appearance **to their advantage**?
4. What is your success in learning English **dependent** on?
5. Have you **adopted** any of your parents' practices?

QUIZ 8

PART A

Choose the word that best completes each item and write it in the space provided.

1. Customers are _____*responsible*_____ for anything their children damage in the store.
   - a. private
   - b. pure
   - c. responsible
   - d. curious

2. A poor hotel and a dirty beach can easily _____ tourists.
   - a. regret
   - b. disappoint
   - c. realize
   - d. possess

3. Knowledge of other languages gives you a(n) _____ in the workplace.
   - a. advantage
   - b. shame
   - c. companion
   - d. manner

4. Whenever I go to the beach, I _____ not learning to swim.
   - a. regret
   - b. depend
   - c. adopt
   - d. observe

5. The _____ did a very good job of organizing the party.
   - a. bargain
   - b. host
   - c. companion
   - d. manner

6. Our _____ neighbors looked in our window to find out what we were doing.
   - a. private
   - b. pure
   - c. responsible
   - d. curious

7. Library books are placed on the shelves in a very organized _____.
   - a. bargain
   - b. tax
   - c. literature
   - d. manner

8. We didn't _____ that our boss was in the room while we were talking about him!
   - a. adopt
   - b. disappoint
   - c. realize
   - d. remind

9. Many people believe that dogs make good _____.
   - a. bargains
   - b. hosts
   - c. companions
   - d. committees

10. Our store _____ on a certain number of customers to stay in business.
    - a. realizes
    - b. depends
    - c. adopts
    - d. possesses

PART B

*Read each statement and write **T** for true or **F** for false in the space provided.*

   _T_   1. Learning another language is a **gradual** process.

   ____   2. **Bargains** help shoppers save money.

   ____   3. One person can be a **committee**.

   ____   4. **Preventing** an accident is the same as causing it to happen.

   ____   5. If I **confess** to making a mistake, I am keeping it a secret.

   ____   6. Pudding, which is made of milk, eggs, and sugar, is an example of a **pure** food.

   ____   7. Illnesses cause people to **suffer**.

   ____   8. When you **possess** something, it is already yours.

   ____   9. Public libraries are **private** places.

   ____ 10. Films are important works of **literature**.

PART C

Each situation shows the meaning of one of the key words. Write the appropriate key word next to the situation. Use the clues in italics.

adopt	desire	observe	remind	~~solve~~
apply	heal	property	shame	tax

1. We needed a lawyer's advice to help *find the answer to our problem.*   ~~solve~~

2. Gail *became part of* Mr. and Mrs. Snyder's *family* when she was only two.   _____

3. The Gibsons *made a written request* for a loan; the bank will give its decision this week.   _____

4. The scientists *watched* the mice *very carefully* to understand their behavior.   _____

5. My brother has a strong *wish* to buy a boat and travel by sea.   _____

6. When you get your paycheck, you'll see that you've already *paid* a certain amount to *the government.*   _____

7. Dasha *felt guilty* for hurting her friend's feelings.   _____

8. After the car accident, it took months for Claude *to become* fully *healthy* again.   _____

9. Students do not *own* the textbooks; the school does.   _____

10. Jason uses notes on his fridge *to make* him *remember* the things he needs to do.   _____

CHAPTER

25

Key Words

command	defeat	enemy	greed	surface
cruel	disgust	faint	owe	whisper

WORDS IN CONTEXT

*Use the sentences to guess what each key word means. Choose the meaning that is closest to that of the key word in **bold**.*

1. **command**
   /kəˈmænd/
   -noun

   - When the general gives a **command**, he expects his soldiers to listen.
   - At the sight of the scared child, I gave my dog the **command** to sit.

   Command means . . .   a. an idea   b. a rule   c. an order

2. **cruel**
   /ˈkruəl/
   -adjective

   - It was **cruel** to make the cat stay in the cold, dark basement.
   - The angry woman had only **cruel** words to say to her ex-husband.

   Cruel means . . .   a. not intelligent   b. surprising   c. causing hurt

3. **defeat**
   /dɪˈfit/
   -verb

   - Our school's football team is strong enough to **defeat** all others.
   - The Native Americans easily **defeated** George Armstrong Custer and his small army at the Battle of the Little Bighorn on June 25, 1876.

   Defeat means . . .   a. to lose a game or battle   b. to win a victory   c. to kill quickly

4. **disgust**
   /dɪsˈgnst/
   -noun

   - The rich woman looked at the cheap hotel with **disgust**.
   - Sitting in heavy traffic filled the driver with **disgust**.

   Disgust means . . .   a. strong dislike   b. fear   c. great excitement

5. **enemy**
   /ˈɛnəmi/
   -noun

   - My sister was once my worst **enemy**, but we grew up to become best friends.
   - The two men were **enemies**; they each tried to hurt the other's career.

   Enemy means . . .   a. someone who steals   b. someone you work with   c. someone who hates you

6. **faint**
   /feɪnt/
   -adjective

   - Grandma did all the baking in the morning, and in the evening there was still the **faint** smell of bread.
   - I'd never spent a night in a forest before, so even a **faint** sound made me jump.

   Faint means . . .   a. difficult to sense   b. easy to sense   c. sudden

7. **greed**
/grid/
-noun

- Rod already had a good job, but **greed** made him take a new one that paid more.
- The girl's **greed** with toys angers other children; she doesn't know how to share.

Greed means . . .   a. boredom   b. a desire for more   c. a plan for one's future

8. **owe**
/oʊ/
-verb

- My roommate still **owes** me $500 because I paid the rent in full last month.
- Earl **owed** several thousand dollars to the bank; it took a year to pay it all back.

Owe means . . .   a. to have to return money   b. to take money   c. to ask for money

9. **surface**
/ˈsɚfəs/
-noun

- The dolphin broke through the **surface** of the water and jumped into the air.
- The **surface** of the rock was flat enough for us to use as a table.

Surface means . . .   a. the top   b. the bottom   c. the side

10. **whisper**
/ˈwɪspɚ/
-verb

- The father doesn't want to wake the baby, so he **whispers** good-bye to his wife.
- The girls stood in a tight circle and **whispered** secrets.

Whisper means . . .   a. to write notes   b. to use your hands to talk   c. to speak quietly

WORDS AND DEFINITIONS

Match each key word with its definition.

1. ___command___ an order for an action that must be followed

2. _____ difficult to see, hear, smell, etc.

3. _____ to speak or say something very quietly, using your breath rather than your voice

4. _____ a strong feeling of dislike and a low opinion of someone or something

5. _____ hurting people or animals or making them feel unhappy on purpose

6. _____ to have to pay someone because s/he has allowed you to borrow money

7. _____ the outside or top layer of something

8. _____ a strong desire to have more money, food, power, etc. than you need

9. _____ to win a victory over someone

10. _____ someone who hates you and wants to harm you or prevent you from being successful

COMPREHENSION CHECK

Choose the best answer.

1. My **greed** made me
   a. thankful for what I had.
   b. ask for more.
   c. want to share with others.

2. An **enemy**
   a. makes a good friend.
   b. is responsible for your safety.
   c. wants to hurt you.

3. Nadine's **cruel** actions
   a. greatly upset Barry.
   b. made Barry love her even more.
   c. showed Barry her softer, kinder side.

4. Connie **defeated** all the other chess players;
   a. she's very good at the game.
   b. she's not very good at the game.
   c. she's not kind to anyone.

5. Gustavo began to **whisper** because
   a. I couldn't hear well with all the noise.
   b. he didn't want the teacher to hear us talk.
   c. he knows how much I enjoy his singing.

6. The **surface** of the wooden box was
   a. smooth.
   b. open.
   c. empty.

7. Heidi **owes** Mike ten dollars;
   a. he loaned her money for lunch last week.
   b. she gave him money for a taxi yesterday.
   c. it was his birthday.

8. Who does NOT give **commands**?
   a. the head of the police department
   b. a new employee
   c. a parent

9. What would most likely fill you with **disgust**?
   a. a man teaching his dog how to sit
   b. a man laughing and playing on the grass with his dog
   c. a man not caring for the needs of his hungry dog

10. When I looked, the faces of the people on the ship were **faint** because
    a. they were so happy to be on their way.
    b. they were getting closer to land.
    c. they were already far away from land.

▌WORD FAMILIES

Now that you have studied the ten key words and their basic definitions, you are ready to learn words that belong to the same family as some of the key words. A word family includes words that look alike but have different functions (noun, verb, adjective, or adverb). Their meanings are related but different.

A. *Look at each model phrase and decide whether the word in **bold** is used as a noun, verb, adjective, or adverb.*

	NOUN	VERB	ADJECTIVE	ADVERB
1. command				
• a strong **command**	✓			
• to **command** others		✓		
2. cruel				
• a **cruel** person				
• to speak **cruelly**				
3. defeat				
• quickly **defeat** the other army				
• learn from **defeat**				
4. disgust				
• will **disgust** you				
• a **disgusting** action				
5. greed				
• act out of **greed**				
• a **greedy** person				
6. whisper				
• to **whisper** a secret				
• must speak in a **whisper**				

B. *Read each sentence and match the word in **bold** with the correct definition.*

<u> b </u> 1. Don't be so **greedy**. You don't need to put so much food on your plate all at once.

_____ 2. In the library, I heard the **whispers** of students who were studying together.

_____ 3. The thought of having to put on yesterday's dirty clothes was **disgusting**.

_____ 4. The fans were upset over their team's unexpected **defeat**.

_____ 5. The leader will **command** his men as they go into war.

_____ 6. The older boy **cruelly** pushed the younger boy and made him fall.

a. very unpleasant or unacceptable

b. wanting more money, food, power, etc. than you need

c. to tell someone to do something, especially if you are in a position of power

d. a very quiet voice

e. failure to win or succeed

f. done in a way to hurt others or make them feel unhappy on purpose

SAME WORD, DIFFERENT MEANING

*Most words have more than one meaning. Study the additional meanings of **command**, **faint**, **owe**, and **surface**. Then read each sentence and decide which meaning is used.*

a.	**command** *n.*	an order for an action that must be followed
b.	**command** *n.*	the total control of a group of people or a situation
c.	**faint** *adj.*	difficult to see, hear, smell, etc.
d.	**faint** *v.*	to fall into a state for a short time in which you are not awake or able to understand what is happening around you
e.	**owe** *v.*	to have to pay someone because s/he has allowed you to borrow money
f.	**owe** *v.*	to feel thankful because someone has done something for you and to want to return the kindness
g.	**surface** *n.*	the outside or top layer of something
h.	**surface** *n.*	the qualities that someone or something seems to have until you learn more about him, her, or it

___*g*___ 1. The **surface** of the glass box had fingerprints all over it.

_____ 2. When young girls saw their favorite singer, they often **fainted** from excitement.

_____ 3. Thanks for picking up my medicine at the pharmacy. How much do I **owe** you?

_____ 4. Robert E. Lee was in **command** of the southern army in the American Civil War.

_____ 5. On the **surface** Maggie seemed calm, but deep down she was very nervous.

_____ 6. I **owe** my teachers a lot for all they taught me. I'll never forget their lessons.

_____ 7. The coach gave the **command** for the team to take a time-out.

_____ 8. As we stood on the balcony, we could hear the **faint** conversations of people down on the street.

WORDS IN SENTENCES

Complete each sentence with one of the words from the box.

commanded	defeat	enemies	greedy	surface
cruel	disgusting	fainted	owe	~~whisper~~

1. The people behind me were speaking in a _____*whisper*_____, but I still had trouble paying attention to the movie.

2. It is _____ to spread lies about others.

3. Shelby thought it was _____ to clean the fish; she especially hated the smell.

4. Even if a leader feels uncertain and afraid, he or she must be strong on the _____.

5. The workers saw each other as _____ and made everything a competition.

6. I _____ Randy for taking the time to teach me this computer program.

7. Minju _____ because she had been exercising in the hot sun.

8. The hockey team of the Soviet Union suffered a(n) _____ in the 1980 Olympics.

9. I don't think it's _____ to ask for higher wages.

10. The captain _____ the sailors to sail the ship to the east.

WORDS IN COLLOCATIONS AND EXPRESSIONS

Following are common collocations (word partners) and expressions with some of the key words. Read the definitions and then complete the conversations with the correct form of the collocations and expressions.

1. **command**
   - **have a command of (sth)** to have knowledge of something, especially a language or the ability to use something
   - **take command (of sb/sth)** to take control of a group of people or a situation

2. **enemy**
   - **make a lot of enemies** to act in such a way, especially during your career, that people become your enemies

3. **owe**
   - **owe it all to (sb)** owing thankfulness to someone

4. **surface**
   - **on the surface** thinking that someone or something has certain qualities until you learn more about him, her, or it
   - **under the surface** seeing the true qualities of someone or something because you had the time to learn more about him, her, or it

1. CAPTAIN: I want you to _____ *take command* _____ of the plane. I'm going on break.

   CO-PILOT: Yes, sir.

2. PLAYER: What a great game! We _____ you, Coach.

   COACH: No. You did it all yourselves. Congratulations on a great game.

3. ANDREA: Rick and Ashley seemed perfect for each other.

   MARGE: But _____ they were an unhappy couple. That explains their divorce.

4. JANETTA: Ravi and Tilak _____ strong _____ English and French.

   GILBERTO: Yes, you might never guess that their native language is Hindi.

5. SAUL: You know, there's a serious side to Lou that not many see.

   PAVEL: Really? _____, Lou is always relaxed and funny.

6. DAUGHTER: It seems like many people who did business with Grandfather feared him or just didn't like him. Why do you think that's so?

   FATHER: To become successful in business it's not unusual to _____.

Read the two articles about history. Complete each one with words and expressions from the boxes.

defeat	faint	on the surface	~~owes~~	whisper

THE MANY PEOPLES OF ITALY

Italy's past belongs to more than one group of people. Each one had their own language, beliefs, and way of life. Thankfully, not all has been lost over the years, and today Italy _____*owes*_____ its
₁ — (1: *owes*) — its
richness to all of the peoples from its past.

Much _____ of Italian history and life is thought of as Roman, but a closer study
(2)
shows another view. For example, a number of groups formed the Italic peoples, and their languages
all came from one mother tongue called Sabellic. The very name "Italy" is a Sabellic word. One group
of the Italic peoples was the Umbrians, and their language is more than just a(n) _____
(3)
_____ in today's Italian; all seven vowel*-sounds spoken in today's Italian are Umbrian
(4)
sounds.

There's more. History shows that the Romans were strong enough to _____ the
(5)
Samnites and all other groups, but it was the Samnites who, through battle, taught the Romans much
about fighting, from how to move in the mountains to which weapons** work best.

There are some very old practices that are still alive today. Many of them, such as the use of snakes
by the Marsians, have religious beginnings. Today these practices go beyond religion; they are part of
the past's gift to present-day Italy.

*A vowel (n.) is the letter a, e, i, o, u, or sometimes y.

**A weapon (n.) is something that you use to fight with.

(Based on information in Erla Zwingle, "Italy Before the Romans." National Geographic, January 2005.)

cruel	disgust	enemy	greedy	took command

BLACKBEARD'S LAST HOME

Blackbeard, like any other pirate*, was _____ and _____ as he stole
(6) (7)
and killed throughout his lifetime. You'd think that people today would remember such a person with
_____, but the people living in Bath, North Carolina, are quite happy to have Blackbeard
(8)
as a part of their town's history.

The famous pirate came to Bath in 1718 to make a home. The people of Bath chose not to see
Blackbeard as a(n) _____; the pirate pleased many of them by spending his money in
(9)

*A pirate (n.) is someone who sails on the oceans, attacking other boats and stealing things from them.

their town and selling stolen goods at low prices. Sadly, this time did not last long. Near the end of 1718, Blackbeard was killed by the British Royal Navy.

Interest in the pirate and his life is still strong today. In 1996 a pirate ship was found near North Carolina, and it's thought to be Blackbeard's. Blackbeard called his ship *The Queen Anne's Revenge*†. He changed the name after he _____ of it from the French. Some like to think that
                                                    10
Blackbeard left more than a ship behind when he died, but he probably spent most of his money and chose not to leave any treasure‡.

†Revenge *(n.) is something you do in order to punish someone who has hurt you.*

‡*A treasure (n.) is gold, silver, jewels, etc.*

(Based on information in Willie Drye, "Blackbeard's Legend, Legacy Live on in North Carolina." National Geographic online, March 7, 2006.)

▌WORDS IN DISCUSSION

Apply the key words to your own life. Read and discuss the questions with a partner. Try to use the key words.

1. Name a situation in which you felt **greedy** or perhaps you seemed **greedy**.

   EXAMPLE

   *In my last job, I wanted more money. Maybe my boss thought I was **greedy**, but I don't think I was.*

2. Have you ever **fainted**?
3. Name a **command** that most dogs can learn.
4. Where is it not unusual for people to **whisper**?
5. Name something in the room with a smooth **surface.**

▌WORDS IN WRITING

Write a short answer (1–2 sentences) for each question. Try to use the key words.

1. What is something you should do if you don't want to **make a lot of enemies**?

   EXAMPLE

   *Be honest. Lies help to **make a lot of enemies**.*

2. Who or what do you think you **owe** most of your happiness to?
3. Can you easily accept **defeat**?
4. Is there a habit some people have that **disgusts** you?
5. If someone is **cruel** to you, are you **cruel** in return?

Key Words

avoid	demand	fit	press	reach
combine	figure	offer	provide	store

WORDS IN CONTEXT

*Use the sentences to guess what each key word means. Choose the meaning that is closest to that of the key word in **bold**.*

1. **avoid**
   /əˈvɔɪd/
   -verb

   - Dress warmly in the winter to **avoid** getting sick.
   - I **avoid** traffic by riding my bike to work.

   Avoid means . . .   a. to make something worse   (b.) to stop from happening   c. to make happen

2. **combine**
   /kəmˈbaɪn/
   -verb

   - Cinnamon and sugar **combine** nicely on top of buttered toast.
   - The musician **combined** two kinds of music to create a very original sound.

   Combine means . . .   a. to put or be put together   b. to compete with each other   c. to be similar

3. **demand**
   /dɪˈmænd/
   -noun

   - There will always be a **demand** for better technology.
   - The **demand** in the United States for big family cars creates a need for more gas.

   Demand means . . .   a. a desire for something   b. a decision to do something   c. a way of doing something

4. **figure**
   /ˈfɪgyɚ/
   -noun

   - Population **figures** in 2005 placed China at the top of the list with 1,306,313,812 people.
   - The **figures** show that our company's sales are increasing each month.

   Figure means . . .   a. a report   b. a number   c. a business

5. **fit**
   /fɪt/
   -verb

   - Jocelyn **fit** the company's needs, so they hired her immediately.
   - The apartment is very modern, so our old furniture doesn't seem to **fit**.

   a. to suit or be suitable   b. to make something better   c. to look nice

6. **offer**
   /ˈɔfɚ, ˈafɚ/
   -verb

   - Ben is wearing a raincoat, so he can **offer** his umbrella to Pamela.
   - When I couldn't stop coughing, my mother **offered** me water.

   Offer means . . .   a. to be willing to sell   b. to be willing to find   c. to be willing to give

7. press
/prɛs/
-verb

- You don't have to knock; just **press** the doorbell.
- Once I got in the elevator, I **pressed** the button for the fifth floor.

Press means . . .   a. to push   b. to hit   c. to turn

8. provide
/prə'vaɪd/
-verb

- Hotels always **provide** towels for guests.
- Will they **provide** a meal on this flight or should I bring my own food on the plane?

Provide means . . .   a. to rent   b. to supply   c. to create

9. reach
/ritʃ/
-verb

- It took the climbers several hours to **reach** the top of the mountain.
- If I send the package today, it should **reach** my grandmother in time for her birthday.

Reach means . . .   a. to deliver to   b. to move toward   c. to arrive at

10. store
/stɔr/
-verb

- We **store** our Christmas decorations in the attic until December 1.
- Mel's parents are letting him **store** boxes in their basement until he moves into an apartment of his own.

Store means . . .   a. to throw away   b. to hide   c. to keep

▌WORDS AND DEFINITIONS

Match each key word with its definition.

1. ___combine___ to put or be put together, or to work together

2. _____ to push something with your finger to make a machine do something

3. _____ to give or supply something to someone especially, because it is expected or needed

4. _____ a number that shows an amount, especially, an officially printed number or an amount of money

5. _____ to say that you are willing to give something to someone (especially out of politeness or kindness), or to hold something out to someone so that s/he can take it

6. _____ to arrive at a place

7. _____ to be suitable, or to seem to have the right qualities for something

8. _____ a need or desire that people have for goods or services

9. _____ to try not to do something, or to stop something from happening

10. _____ to put things away and keep them there until you need them

Choose the best answer.

1. People plan vacations to **fit** all of the following EXCEPT
   a. their schedules.
   b. their diet.
   c. the amount of money they can spend.

2. Kathy wants to be healthy, so she **avoids**
   a. exercising regularly.
   b. getting enough sleep.
   c. eating lots of candy.

3. We **store** things in all of the following EXCEPT
   a. mailboxes.
   b. jars.
   c. closets.

4. Artists often **combine**
   a. brushes.
   b. colors.
   c. paintings.

5. There's a **demand** for boots, so
   a. the shoe store will be selling a lot of them.
   b. no one needs them right now.
   c. customers are buying other footwear like sneakers.

6. Raymond lost his wallet, so Jessi **offered** him
   a. her purse.
   b. money for lunch.
   c. responsibility.

7. **Figures** help us understand all of the following EXCEPT
   a. population.
   b. poetry.
   c. business sales.

8. We **press** all of the following EXCEPT
   a. a doorknob.
   b. the buttons on a calculator.
   c. the keys on a computer.

9. When the hikers **reached** the cabin, they
   a. turned on the lights and started a fire.
   b. felt sad to leave it.
   c. looked at a map to find their way.

10. The school **provides** all textbooks;
    a. students don't have to buy them.
    b. teachers sell the books needed for each class.
    c. most students are able to find the books they need in local libraries.

WORD FAMILIES

Now that you have studied the ten key words and their basic definitions, you are ready to learn words that belong to the same family as some of the key words. A word family includes words that look alike but have different functions (noun, verb, adjective, or adverb). Their meanings are related but different.

A. *Look at each model phrase and decide whether the word in **bold** is used as a noun, verb, adjective, or adverb.*

	NOUN	VERB	ADJECTIVE	ADVERB
1. **avoid**				
• to **avoid** illness		✓		
• an **unavoidable** problem			✓	
2. **combine**				
• will **combine** companies				
• a good **combination**				
3. **demand**				
• a **demand** for technology				
• must **demand** changes				
• a **demanding** job				
4. **offer**				
• never **offer** money				
• a good **offer**				

B. *Read each sentence and match the word in **bold** with the correct definition.*

___b___ 1. You're in no position to **demand** more money.

_____ 2. An argument with my parents about moving to another city was **unavoidable**.

_____ 3. Thank you for the **offer** to drive me home, but I'd like to walk.

_____ 4. Drinking and driving are a deadly **combination**.

_____ 5. My teacher is very **demanding**, but I enjoy his lessons and I learn a lot.

a. a statement that you are willing to give something to someone or to do something for someone

b. to ask strongly for something because you think you have a right to do this

c. two or more different things that are used or put together

d. making you use a lot of your time, skill, attention, etc.

e. impossible to stop or prevent

SAME WORD, DIFFERENT MEANING

*Most words have more than one meaning. Study the additional meanings of **offer**, **reach**, and **store**. Then read each sentence and decide which meaning is used.*

a.	**offer** *v.*	to say that you are willing to give something to someone, or to hold something out to someone so that s/he can take it
b.	**offer** *v.*	to say that you are willing to do something
c.	**reach** *v.*	to arrive at a place
d.	**reach** *v.*	to move your hand or arm in order to touch, hold, or pick up something
e.	**reach** *v.*	to make contact with someone by speaking on the phone, sending a message electronically, etc.
f.	**store** *v.*	to put things away and keep them there until you need them
g.	**store** *v.*	to keep facts or information in a computer or other electronic instrument

___c___ 1. Many astronauts have been to space, but no human has **reached** Mars.

_____ 2. Charlie **offered** his hand to Brenda to help her get out of the car.

_____ 3. You have too much in your closet. Why not **store** some things in the attic?

_____ 4. While I visited my aunt, I **offered** to take the dog for his morning walk.

_____ 5. Ahmet **reached** for a pen so that he could take a message.

_____ 6. Don **stores** contact information for all his friends and family on his cell phone.

_____ 7. I couldn't **reach** you at home last night, so I sent a message by e-mail.

WORDS IN SENTENCES

Complete each sentence with one of the words from the box.

combination	figures	offer	provides	stores
~~demanding~~	fits	pressed	reach	unavoidable

1. Being a lifeguard on a beach can be physically _____demanding_____ work.

2. Our office _____ coffee, tea, and water for all workers.

3. The hospital _____ information about its patients on the main computer.

4. Judy said she could take me to the bus station. It's a kind _____.

5. The police found a man who _____ the description of the robber.

6. The business owner studied the sales _____.

7. Firefighters must be well-trained because some dangers are _____.

8. I'm going out of town. Here's the number where you can _____ me.

9. Is the microwave working? I _____ the start button, but nothing happened.

10. Miss Sweden had the winning _____ of good looks, talent, and a sharp mind. That's why she won the contest.

WORDS IN COLLOCATIONS AND EXPRESSIONS

Following are common collocations (word partners) and expressions with some of the key words. Read the definitions and then complete the conversations with the correct form of the collocations and expressions.

1.	**combine**	
	• **in combination with**	placing or using two or more different things together
2.	**demand**	
	• **on demand**	to be ready for use when you need it
3.	**figure**	
	• **figure (sb)/ (sth) out**	to understand someone or something after thinking about him, her, or it
4.	**fit**	
	• **fit in**	to be accepted by other people in a group because you have similar interests and views
5.	**press**	
	• **the press**	the people who write news reports for newspapers, radio, or television, or the reports that are written
6.	**provide**	
	• **provide for (sb)**	to give someone the things s/he needs, such as money, food, or clothing

1. ROBERTO: Did you visit colleges this summer?

   ED: Yeah, I visited several. I really liked Swarthmore College out near Philadelphia. After taking a tour, having an interview, and meeting some students, I felt I could _____*fit in*_____ there.

2. HEE-JUNG: Do you still need help with your math homework?

   PAT: Yes, please. I keep looking at this one problem, and I can't _____ it _____.

3. DENIS: Why are you taking computer classes?

   MATVEI: I want a better job. I think my experience _____ a better understanding of computers will give me more opportunities and higher wages.

4. SHIRLEY: All the newspapers say that this movie is terrible, but I still want to see it. My favorite actor is in it.

   ELAINE: Well, you can't believe everything _____ writes. Some of my friends at work really liked the movie.

5.   EVAN: Do you like the company you work for?

     VALENTINE: I enjoy the work, but the pay isn't very good. I worry that if I ever get married,
                  I won't make enough money to _____ a family.

6.   JEAN: Why do you have so many books, Grandma? You know with the Internet you can get
                  almost anything _____. Facts, maps, definitions, stories . . .

     GRANDMA: That may be so, but I still like the look and feel of books.

WORDS IN READINGS

Read the two articles about the media. Complete each one with words and expressions from the boxes.

combine	figures	offer	~~on-demand~~	reach

TAKING TELEVISION IN A NEW DIRECTION

The computer age is quickly changing television. As we all know, the Internet gives information and
entertainment ___*on demand*___ . Now when Internet users turn on the TV, they want similar choices.
Television companies have already begun to _____ video-on-demand (VOD) services, so
viewers can see what they want when they want. _____ paint a clearer picture: by the end
of 2005, 38 million American homes had high-speed Internet and 24 million had VOD on their television.

These changes create new problems. Advertisements*, which help keep television companies in
business, have always been created for a large audience**. The VOD service breaks that audience into
smaller groups. Advertisers cannot _____ the number of viewers they once did with
regular TV ads, so they are using new ways like Internet ads. TV companies, which lose business to the
Internet, are looking for ways to make money from VOD services. ABC, for example, will let people
watch the popular program *Desperate Housewives* on Apple iPods for $1.99 a show.

It should be noted, though, that a lot of entertainment on the Internet does not cost anything.
Advertiser Rishad Tobaccowala sees all these changes happening and believes that the TV set will
certainly _____ with the World Wide Web in the future.

*An advertisement (n.), "ad" for short, is a set of words or pictures that gives information about a product, event, or service that tries to
get people to buy or use it. Advertisers are the people or companies that put together such words or pictures.

**An audience (n.) is the people watching or listening to a concert, speech, movie, etc.

(Based on information in David Kiley and Tom Lowry, "The End of TV (As You Know It)." Business Week, November 21, 2005.)

avoid	fit	pressing	provide	store

THE RADIO OF TOMORROW—TODAY

You're listening to the radio in your car, and a good song comes on. You want a copy of this song to
listen to later. If you have satellite* radio, you can record the whole song just by _____
a button.

Do you want to _____ traffic and always have an easy ride to wherever you're going? No problem. Satellite radio can _____ drivers with traffic and weather information along with road maps. Also, those in the backseat will soon be able to enjoy films and music videos—all through satellite radio.

In less than four years about 8 million people have signed up for satellite radio service, and they're not just car owners. Many new cars do have satellite radio, but the radios themselves have become small enough and cheap enough for people to enjoy outside the car. In fact, there are even satellite radios you can hold in your hand. Everything that you _____ can be played back at any time.

The next step is to create radio channels that _____ people's interests, from Frank Sinatra to Bruce Springsteen. There will be a channel for everyone to enjoy, front seat or backseat, in the car or in your hand.

A satellite (n.) is a machine that has been sent into space and goes around the Earth. It is used for electronic communication.

(Based on information in Adam Aston, "All Bruce, All the Time," Business Week. November 7, 2005.)

█ WORDS IN DISCUSSION

Apply the key words to your own life. Read and discuss the questions with a partner. Try to use the key words.

1. What kind of information do you **store** on the computer?

    EXAMPLE

    *I **store** pictures, songs, and some school work on my computer.*

2. Do you know which three countries have the largest populations? Can you give any **figures**?

3. You enter a crowded elevator and must stand far from the door. What's a polite way to ask someone to **press** the button for the floor you need?

4. What kinds of foods would you like airlines to **provide** passengers?

5. Name something that tastes good **in combination with** fresh fruit.

█ WORDS IN WRITING

Write a short answer (1–2 sentences) for each question. Try to use the key words.

1. Are you easy to **reach** by phone? Is it better to reach you by e-mail?

    EXAMPLE

    *I check e-mail throughout the day, but it's best to **reach** me by phone in the evenings. During the day I have classes at the university.*

2. Name a job that's very **demanding**. Would you ever consider doing this job?

3. When was the last time you **offered** to help someone?

4. Are there any foods you try to **avoid**?

5. Name a city that **fits** your way of life and that you would consider moving to.

Key Words

admire	civilize	remain	soil	tame
attract	crop	society	steep	voyage

WORDS IN CONTEXT

*Use the sentences to guess what each key word means. Choose the meaning that is closest to that of the key word in **bold**.*

1. admire
/əd'maɪɚ/
-verb

- I **admire** Piper's strength; she never quits even when things get difficult.
- Children often **admire** an older brother or sister and even try to be like them.

Admire means . . .   a. to respect ⓐ   b. to question   c. to copy

2. attract
/ə'trækt/
-verb

- The company hopes that higher wages will **attract** good workers to apply for the job.
- The art program here is very good. That's what **attracted** me to this school.

Attract means . . .   a. to make you remember   b. to give you a chance   c. to interest you

3. civilize
/'sɪvə,laɪz/
-verb

- Europeans who first arrived in Australia felt the need to **civilize** the natives, the Aborigines.
- Farming played an important part in **civilizing** people like the Egyptians.

Civilize means . . .   a. to make war on a group of people   b. to feed and take care of a group of people   c. to help a group of people develop and improve

4. crop
/krap/
-noun

- The farmer planted a **crop** of wheat.
- **Crops** of corn are important to farms in the American Midwest.

Crop means . . .   a. a farm   b. a group of plants   c. a meal

5. remain
/rɪ'meɪn/
-verb

- My sister will **remain** angry until I replace the CD I lost.
- Marlene and Louisa moved to different cities after college, but they **remained** friends.

Remain means . . .   a. to stay the same way   b. to grow stronger   c. to stop doing or being something

6. society
/sə'saɪəti/
-noun

- In history class, we're now studying Roman **society**.
- It was difficult for Krishna to understand all the ways of American **society**.

Society means . . .   a. a country   b. a large group of people   c. a period in history

7. soil
/sɔɪl/
-noun

- The rich black **soil** in the central and southern parts of Ukraine is good for farming.
- We bought **soil** to plant a flower garden behind our house.

Soil means . . .   a. earth or dirt   b. water   c. a plant or flower

8. steep
/stip/
-adjective

- Meiko was out of breath after she walked up the **steep** hill.
- Be careful. These stairs are **steep**.

Steep means . . .   a. very high   b. poorly built   c. very long

9. tame
/teɪm/
-adjective

- The horses weren't **tame**; they lived as wild animals on the open land.
- People shouldn't try to make animals such as lions and wolves **tame**.

Tame means . . .   a. safe   b. smart   c. trained

10. voyage
/ˈvɔɪ-ɪdʒ/
-noun

- Ferdinand Magellan led the first **voyage** around the world from 1519 to 1522.
- The first **voyages** to the moon were important steps in history.

Voyage means . . .   a. a group of travelers   b. a long trip   c. a ship

▌WORDS AND DEFINITIONS

Match each key word with its definition.

1. ___civilize___ to improve a group of people so that they are more organized and developed

2. _____ to make someone interested in something, or to make him/her want to be a part of something

3. _____ rising up high and quickly (said of roads, hills, etc.)

4. _____ trained to live with people and do work (said of animals)

5. _____ a long trip, especially in a ship or a spaceship

6. _____ to respect and have a high opinion of someone or something

7. _____ plants such as corn or wheat that are grown by a farmer and used as food

8. _____ the top layer of earth (dirt) in which plants grow

9. _____ a large group of people who share the same laws, way of doing things, religion, etc.

10. _____ to continue to be the same way (said of feelings, situations, or conditions)

Choose the best answer.

1. You can take a **voyage**
   a. on a bike.
   b. to another country.
   c. in a few minutes.

2. Each of the following can help **civilize** a people EXCEPT
   a. a written language.
   b. tools.
   c. disease.

3. Many shoppers were **attracted** by
   a. the good bargains.
   b. the high prices.
   c. the poor quality.

4. People in a **society** do NOT share
   a. the same religion.
   b. the same holidays.
   c. the same family name.

5. A farmer can have a **crop** of
   a. cows.
   b. potato plants.
   c. fields.

6. The road is **steep**;
   a. many cars have trouble going up in the snow.
   b. it's easy to get lost.
   c. there's little room to park.

7. The **soil** was very dry;
   a. plants grew well.
   b. nothing grew.
   c. we planted some flowers.

8. Which animals are unusually **tame**?
   a. horses
   b. alligators
   c. penguins

9. The patient **remained** sick;
   a. the doctor kept her in the hospital for another week.
   b. the doctor was pleased.
   c. the doctor allowed her to go home.

10. I **admire** your
    a. bad habits.
    b. rudeness.
    c. writing skills.

WORD FAMILIES

Now that you have studied the ten key words and their basic definitions, you are ready to learn words that belong to the same family as some of the key words. A word family includes words that look alike but have different functions (noun, verb, adjective, or adverb). Their meanings are related but different.

A. *Look at each model phrase and decide whether the word in **bold** is used as a noun, verb, adjective, or adverb.*

	NOUN	VERB	ADJECTIVE	ADVERB
1. **admire**				
• greatly **admire** an artist		✓		
• to feel **admiration**	✓			
2. **attract**				
• will **attract** tourists				
• an **attractive** woman				
• feel an **attraction**				
3. **civilize**				
• to **civilize** the people				
• a **civilized** country				
4. **remain**				
• can **remain** safe				
• our **remaining** time				
5. **society**				
• Chinese **society**				
• **social** questions				
6. **tame**				
• a **tame** elephant				
• to **tame** a lion				

B. *Read the first half of each sentence and match it with the appropriate ending.*

___g___ 1. With his new haircut, Murray looked

_____ 2. Many workers left the company after the changes were made;

_____ 3. As humans moved from hunting to farming, they began

_____ 4. Jonas, a movie lover, said he has

_____ 5. Many people in the United States did not think the American West was

_____ 6. The existence of homeless, jobless people continues to be

_____ 7. Nora admitted there is

a. the **remaining** ones decided to accept the new president and his new ways.

b. to **tame** goats, sheep, and pigs.

c. very **civilized** until the late 1800s.

d. an **attraction** between her and Shawn.

e. a **social** problem around the world.

f. **admiration** for the work of older filmmakers like Alfred Hitchcock.

g. very **attractive**; I was not the only woman who took notice of him.

SAME WORD, DIFFERENT MEANING

Most words have more than one meaning. Study the additional meanings of **admire**, **attraction**, and **remain**. Then read each sentence and decide which meaning is used.

a.	**admire** *v.*	to respect and have a high opinion of someone or something
b.	**admire** *v.*	to look at someone or something because you think s/he or it is beautiful or special
c.	**attraction** *n.*	the feeling of liking someone or something very much
d.	**attraction** *n.*	something interesting or fun to see or do
e.	**remain** *v.*	to continue to be the same (said of feelings, situations, or conditions)
f.	**remain** *v.*	to stay in the same place or position without moving or leaving

_b_ 1. I stood on the shore and **admired** the sunrise over the ocean.

____ 2. Larys felt a strong **attraction** to Winona, but he tried not to show his feelings.

____ 3. The children **admire** Mr. Holland; they say he's the best teacher they ever had.

____ 4. Bella didn't plan to **remain** in London for more than a few hours, but the next flight home wasn't until tomorrow.

____ 5. Niagara Falls is a popular **attraction**; lots of tourists go to Canada to see it.

____ 6. The two countries **remained** enemies for many years after the war.

WORDS IN SENTENCES

Complete each sentence with one of the words from the box.

admiration	civilizations	remaining	soil	tame
attraction	crop	~~social~~	steep	voyage

1. Children learn _____social_____ rules at home and by watching how others act.

2. Gordon has a(n) _____ to red-haired women.

3. The _____ streets of San Francisco make trolley rides exciting for tourists.

4. My great-grandfather kept a diary of his _____ from Hamburg to New York.

5. American, Australian, and Canadian _____ developed from Europe.

6. Humans learned to _____ animals for food, transport, and physical work.

7. Which painter do you have the greatest _____ for?

8. Plants need good _____, water, and sun.

9. Yesterday I started to review my notes for the history test; I'll finish with the _____ notes this evening.

10. This farm has only one _____: wheat.

▌WORDS IN COLLOCATIONS AND EXPRESSIONS

Following are common collocations (word partners) and expressions with some of the key words. Read the definitions and then complete the conversations with the correct form of the collocations and expressions.

1. **admire**
   - **have (a deep or great) admiration for (sb)/(sth)**   to have respect for and a high opinion of someone or something

2. **attract**
   - **attract attention**   to make someone give their attention to something or someone else
   - **attraction to (sb)/(sth)**   the feeling of liking someone or something very much
   - **be attracted to (sb)**   to like someone and want to have a romantic or sexual relationship with him/her

3. **crop**
   - **crop up**   to happen or appear suddenly in an unexpected way

4. **society**
   - **high society**   the smaller group of people within a larger society that has the most money and power and is thought to have a fashionable life

1. JASON: My brother has a(n) _____*attraction to*_____ women in the arts.

   NORBERT: He told you that?

   JASON: No, but his past girlfriends include a poet, a dancer, and a painter.

2. TERESE: Leanne's hair is no longer orange. It's blue. Did you see her?

   LEO: No, but it's not unusual for her. She likes to _____ with bright hair colors.

3. PARENT 1: I sometimes have trouble understanding what my teenager is talking about.

   PARENT 2: I do, too. New expressions _____ all the time among teenagers.

4. SAUL: There were quite a lot of people from _____ at Dana's wedding.

   DALE: That's not surprising. Dana's father is an important businessman in this city.

5. TEACHER: Who will you write your essay about?

   STUDENT: Jane Goodall. I _____ her and all the work she's done with chimpanzees.

6. HEATH: You're not the first to notice how different Betsy and I are.

    PRASIT: Yes, but people are often _____ someone who's very different from themselves. For example, my mom is fun-loving and my dad is very serious.

▌WORDS IN READINGS

Read the two articles about geography. Complete each one with words and expressions from the boxes.

admire	attract	attraction	soil	steep	~~voyage~~

MUCH MORE THAN A GARDEN

If you like the sights and smells of a rich green garden, you might take a(n) ___*voyage*___ to
                                                                              1
the Portuguese island of Madeira, which rests out in the Atlantic among a group of islands. People call

it the "floating* flower pot" because it holds so much beauty. With the temperature almost always

around 68 degrees Fahrenheit, plants grow very well in the Madeiran _____. The island
                                                                        2
has over 3,000 kinds of flowering plants. Many of them were brought by sailors and immigrants†.

Madeira and its beauty continue to _____ people from all over the world. Besides the
                                      3
many plants, Madeira has almost 55,000 acres of forest. Nature lovers can visit the Monte Palace

Tropical Gardens, which have seventeen acres of nature to _____. Also, grapes are
                                                            4
grown on the island, and the wine made from these grapes is well-known.

For those who enjoy city life, there's the capital,‡ Funchal. One _____ there is the
                                                                    5
Monte sleigh§ ride. Passengers experience a quick one-mile ride down a _____ street. It's
                                                                          6
one more reason to say Madeira is more than just an island garden.

*To float (v.) is to stay or move on the surface of a liquid.

†An immigrant (n.) is someone who enters another country to live there.

‡A capital (n.) is the city where a country or state's central government is.

§A sleigh (n.) is a large vehicle that is usually pulled by animals such as horses. Note: the sleigh in Funchal is pulled by men.

(Based on information in "This Week's Dream: A Tropical Portuguese Garden." The Week, January 27, 2006.)

civilized	crops	remained	societies	tame	tamed

AFRICA UNDER GEOGRAPHY'S CONTROL

At first it may be difficult to understand why Africa as a whole faces so many difficulties today.

After all, this continent is where human history began, so Africans got an early start in the world. How

then did Europe, Asia, North and South America, and Australia get so far ahead? Part of the answer

lies in geography.

The type of land decided where _____ would form and grow. About 10,000 years ago,
7

humans learned to farm and _____ animals for everyday use. For example, people in
8

Asia had _____ of wheat and barley, and Europeans had sheep and horses. All of this
9

meant that they could stop hunting for food; those people _____ in one place and grew
10

in number as well as in skill. Soon after humans learned to control land and animals, they learned how

to make metal tools and how to write. Groups of people became organized and _____.
11

But in Africa, geography worked against such growth. Places like South Africa didn't have natural

food crops such as wheat and barley. Also, the kinds of large animals living in Africa couldn't be

_____ like the smaller ones on other continents.
12

The good news is that the past doesn't have to be the future. With money from other countries

to help, Africans can control their development instead of letting geography shape it.

(Based on information in Jared Diamond, "The Shape of Africa." National Geographic, September 2005.)

▌ WORDS IN DISCUSSION

Apply the key words to your own life. Read and discuss the questions with a partner. Try to use the key words.

1. Name a place you know that has a **steep** hill.

   EXAMPLE

   *My street is very **steep**. When I'm tired, it's hard to walk up the hill to get home.*

2. Have you ever planted flowers or vegetables in **soil**?
3. What kinds of problems can **crop up** during a trip?
4. Are you interested in the lives of **high society**? Does news about them **attract** your **attention**?
5. Name an animal that is difficult to **tame**.

▌ WORDS IN WRITING

Write a short answer (1–2 sentences) for each question. Try to use the key words.

1. Do you plan to **remain** where you are right now, or will you move to another city?

   EXAMPLE

   *I plan to **remain** here for a long time. This is where my friends and family are.*

2. Where's a good place to **admire** a sunset?
3. You can take a **voyage** to any island for a one-week vacation. Where will you go?
4. What country are you from? When did **civilization** of your country begin?
5. Name a popular **attraction** in your hometown or native country. Have you visited this place?

QUIZ 9

PART A

Choose the word that best completes each item and write it in the space provided.

1. Corn is the main _____*crop*_____ on this farm.
   - a. society
   - b. crop
   - c. figure
   - d. soil

2. Even after the war, the two countries considered each other _____.
   - a. enemies
   - b. voyages
   - c. figures
   - d. demands

3. Todd _____ an extra pencil to Helen because she had nothing to write with.
   - a. stored
   - b. demanded
   - c. offered
   - d. owed

4. The newspaper printed _____ that showed which companies made the most money last year.
   - a. societies
   - b. commands
   - c. figures
   - d. surfaces

5. The Amish are a small _____ in North America that share a religion and a way of life.
   - a. society
   - b. voyage
   - c. demand
   - d. soil

6. _____ this button to turn the TV on and off.
   - a. Whisper
   - b. Offer
   - c. Press
   - d. Combine

7. The flowers did not grow well because the _____ was too dry.
   - a. disgust
   - b. enemy
   - c. figure
   - d. soil

8. During the spring and summer, we _____ our skis and winter clothing.
   - a. store
   - b. demand
   - c. press
   - d. combine

9. Because the library is a quiet place, my friend and I _____ to each other.
   - a. whispered
   - b. demanded
   - c. pressed
   - d. combined

10. There is usually a strong _____ for housing in large cities.
    - a. voyage
    - b. enemy
    - c. demand
    - d. command

PART B

*Read each statement and write **T** for true or **F** for false in the space provided.*

_T_ 1. A dirty, smelly restaurant would make customers feel **disgust**.

_____ 2. We **admire** weakness in other people.

_____ 3. An employee gives an employer a **command**.

_____ 4. Students don't have to bring food from home if the school **provides** lunch.

_____ 5. If a bank gives you a loan, you then **owe** it money.

_____ 6. A large, well-trained army is not easy to **defeat**.

_____ 7. The **surface** of a pillow is soft.

_____ 8. A bicycle cannot help you **reach** other places.

_____ 9. Companies need workers who **fit** their needs.

_____ 10. A shout from far away sounds **faint**.

PART C

Each situation shows the meaning of one of the key words. Write the appropriate key word next to the situation.
Use the clues in italics.

attract	civilize	cruel	remain	tame
avoid	combine	greed	steep	~~voyage~~

1. The small ship made a *long* and difficult *trip* across the Atlantic.   _____voyage_____

2. Jack *hurt* Lisa *on purpose*; his *unkind* words made her very *unhappy*.   _____

3. The house sat on a *high hill*, and it took me several minutes to climb it.   _____

4. Some rulers are not happy with having power in their own countries;
   they want *more power*.   _____

5. The doctor hoped to see a change for the better, but the patient's
   condition stayed the same.   _____

6. Horses, mules, elephants, and camels can be *trained* to carry and
   work for people.   _____

7. Developing a writing system helps to *organize a group of people*.   _____

8. Even very careful people cannot *stop* accidents *from happening*.   _____

9. The lively music *made* people stop and *take interest* in the street
   artist's performance.   _____

10. The two schools closed, and in the fall they *began to work together*
    as one large school.   _____

▌ WORDS IN CONTEXT

Use the sentences to guess what each key word means. Choose the meaning that is closest to that of the key word in **bold**.

1. advance
/əd'væns/
-noun

- Learning about electricity led to many other **advances** in science, from the light bulb to the radio.
- Alexander Fleming's finding of penicillin was a great **advance** in medicine.

Advance means . . .   (a.) a development   b. an important question   c. a danger

2. afford
/ə'fɔrd/
-verb

- I'd like a new computer, but I can't **afford** one on my wages.
- You can't **afford** to buy those new boots. You still have to pay this month's rent.

Afford means . . .   a. to borrow money   b. to have enough money   c. to lose money

3. case
/keɪs/
-noun

- In most **cases,** a store will allow you to return or exchange clothes.
- It's usually best to ask questions during your professor's office hours. In your **case** there's no time, so why don't you send a message by e-mail?

Case means . . .   a. a situation   b. a request   c. a place of business

4. discover
/dɪ'skʌvɚ/
-verb

- While I was cleaning the attic, I **discovered** old love letters from my grandfather to my grandmother.
- The police **discovered** the criminal's hiding place and arrested him.

Discover means . . .   a. to explain   b. to doubt   c. to find

5. edge
/ɛdʒ/
-noun

- Move the vase away from the **edge** of the table or it might fall.
- I stayed toward the **edge** of the ice and let faster skaters pass me.

Edge means . . .   a. far from the center   b. the center   c. the top

6. manufacture
/ˌmænyə'fæktʃɚ/
-verb

- Some companies already **manufacture** cars that use both gas and electricity.
- This factory **manufactures** children's toys and games.

Manufacture means . . .   a. to make   b. to sell   c. to fix

7. recent
/ˈrisənt/
-adjective

- In a **recent** meeting with the press, the politician explained the new tax law.
- *The Catcher in the Rye*, written in 1951, isn't a **recent** novel, but it's a good one.

Recent means . . .
a. happening in the future
b. happening in the distant past
c. happening not long ago

8. satisfy
/ˈsætɪsˌfaɪ/
-verb

- George eats a lot. It took three hamburgers to **satisfy** his appetite.
- This is a good hotel. The staff does everything they can to **satisfy** the guests.

Satisfy means . . .
a. to make you happy
b. to make you want more
c. to feed you

9. spill
/spɪl/
-verb

- The cup was very full; Michelle was careful not to **spill** any coffee.
- The bottle fell over and red wine **spilled** across the white tablecloth.

Spill means . . .
a. to flow out of something by accident
b. to prepare a drink
c. to serve a drink to others

10. stain
/steɪn/
-verb

- I dropped my cup, and the tea **stained** the carpet.
- Don't wear white pants to the picnic. They can easily **stain**.

Stain means . . .
a. to mark by accident
b. to fall
c. to smell bad

▌WORDS AND DEFINITIONS

Match each key word with its definition.

1. _____stain_____ to accidentally make a colored mark on something, especially one that is difficult to remove

2. _____ to flow out of something such as a cup, bowl, etc. by accident (mostly said of liquids)

3. _____ a new understanding or creation that makes something develop or improve

4. _____ having happened or begun to exist only a short time ago

5. _____ the part of something that is farthest from the center

6. _____ to find something that was hidden or that people did not know about before

7. _____ a situation that exists, or an example of that situation

8. _____ to use machines to make goods, usually in large numbers

9. _____ to make someone happy by providing what s/he wants or needs

10. _____ to have enough money to buy something

Choose the best answer.

1. Which of the following items does NOT have an **edge**?
   a. a box
   (b.) a ball
   c. a chair

2. If a restaurant **satisfies** its customers,
   a. the food and service must be good.
   b. the customers must pay too much.
   c. the food must be free.

3. The box of rice **spilled**
   a. when I hit it with my elbow.
   b. because it was so old.
   c. for only $2.00; it was a bargain.

4. We can **manufacture** each of the following EXCEPT
   a. fruit.
   b. cars.
   c. coats.

5. The Murphy family cannot **afford** a big house, so
   a. they live in a small apartment.
   b. they chose to build the largest house in the neighborhood.
   c. they need more space for their four children.

6. The man **discovered** gold;
   a. people sold him everything from rings to watches.
   b. he then became very rich.
   c. he liked it better than silver.

7. Which of the following is a **case** of envy?
   a. money
   b. a cruel person
   c. John would like to have Greg's exciting job.

8. What does NOT **stain** clothing?
   a. blue paint
   b. clean water
   c. tomato sauce

9. Here's a **recent** letter from Rick; I received it
   a. a few years ago.
   b. a few months ago.
   c. a few days ago.

10. All of the following are **advances** in technology EXCEPT
    a. keeping cars that use too much gas.
    b. moving from regular phones to cell phones.
    c. making computers smaller and lighter.

▌WORD FAMILIES

Now that you have studied the ten key words and their basic definitions, you are ready to learn words that belong to the same family as some of the key words. A word family includes words that look alike but have different functions (noun, verb, adjective, or adverb). Their meanings are related but different.

A. *Look at each model phrase and decide whether the word in **bold** is used as a noun, verb, adjective, or adverb.*

	NOUN	VERB	ADJECTIVE	ADVERB
1. **advance**				
• an **advance** in science	✓			
• an **advanced** math class			✓	
2. **afford**				
• can't **afford** a house				
• an **affordable** car				
3. **discover**				
• to **discover** a new land				
• an important **discovery**				
4. **recent**				
• a **recent** film				
• see a friend **recently**				
5. **satisfy**				
• to **satisfy** the boss				
• to be **satisfied** with the results				
6. **stain**				
• **stain** your shirt with coffee				
• a large **stain**				

B. *Read the first half of each sentence and match it with the appropriate ending.*

_b_ 1. I washed my pants two times, but

_____ 2. Shanna wants to have a dinner party because she finished

_____ 3. California's population increased after

_____ 4. Kristi studied French in high school, so now in college she's

_____ 5. We'd really like to buy an apartment in the city, but the suburbs are

_____ 6. I rewrote my essay, and now the teacher is

a. a cooking class **recently**.

b. the **stain** is still there.

c. **satisfied** with my work.

d. the **discovery** of gold.

e. more **affordable**.

f. an **advanced** student.

SAME WORD, DIFFERENT MEANING

Most words have more than one meaning. Study the additional meanings of **case**, **discover**, and **satisfy**.
Then read each sentence and decide which meaning is used.

a.	**case** *n.*	a situation that exists, or an example of that situation
b.	**case** *n.*	a question that must be decided in a court of law
c.	**discover** *v.*	to find something that was hidden or that people did not know about before
d.	**discover** *v.*	to learn a fact or the answer to a question
e.	**satisfy** *v.*	to make someone happy by providing what s/he wants or needs
f.	**satisfy** *v.*	to provide someone with enough information to show that something is true or has been done correctly

___e___ 1. This pizza has enough meat to **satisfy** any meat lover.

_____ 2. Behind the bookcase we **discovered** a secret room. Who else knew about it?

_____ 3. The lawyer prepared well for the **case.**

_____ 4. The teacher wasn't **satisfied** with my answer. He asked me for an example.

_____ 5. The car accident was a **case** of a new driver who made a careless mistake.

_____ 6. Through the voyages of Magellan and Columbus, people **discovered** that the world was round.

WORDS IN SENTENCES

Complete each sentence with one of the words from the box.

advanced	case	edge	recently	spilled
affordable	discovery	manufactures	satisfy	~~stain~~

1. I'm glad I saw the _____stain_____ on the back of the shirt before I bought it.

2. Reiko stood on the _____ of the sidewalk to catch a taxi.

3. How's Mehmet doing? Have you talked to him _____?

4. Gas prices are so high that driving isn't _____ for everyone.

5. As a kid, I made the _____ that chocolate and potato chips go very well together.

6. Kent and I do yoga, but I'm a beginner and he's in the _____ class.

7. The Nike company _____ athletic clothes and shoes.

8. The waitress _____ the drink before she got to the table.

9. The young lawyer was very pleased to win his first _____.

10. Answers _____ people's need to know the facts.

WORDS IN COLLOCATIONS AND EXPRESSIONS

Following are common collocations (word partners) and expressions with some of the key words. Read the definitions and then complete the conversations with the correct form of the collocations and expressions.

1. **advance**
   - **in advance** — before something happens or is expected to happen
2. **afford**
   - **can afford (sth/to do sth)** — to have enough money to buy something
3. **case**
   - **(just) in case** — used in order to say that someone should do something because something else might happen or be true
   - **in any case** — used in order to say that a fact or situation remains the same even if other things change
4. **edge**
   - **give (sb) an edge** — to give someone an advantage in a competition, game, or fight
5. **satisfy**
   - **be satisfied with (sth)** — to be pleased with something

1. RORY: Why do you keep money in your shoe?!

   SHANNON: It may seem funny, but I always keep twenty dollars in my shoe _____*just in case*_____. You never know if you'll lose your wallet or if someone will steal it.

2. THAWORN: I'm taking a public speaking class at my local college. I'd like more confidence in expressing my ideas at work.

   RYAN: That's not a bad idea. Speaking skills can _____ you _____ in our field.

3. TOM: Dean says he wants a sports car.

   DONNY: Lucky for him, he _____ one.

4. SHARON: I don't have a passport, but then again I don't plan to travel any time soon.

   EMINE: I think _____, getting a passport is a good idea. It never hurts to have it.

5. BOSS: If you cannot come to the meeting, you need to let me know

   _____.

   EMPLOYEE: Yes, ma'am.

6. MARIA: Reginald's company has built some beautiful homes in this city.

   WES: He's a good architect, and he wants people to _____ his work. That's why he asks for opinions of the houses and buildings he creates.

WORDS IN READINGS

Read the two articles about fashion. Complete each one with words and expressions from the boxes.

| case | give him an edge | ~~recent~~ | satisfy | stain |

TODAY'S MAN IS LOOKING GOOD

There was a time when women did all the shopping, and many young men let their moms choose their clothes. A _____*recent*_____ study shows that this is no longer the _____:
1   2
74 percent of men shop for themselves, and men especially in their twenties are taking great care in choosing from the latest fashions. Men today are interested in looking good.

Businesses are following the change in men's shopping habits. More and more male personal care products are being sold, from aftershave to face care lotions. Companies like Procter & Gamble and Johnson & Johnson want to _____ mens' new needs.
                                  3

Today's man wants his clothes to fit right and look stylish, so he chooses a dress shirt to go with a suit or blazer made just for him. He is likely a white-collar* worker, and he knows that dressing well can _____ in the professional world.
       4

The clothes must also be "smart." He wants shirts that never have wrinkles** and pants with a waist size that changes with his weight. Clothes that don't _____ or get wet very easily
                                                                    5
are another example of what men want these days. The changes are making everyone happy. The stores make more money, and the men look their best.

*A white-collar worker (n.) is someone who has a job in an office, bank, etc., and who often has a higher position over others.

**Wrinkles (n.) are small folds; wrinkles in clothes must be ironed.

(Based on information in Pallavi Gogoi, "Men Dress for [Retail] Success." Business Week online, January 20, 2006.)

| advances | can afford | discovering | manufacture | spill |

COOL CLOTHES

Fashion and technology are combining, and the way we shop for clothes will soon change. We'll be asking a salesperson, "What does it *do*?" We won't just wear our clothes; we'll use our clothes. Clothing makers are _____ how science can change everything from our hats down to our shoes.
                   6

Don't worry about taking your cell phone or MP3 player with you in the future. Motorola is working with one clothing company to _____ ski jackets and helmets that will let you
                                          7
make phone calls. As for clothes with MP3 players, they're already here. Of course, not everyone _____ a Burton Snowboards jacket for $499, but with more _____ in
       8   9
technology, the prices will come down.

A California company called Nano-Tex is working with popular clothing lines like Gap and Hugo Boss to give us clothes that hold in heat and keep out dirt. There is talk of $1,000 evening gowns that won't stain if you _____ red wine on them.
10

The world of fashion is changing. It's not enough anymore to have cool clothes. You need clothes that do cool things. Just wait. In a short time, we'll all be talking to our color-changing clothes as we turn up the volume for our favorite song.

(Based on information in Booth Moore, "So Plugged In." LA Times online, January 28, 2006.)

WORDS IN DISCUSSION

Apply the key words to your own life. Read and discuss the questions with a partner. Try to use the key words.

1. Do you know how to remove a difficult **stain**?

   EXAMPLE

   *Toothpaste can help remove a difficult **stain**.*

2. Name something in the room with **edges**.

3. Name a **recent** film that you haven't seen yet but want to.

4. Name a company that **manufactures** good clothing. Do you often buy clothes from this company?

5. You **spill** a cold drink on someone's shoes in the movie theater. What do you do?

WORDS IN WRITING

Write a short answer (1–2 sentences) for each question. Try to use the key words.

1. Name something you bought **recently**. Are you **satisfied with** it?

   EXAMPLE

   *I bought a mystery novel **recently**. I'm not finished reading it, but so far I'm very **satisfied with** it.*

2. Name something you take with you on trips **just in case**.

3. What is something you want but **cannot afford** right now?

4. Name an important **discovery** in science.

5. How long will it take you to reach an **advanced** level of English?

Key Words

common	force	multiply	particular	sort
detail	miss	object	rapid	value

WORDS IN CONTEXT

Use the sentences to guess what each key word means. Choose the meaning that is closest to that of the key word in **bold**.

1. **common**
   /ˈkamən/
   -adjective

   • Blond-haired children are **common** among Scandinavian families.
   • It's **common** to feel nervous before flying by plane for the first time.

   Common means . . .   a. not interesting or important   b. unusual or surprising   (c.) happening or appearing often

2. **detail**
   /ˈditeɪl, dɪˈteɪl/
   -noun

   • Chad told us every **detail** about his trip to California; it sounded exciting.
   • You need to add more **details** to your paragraph. It's too general.

   Detail means . . .   a. a word   b. a piece of information   c. an activity

3. **force**
   /fɔrs/
   -verb

   • Parents shouldn't **force** their children to eat if they're not hungry.
   • I **force** myself to exercise every morning, even if I'm really tired.

   Force means . . .   a. to make someone do something   b. to tell someone not to do something   c. to politely ask someone to do something

4. **miss**
   /mɪs/
   -verb

   • Come to the party tonight. It'll be so much fun. You can't **miss** it!
   • I **missed** class yesterday. May I borrow your notes?

   Miss means . . .   a. to not go somewhere   b. to forget about something   c. to plan to go somewhere

5. **multiply**
   /ˈmʌltəˌplaɪ/
   -verb

   • As the city's population grows, the number of cars on the road will **multiply**.
   • With less and less money, the family's problems have **multiplied**.

   Multiply means . . .   a. to decrease   b. to increase   c. to stop growing

6. **object**
   /ˈabdʒɪkt, ˈabdʒɛkt/
   -noun

   • During the storm, a hard **object** hit against the window and broke it.
   • Do not give small **objects** to babies; they'll put almost anything in their mouths.

   Object means . . .   a. a sound   b. a food   c. a thing

7. **particular**
/pɚˈtɪkyələ/
-adjective

- Rasool needs **particular** spices to make a dish from his native country.
- You need a **particular** kind of battery for this watch.

Particular means . . . a. expensive b. strong c. certain

8. **rapid**
/ˈræpɪd/
-adjective

- When the deer saw us, it made a **rapid** exit.
- For many, **rapid** changes are difficult to accept. Time is needed to understand them.

Rapid means . . . a. very quick b. difficult c. large

9. **sort**
/sɔrt/
-noun

- You're a lawyer? What **sort** of law do you practice?
- Brie is a **sort** of French cheese. It's light in color and soft enough to spread.

Sort means . . . a. a rule b. a kind c. a piece

10. **value**
/ˈvælyu/
-noun

- The ten-year-old car had a **value** of only $2,500.
- When Denise travels, she doesn't take things of great **value**, such as her gold watch.

Value means . . . a. the cost of something b. a tax c. a loan

WORDS AND DEFINITIONS

Match each key word with its definition.

1. _____multiply_____ to increase greatly, or to make something do this

2. _____ to not go somewhere or do something, especially when you want to but cannot

3. _____ a certain one, and not any other

4. _____ a single fact or piece of information about something

5. _____ the amount of money something costs if you sell it

6. _____ a kind of person, thing, action, etc.

7. _____ a thing that you can see, hold, or touch

8. _____ existing in large numbers, or happening often

9. _____ to make someone do something s/he does not want to do

10. _____ done very quickly, or happening in a short time

Choose the best answer.

1. Of the following, which is an **object** you can find in a college dormitory?

   a. a lecture

   (b.) a textbook

   c. a party

2. Each of the following are **common** behaviors within a family EXCEPT

   a. taking a vacation together.

   b. living alone.

   c. sharing a meal.

3. The number of forest fires has **multiplied** because

   a. people understand the danger.

   b. campers are more responsible about their campfires.

   c. the weather is hot, and the trees and grass are very dry.

4. If Hugh likes the **sort** of games that have a lot of physical activity, he might enjoy

   a. a crossword puzzle.

   b. chess.

   c. volleyball.

5. Each of the following statements give a **detail** about Sharice's job EXCEPT

   a. she works for a bank in Chicago.

   b. she recently became a vice-president.

   c. she likes her work.

6. Helder will **miss** his bus if he

   a. rushes to the bus stop.

   b. stops to buy a newspaper on the way to the bus stop.

   c. arrives on time at the bus stop.

7. Renata needs a **particular** shoe;

   a. she'll be happy to borrow any pair her roommate lends her.

   b. it will be difficult to find the exact color to match her blue dress.

   c. she'll be comfortable in either high-heeled or low-heeled shoes.

8. Theo's mother **forced** him to get up because

   a. she didn't want him to be late for school again.

   b. Theo has an alarm clock.

   c. he was sick and needed to rest.

9. Which of the following has the greatest **value**?

   a. a new dictionary with a CD-ROM

   b. a small box of chocolates

   c. a plane ticket from New York to Sydney, Australia

10. Who does NOT make **rapid** movements?

    a. a worker carrying a heavy box

    b. a robber trying to get away from the police

    c. a soccer player trying to score a point

WORD FAMILIES

Now that you have studied the ten key words and their basic definitions, you are ready to learn words that belong to the same family as some of the key words. A word family includes words that look alike but have different functions (noun, verb, adjective, or adverb). Their meanings are related but different.

A. *Look at each model phrase and decide whether the word in **bold** is used as a noun, verb, adjective, or adverb.*

	NOUN	VERB	ADJECTIVE	ADVERB
1. force				
• will **force** him to leave		✓		
• a strong **force**	✓			
• **forceful** words			✓	
2. rapid				
• her **rapid** growth				
• is changing **rapidly**				
3. sort				
• a new **sort** of shoe				
• must **sort** the laundry				
4. value				
• a **value** of $100				
• to **value** your time				
• a **valuable** car				

B. *Read each sentence and match the word in **bold** with the correct definition.*

__d__ 1. Mrs. Davis placed the **valuable** vase on a high shelf where the children couldn't touch it.

_____ 2. Hyewon **sorted** the bills. Some she had to pay right away; others could wait.

_____ 3. Martin Luther King, Jr. was a **force** for social change in America.

_____ 4. Once Jared turned thirteen, he began to grow **rapidly** and soon became very tall.

_____ 5. The hockey player took a **forceful** swing with his stick.

_____ 6. I **value** the lessons about life that my grandfather taught me.

a. to think that something is important to you

b. powerful and strong

c. very quickly

d. costing a lot of money

e. to put things in a certain order, or to place them in groups

f. something or someone that has a strong influence or a lot of power

SAME WORD, DIFFERENT MEANING

*Most words have more than one meaning. Study the additional meanings of **common**, **miss**, and **value**.*
Then read each sentence and decide which meaning is used.

a.	**common** *adj.*	existing in large numbers, or happening often
b.	**common** *adj.*	belonging to, shared by two or more people or things
c.	**miss** *v.*	to not go somewhere or do something, especially when you want to but cannot
d.	**miss** *v.*	to feel sad because someone or something is no longer with you, or you are no longer doing something you enjoy
e.	**miss** *v.*	to not see, hear, or notice something
f.	**value** *n.*	the amount of money something costs if you sell it
g.	**values** *pl. n.*	your personal rules or ideas about what is right and wrong or what is important

_c_ 1. I don't feel well, but I can't **miss** the final exam.

____ 2. Karel now lives in Boston, and she **misses** the warmer weather in Florida.

____ 3. The owners say the **value** of their home is half a million dollars, but I think it's much less.

____ 4. It's **common** for cats to take many naps throughout the day.

____ 5. Getting into a good college is a **common** concern among high school students.

____ 6. Jacques **missed** the point of the joke, so he didn't laugh along with us.

____ 7. I love and respect my parents, but I don't share all of their **values**.

WORDS IN SENTENCES

Complete each sentence with one of the words from the box.

common	forceful	~~multiply~~	particular	sort
details	miss	object	rapidly	valuable

1. When conditions aren't clean, sickness and disease will _____*multiply*_____.

2. I'm looking for a(n) _____ book on training dogs. Can you help me find it?

3. Don't hide _____ things in a drawer. Thieves know to look there.

4. Fedya has a new girlfriend, but he hasn't given any _____ about her.

5. As night came, the air _____ turned colder.

6. Mi-Young says she saw a strange _____ flying in the sky last night.

7. Keva gave her brother a(n) _____ push to make him stop laughing at her.

8. This is a(n) _____ kitchen. All the students on this floor can use it.

9. You haven't seen your family in two years. Do you _____ them?

10. When I _____ the mail, I throw away anything that's not a bill or a personal letter.

▌WORDS IN COLLOCATIONS AND EXPRESSIONS

Following are common collocations (word partners) and expressions with some of the key words. Read the definitions and then complete the conversations with the correct form of the collocations and expressions.

1. common	
• **common for (sb/sth) to (do sth)**	existing in large numbers, or happening often
• **have (sth) in common**	to have the same qualities and interests as another person or group
2. detail	
• **in detail**	using a lot of details
• **go into detail**	to give a lot of details
3. sort	
• **sort of**	used when you cannot be exact or do not want to give details
• **sort (sth) into**	to place things in groups (by size, kind, etc.)

1. ROOMMATE 1: You're home late. Problems at work?

   ROOMMATE 2: Yeah. But if you don't mind, I really don't want to ___*go into detail*___ right now. I'll tell you about it later.

2. TANNER: I didn't know many students in my high school class. There were over four hundred of us.

   WILL: Four hundred in one class? That's a lot.

   TANNER: It's _____ public schools _____ be large, especially in the city.

3. JOURNALIST: Have you and your fiancé chosen a wedding date?

   FILM STAR: Yes. Our wedding is planned for this coming September.

   JOURNALIST: Will you tell me about your wedding plans _____? Our readers will want to know everything.

4. HUSBAND: What's this? Pudding?

   WIFE: _____. It's not heavy like a pudding; it's much lighter. This is called *leche flan*. Maria, my friend from the Philippines, gave it to me.

5. FATMA: What are you doing?

   BRENDON: I want to _____ these books _____ three boxes: what I want to keep, what I plan to give to the local library, and what I can sell on the Internet.

6. SENIOR: Are you going to live in the dorm your first year?

FRESHMAN: Yes. I just hope to _____ something
_____ with my roommate.

SENIOR: Don't worry. Your roommate doesn't have to be your best friend.

WORDS IN READINGS

Read the two articles about cross-cultural communication. Complete each one with words and expressions from the boxes.

detail	rapidly	value (*v.*)
object	sort . . . into	~~values~~ (*n.*)

SEEING THE WORLD THROUGH DIFFERENT EYES

How do you view the world? A study in *New Scientist* magazine shows that a person's

_____values_____ likely tell the eyes what to see.
1

In the East, people _____ togetherness, explains Richard Niesbett of the University
2

of Michigan. For them it's important to see how smaller things connect to the whole. In the study,

Chinese people took their time when they looked at a picture of a jungle. They let their eyes rest on

every _____, and came to understand that each thing had its place in the picture.
3

In the same study, Americans' eyes went quickly to the tiger that was in the center of the picture.

Why? Because Westerners have a need to _____ everything _____ groups,
4

and in doing this, they decide some things are more important than others. Just as their eyes go straight

to one main _____, they want their lives to move ahead toward something important.
5

Another part of the study used a picture of underwater life. The Asians talked about the stream and

its color; the Westerners wanted to tell about the brightest object in the picture or the fish that swam

more _____ than any other thing in the water. The picture never changed, but what
6

people wanted to look at did.

(Based on information in "The Yin and Yang of Seeing." The Week, September 16, 2005.)

common	forces	miss	multiply	particular

WHICH ENGLISH DO YOU SPEAK?

Canada and the United States are both English-speaking countries, but a careful listener won't

_____ the differences in the way they speak. This is because there are different *dialects* of
7

English. A dialect is a form of a language that's spoken in one area in a way that's different than it's

spoken in other areas. Canadians and Americans may talk with one another every day, but they have

their own dialects.

South of Canada, the North American dialects _____ 8 : northwestern New England, eastern New England, southwestern New England, Middle Atlantic, North, Midland, and South. Each area has a _____ 9 way of speaking. For example, southerners say *pens* like *pins*.

Those who study languages thought at one time that dialects would be lost and a _____ 10 way of speaking English would develop with the growing popularity of TV and radio. But there are stronger _____ 11 that make people want to keep their dialects. For many, one's way of speaking is part of who they are. So Canadians will continue to make the *a* in *back* sound like the *o* in *stock,* and people in western Pennsylvania will read *cot* and *caught* the same way. Everyone will still understand one another, won't they?

(Based on information in "North American Dialects." National Geographic, December 2005.)

▌WORDS IN DISCUSSION

Apply the key words to your own life. Read and discuss the questions with a partner. Try to use the key words.

1. Name a relative you **have** a lot **in common** with.

   EXAMPLE

   > *I **have** much **in common** with my grandmother. We have a similar sense of humor, and we both love music and dancing.*

2. Is there a **particular** song you could listen to every day?

3. Name a musical group whose fans continue to **multiply**.

4. Is your natural walk **rapid** or slow?

5. What are **common objects** that you find on a desk?

▌WORDS IN WRITING

Write a short answer (1–2 sentences) for each question. Try to use the key words.

1. Do you **sort** your clothes when you put them away?

   EXAMPLE

   > *I'm not very organized, but I do **sort** my clothes **into** things for warmer weather and things for colder weather.*

2. Is there someone or something from your childhood that you **miss**?

3. Name a **valuable** lesson you have learned from your parents.

4. If you are on a crowded bus or train and you need to get off, are you **forceful**?

5. When people ask about your family, do you usually **go into detail**?

Key Words

dive	gentle	height	solid	trade
fold	harvest	pipe	steer	wrap

WORDS IN CONTEXT

Use the sentences to guess what each key word means. Choose the meaning that is closest to that of the key word in **bold***.*

1. **dive**
/dəɪv/
-verb

   - At the start of the race, the swimmers **dive** into the water.
   - Jorge stood on the high rock and **dove** into the lake.

   Dive means . . .

   (a.) to jump into water head first
   b. to get out of the water
   c. to lie on the surface of water

2. **fold**
/foʊld/
-verb

   - Mother asked me to **fold** the clean towels.
   - Chas **folded** the letter two times before he put it in the envelope.

   Fold means . . .

   a. to wash and dry
   b. to make one part cover another
   c. to put away for future use

3. **gentle**
/ˈdʒɛntəl/
-adjective

   - You must be **gentle** with eggs because they can easily break.
   - Narin was very **gentle** as he picked up the small kitten.

   Gentle means . . .

   a. very slow
   b. very quiet
   c. very careful

4. **harvest**
/ˈhɑrvɪst/
-noun

   - The families of the farmers gathered to celebrate the **harvest**.
   - **Harvest** is a busy time when many workers are needed in the fields.

   Harvest means . . .

   a. gathering crops
   b. planting crops
   c. selling crops

5. **height**
/haɪt/
-noun

   - The **height** of the bookcase was seventy-two inches. It's hard for short people to reach the top shelf.
   - The great **height** of the buildings in New York City made me look up to the sky.

   Height means . . .

   a. how wide something is
   b. how tall something is
   c. how heavy something is

6. **pipe**
/paɪp/
-noun

   - There are long **pipes** that carry gas to all the homes in our neighborhood.
   - The **pipes** were old, so when the water was turned on, they shook and made noise.

   Pipe means . . .

   a. long tubes
   b. long roads
   c. a long time

7. solid
/salɪd/
-adjective

- Ice must be **solid** for people to skate safely on it.
- The workers dug in the ground until they hit **solid** rock.

Solid means . . .　　a. hard　　　　b. rough　　　　c. flat

8. steer
/stɪr/
-verb

- My driving instructor told me to use two hands to **steer** the car.
- Tyra **steered** her shopping cart over to the fruit and vegetables section.

Steer means . . .
a. to make something　　b. to control the　　c. to stop something
　　start to move　　　　　direction of something　　from moving

9. trade
/treɪd/
-noun

- **Trade** with the United States has helped Taiwan's economy; U.S. companies buy a lot of Taiwanese goods.
- The euro has made **trade** easier among the countries that use it.

Trade means . . .　　a. receiving a loan　　b. traveling　　c. buying and selling

10. wrap
/ræp/
-verb

- Do you want to take some of these cookies home? I'll **wrap** some in plastic for you.
- The salesman **wrapped** the painting in thick paper and tied it with string.

Wrap means . . .　　a. to protect　　b. to cover　　c. to hide

▌WORDS AND DEFINITIONS

Match each key word with its definition.

1. ___*harvest*___ the time when crops are gathered from the fields, or the act of gathering them

2. _____ careful enough so that you do not hurt or damage anyone or anything

3. _____ the activity of buying, selling, or exchanging goods, especially between countries

4. _____ to control the direction of a car, truck, etc.

5. _____ hard, without spaces or holes

6. _____ to place cloth, paper, etc. around something in order to cover it

7. _____ to make a line in a piece of paper, cloth, etc. by making one part cover another

8. _____ a tube (made of metal, plastic, or glass) through which a liquid or gas moves

9. _____ how tall something or someone is

10. _____ to jump into the water with your head and arms going in first

Choose the best answer.

1. Which of the following measurements can be a person's **height**?

    (a.) five feet and eleven inches

    b. 160 pounds

    c. 98.6°F

2. During **harvest** farmers are busy

    a. planting crops.

    b. watering crops.

    c. gathering crops.

3. Because I wasn't **gentle**,

    a. I broke the thin chain.

    b. I was able to close the chain carefully.

    c. I lost my chain.

4. Which of the following objects is NOT **solid**?

    a. a metal ring

    b. warm milk

    c. a tree

5. You CANNOT **steer**

    a. a bus.

    b. a boat.

    c. a bird.

6. Which of the following is an example of **trade**?

    a. an Australian family visiting Spain

    b. a Canadian businessman learning the Chinese language

    c. Ireland selling wool to the United States

7. Severa is going to **wrap**

    a. a birthday present for her friend.

    b. a glass of water for her younger brother.

    c. her homework for her teacher.

8. We CANNOT **fold**

    a. paper.

    b. wood.

    c. a blanket.

9. If Kane **dives** into the water, which part of his body gets wet first?

    a. his back

    b. his feet and legs

    c. his hands and head

10. **Pipes** do NOT carry

    a. electricity.

    b. hot water.

    c. gas.

WORD FAMILIES

Now that you have studied the ten key words and their basic definitions, you are ready to learn words that belong to the same family as some of the key words. A word family includes words that look alike but have different functions (noun, verb, adjective, or adverb). Their meanings are related but different.

A. *Look at each model phrase and decide whether the word in **bold** is used as a noun, verb, adjective, or adverb.*

	NOUN	VERB	ADJECTIVE	ADVERB
1. fold				
• **fold** the paper		✓		
• to **unfold** the paper		✓		
2. gentle				
• must be **gentle**				
• put it down **gently**				
• speaking with **gentleness**				
3. height				
• the **height** of the building				
• to **heighten** their excitement				
4. trade				
• the **trade** between two countries				
• decided to **trade** places				
5. wrap				
• should **wrap** your food				
• **unwrap** your gift quickly				

B. *Read each sentence and match the word in **bold** with the correct definition.*

___*e*___ 1. Kaylee knows I don't like soda, so she offered to **trade** her iced tea for my Coca-Cola.

_____ 2. The movie sometimes used silence to **heighten** your fear.

_____ 3. The smell of fresh soap filled the room when Jana **unfolded** the clean sheets.

_____ 4. My broken nose hurt very much even when the doctor **gently** touched it.

_____ 5. Hae Min needed scissors to help him **unwrap** the package.

_____ 6. Because we knew Mitch to be a tough athlete, we were surprised by his **gentleness** with his nephew when they played.

a. to remove the paper, cloth, etc. that covers something

b. the quality of being careful enough so that you do not cause hurt or damage

c. done with enough care so that you do not cause hurt or damage

d. to raise or increase, or to make something rise or increase

e. to exchange one thing for another

f. to open something up such as paper, cloth, etc.

SAME WORD, DIFFERENT MEANING

Most words have more than one meaning. Study the additional meanings of **gentle**, **solid**, and **steer**.
Then read each sentence and decide which meaning is used.

a.	**gentle** *adj.*	careful enough so that you do not hurt or damage anyone or anything
b.	**gentle** *adj.*	not strong, loud, or forceful
c.	**solid** *adj.*	hard, without spaces or holes
d.	**solid** *adj.*	able to be trusted or depended on
e.	**steer** *v.*	to control the direction of a car, truck, etc.
f.	**steer** *v.*	to influence someone's actions or the way a situation develops

___e__ 1. How can you **steer** the car while you're holding a phone and drinking coffee?

_____ 2. The **gentle** waves softly rocked our little boat, and soon I fell asleep.

_____ 3. Companies work hard to beat the competition and build a **solid** name.

_____ 4. Mia's parents tried to **steer** her toward a career in law, but she chose business.

_____ 5. Monique is warm and **gentle**, so it's easy to see her as a kindergarten teacher.

_____ 6. The actor forgot that the tree on stage wasn't **solid**, and they both fell over.

WORDS IN SENTENCES

Complete each sentence with one of the words from the box.

dove	harvest	pipes	steered	unfolded
gentleness	heightened	solid	trade	~~unwrapped~~

1. Mother _____unwrapped_____ the package, and by the smell I knew we were having fish for dinner.

2. Tudsanee's hands shook with excitement as she _____ the letter.

3. This is a(n) _____ group of students; I know they'll all do their very best on the exam.

4. The farmers came in from the fields; the _____ was finished.

5. We have to clean out the _____ so the water in the sink can flow down easily.

6. The politician skillfully _____ the questions away from subjects she didn't want to talk about.

7. I know you like sitting next to the window, so do you want to _____ seats with me?

8. Watching my favorite boxer shake the winner's hand _____ my respect for him.

9. Kazuyuki took a deep breath before he _____ to the bottom of the pool.

10. I remember the _____ of the nurse who took care of me after my operation.

WORDS IN COLLOCATIONS AND EXPRESSIONS

Following are common collocations (word partners) and expressions with some of the key words. Read the definitions and then complete the conversations with the correct form of the collocations and expressions.

1. **dive**
   - **dive into (sth)**   to enter an activity, usually suddenly and unexpectedly

2. **fold**
   - **twofold/threefold/etc.**   having two parts/three parts/etc.

3. **height**
   - **at the height of (sth)**   during the period when something is the strongest, best, etc. it can ever be

4. **steer**
   - **steer the conversation**   to control the direction of a conversation toward or away from a certain subject

5. **trade**
   - **trade (sth) for (another thing)**   to exchange one thing for another

6. **wrap**
   - **wrap (sth) up**   to completely cover something by folding paper, cloth, etc. around it

---

1. REPORTER: The number of jobless people is growing. What are your plans to help?

   MAYOR: I've put together a _____ *twofold* _____ plan for the city to consider: a new center for job training and a way to bring in new businesses.

2. DEREK: Sometimes it's hard to remember which players are on which teams.

   THORN: Every season sports teams _____ one player _____ another. It's common for players to be on more than one team throughout their careers.

3. JAKE: Have you heard how Quinn's new job is going?

   SEONJU: He had to _____ the position with little training, but luckily he deals well with unexpected changes and learns new skills quickly.

4. FADIMATA: Do you go out for lunch?

   KIM: Not anymore. I'm trying to save a little money. Every morning I make a sandwich, _____ it _____, and bring it to the office.

5. ALLISON: _____ her popularity, that actress was on a lot of magazine covers.

   LIZ: I guess that time has passed because you don't hear much about her anymore.

6. GREG: Rafael doesn't share much about his personal life with his co-workers.

   EVE: No, he doesn't. He chooses to _____ back toward business even during lunch and coffee breaks.

Read the two articles about world economics. Complete each one with words and expressions from the boxes.

heightened	pipes	~~steering~~	trade	twofold

THE IMPORTANCE OF LATIN AMERICAN ECONOMIES

New leaders in Latin America are _____*steering*_____ their countries toward change—not just
1

political, but social. To move closer to such change, these countries must face an important question:
how can they make their economies grow? Julia E. Sweig, director of Latin American studies at the
Council on Foreign Relations, has a _____ answer to that question.
2

To begin with, interest in helping society needs to be _____ among the upper classes.
3

If the upper classes begin to pay higher taxes, they'll help their countries build and care for roads,
hospitals, education, and technology. Putting more money into one's economy can help social growth.

Also, the United States can rethink its use of oil from the Middle East. The United States already
gets almost 50 percent of its oil from Canada and Latin America. Venezuela alone sells half of its oil to
the United States, and Washington spends millions to keep Colombian oil _____ safe.
4

If the United States increases its oil _____ with Latin America, the countries can have
5

more money to help their social growth.

(Based on information in Julia E. Sweig, "Continental Drift." International Herald Tribune online, January 20, 2006.)

dive into	gentle	solid	unwrap

IKEA WELCOMED AROUND THE WORLD

With 226 stores in 33 countries, Ikea has built a _____ name and business. Its
6

furniture and other products are in homes all around the world. But this Swedish company does more
than sell furniture; it sells a lifestyle. Ikea makes it simple and inexpensive to live fashionably. The
people who happily _____ this lifestyle are from the middle classes of those two
7

hundred-some countries. No other store has had as much success.

How do they do it? First, there's the idea of using _____ force. In other words, the
8

stores do everything they can to keep people there as long as possible. For example, there's a playroom
for kids, and restaurants help shoppers keep up their energy as they look at the 7,000 items placed
throughout the huge blue-and-yellow building.

The company also knows how to _____ surprises to keep its customers happy. There
9

are small surprises like nice-smelling candles and picture frames for less than $2 (right next to the free
pencils), and there are big surprises: a third of Ikea's product line is replaced every year.

In all their excitement, people tell other people about Ikea. Ingvar Kamprad, the man who started the company back in 1943, seems to have done what he always wanted to do: create "a better life for many."

(Based on information in Kerry Capell, "Ikea: How the Swedish Retailer Became a Global Cult Brand." Business Week, November 14, 2005.)

█ WORDS IN DISCUSSION

Apply the key words to your own life. Read and discuss the questions with a partner. Try to use the key words.

1. Do you always take the time to **fold** clothes before putting them away?

   EXAMPLE

   *I **fold** T-shirts, but not socks or shorts. Other things I put on hangers.*

2. Name a college or university with a **solid** academic program.

3. Do you like to **dive** into a pool or enter slowly?

4. Have you ever fixed any **pipes** in your home?

5. Have you ever been to a celebration of the **harvest**?

█ WORDS IN WRITING

Write a short answer (1–2 sentences) for each question. Try to use the key words.

1. Name a famous artist or athlete still alive today. Is this person already **at the height of** his or her popularity?

   EXAMPLE

   *Nicole Kidman became a famous actress more than ten years ago, but I think she gets better with every film. I don't think she's past the **height** of her popularity.*

2. Would you like to **trade** your present home **for** another if you could?

3. When should you speak in a **gentle** voice?

4. What kinds of foods are important to **wrap up** before you put them in the refrigerator?

5. Name at least two reasons why a driver might **steer** the car with only one hand.

QUIZ 10

PART A

Choose the word that best completes each item and write it in the space provided.

1. Be careful. That box isn't _____*solid*_____ enough to sit on.
   - a. particular
   - b. solid
   - c. gentle
   - d. rapid

2. Mozart's ability to play music at the age of three is a(n) _____ of a very talented child.
   - a. object
   - b. harvest
   - c. case
   - d. height

3. Mitsuru sat on the _____ of the chair and waited nervously.
   - a. height
   - b. trade
   - c. detail
   - d. edge

4. This is an important meeting. Please don't _____ it.
   - a. miss
   - b. afford
   - c. stain
   - d. manufacture

5. Throughout history water has helped _____ by making it easier to move products from one place to another.
   - a. sort
   - b. trade
   - c. case
   - d. edge

6. You must be rich to _____ a house in this neighborhood.
   - a. discover
   - b. afford
   - c. stain
   - d. multiply

7. Red, black, and blue are _____ colors for cars.
   - a. recent
   - b. solid
   - c. common
   - d. rapid

8. The company _____ products for the home such as toasters and lamps.
   - a. discovers
   - b. affords
   - c. manufactures
   - d. misses

9. A viola is a(n) _____ of stringed instrument, a little bigger than a violin.
   - a. object
   - b. trade
   - c. sort
   - d. edge

10. Because of Salah's great _____, it's difficult for him to get in and out of small cars.
    - a. object
    - b. detail
    - c. sort
    - d. height

PART B

*Read each statement and write **T** for true or **F** for false in the space provided.*

__T__   1. Yesterday's newspaper has **recent** news.

_____   2. A very full glass of water can easily **spill** when you carry it across the room.

_____   3. **Pipes** bring light into a room.

_____   4. Cows are known for their **rapid** movements.

_____   5. When you are done reading a book, you **fold** it.

_____   6. Sending a human into space was an **advance** in science and technology.

_____   7. If I **discover** your secret, it was your choice to tell it to me.

_____   8. The **value** of a gold ring is likely more than the **value** of a new magazine.

_____   9. People **wrap** pictures on the walls of their homes.

_____ 10. Good food and polite service **satisfy** customers in restaurants.

PART C

Each situation shows the meaning of one of the key words. Write the appropriate key word next to the situation. Use the clues in italics.

common	dive	gentle	multiply	stain
detail	force	harvest	~~object~~	steer

1. We all *saw* a dark *thing* in the night sky, but we didn't know what it was. Maybe some kind of plane?   *object*

2. Please don't *make me* go. I really *don't want to* see a ballet.   _____

3. It was a hot summer day, and I happily *jumped into* the cool water *headfirst*.   _____

4. The name "Maria" *exists in many* different languages. It's a popular name for girls.   _____

5. Antonio *accidentally* got *marks* of dark dirt and green grass on his clothes while he was playing soccer.   _____

6. The *crops* will be *gathered* in the fall.   _____

7. Vera could *control the direction* of the bike without using her hands.   _____

8. Bob told the police every *piece of information* about the crime he had seen.   _____

9. The movers promised to be *careful* with the piano so that there would be *no damage* during the long climb to the third floor.   _____

10. After the actor's first film, his success and fortune *increased greatly*.   _____

Use the chart below to help you understand the parts of speech.

PART OF SPEECH	DESCRIPTION	EXAMPLES
NOUN	A noun is a person, place, or thing such as an animal, idea, activity, feeling, or state. (Note: A state is how something is or seems. *Hunger* is the state of being hungry. *Happiness* is the state of being happy.) It answers the questions: *Who?* *What?*	*a **doctor**, a **cat**, a **school**, the **United States of America**, your **health**, **sports**, no **sickness***
VERB	A verb describes an action, experience, or state. It answers the question: *What happens?*	*to **walk**, can **learn**, will **strengthen**, must **try**, not **die***
ADJECTIVE	An adjective describes a person, place, or thing. It answers the questions: *Which?* *What kind?*	*a **brown** house, the **larger** one, **fun** games, a **scared** child*
ADVERB	An adverb describes the way something is done, or how strong an experience is or seems. It answers the questions: *How?* *How much?*	*be **terribly** difficult, run **fast**, feel **deeply** hurt*

APPENDIX B: Spell and Grammar Checks

Understanding the meaning of a new word is only part of the process of learning it; you must also know how the word is used. When you speak or write a word, you should be able to use correct grammar and spelling. The following exercises will give you additional practice to help you fully master the new words in this book. Look back to the word lists in each chapter to help you complete the Spell Checks. Before you complete the Grammar Checks, review the use of the key words in the chapters. Those sentences can be your model; through them you can understand the correct grammar and then find the mistakes in the exercises below. You may also use the *Longman Dictionary of American English* as needed.

CHAPTER 1

Spell Check

If a word is spelled incorrectly, rewrite it with the correct spelling in the space provided.

1. _____ consider

2. _____occasion_____ ocassion

3. _____ gilt

4. _____ mean

5. _____ load

6. _____ settel

7. _____ feest

8. _____ spirit

9. _____ generus

10. _____ proof

CHAPTER 2

Spell Check

Circle the correctly spelled word in each group.

1. attemt   (attempt)   atempt

2. disease   desease   diseaze

3. rekord   reccord   record

4. cure   kure   cyure

5. shure   shour   shore

6. raize   raisse   raise

7. allow   alow   allaw

8. cuase   caus   cause

9. risc   rizk   risk

10. damage   damidge   dammage

CHAPTER 3

Spell Check

If a word is spelled incorrectly, rewrite it with the correct spelling in the space provided.

1. _____develop_____ develope

2. _____ sense

3. _____ kontain

4. _____ effekt

5. _____ coast

6. _____ publik

7. _____ compair

8. _____ expariment

9. _____ skill

10. _____ systim

CHAPTERS 1-3

Grammar Check

Correct the mistakes. In some items there may be more than one mistake.

1. I made **attempt** to **set a new record**.
   (an)

2. At the baseball game, we **feasted** hot dogs and peanuts.

3. Nick has helped me at several **occasions**; I **consider** him as a good friend.

4. My sister and I are very different people. Please don't **compare** me her.

5. Stop! I won't **allow** you take **risk**.

6. We need to find a **cure** to cancer.

CHAPTER 4

Spell Check

Circle the correctly spelled word in each group.

1. pattern	patern	pattarn		6. eksist	exist	exsist
2. creeture	creature	creacher		7. bold	bould	bauld
3. serve	sirve	surve		8. stick	stik	stikt
4. shalow	shallow	shallo		9. dagree	digree	degree
5. certen	certain	sertain		10. rize	riase	rise

CHAPTER 5

Spell Check

If a word is spelled incorrectly, rewrite it with the correct spelling in the space provided.

1. ___improve___ improof

2. _____ doubt

3. _____ handel

4. _____ lead

5. _____ gain

6. _____ habit

7. _____ result

8. _____ reduse

9. _____ origen

10. _____ reward

CHAPTER 6

Spell Check

Circle the correctly spelled word in each group.

1. distroy	(destroy)	dastroy		6. beem	beme	beam
2. baord	bord	board		7. raip	riap	ripe
3. population	popyulation	populaition		8. crime	krime	craim
4. wern	warnn	warn		9. fayth	faith	feith
5. admitt	admit	admidt		10. disterb	disturb	distturb

CHAPTERS 4-6

Grammar Check

Correct the mistakes. In some items there may be more than one mistake.

1. <u>The **certain**</u> people can be trusted more than others.
   Certain
2. This story isn't new. The **origin** movie was made in 1960.
3. I **admitted** to driving fast, and my father **warned** the dangers.
4. His question was too bold. Claire's voice **rise** in anger and she asked him to leave.
5. You can **stick on** the map to the wall.
6. I have the **habit** to **gain** in weight during the winter because I exercise less.

CHAPTER 7

Spell Check

If a word is spelled incorrectly, rewrite it with the correct spelling in the space provided.

1. ___miserable___ **miserabel**
2. _____ **exact**
3. _____ **simpathy**
4. _____ **blow**
5. _____ **duty**

6. _____ **compoze**
7. _____ **proper**
8. _____ **probabal**
9. _____ **pity**
10. _____ **inquier**

CHAPTER 8

Spell Check

Circle the correctly spelled word in each group.

1. bleam   blaim   (blame)
2. perpose   purpose   purpoze
3. practical practicle praktical
4. gathre   gatheir   gather
5. ancient   anchient   anchent

6. thret   threat   threadt
7. mosion   moshion   motion
8. entair   entire   entier
9. ruen   ruinn   ruin
10. course   kourse   corse

CHAPTER 9

Spell Check

If a word is spelled incorrectly, rewrite it with the correct spelling in the space provided.

1. _____ divide
2. ____dismiss____ dismis
3. _____ field
4. _____ produse
5. _____ opinion

6. _____ indistry
7. _____ treat
8. _____ includ
9. _____ train
10. _____ compete

CHAPTERS 7-9

Grammar Check

Correct the mistakes. In some items there may be more than one mistake.

1. The test was ~~entire~~ *entirely* too difficult; we **gathered ~~up~~** after class to talk to the teacher.
2. You shouldn't **blame** your parents with their decision to move to a new town.
3. **In my opinion**, Ouri is a terrific hostess. She **treats** everyone as family.
4. Gordon and Saul are strong swimmers. They'll **compete** at first place in today's race.
5. Is it **proper** for showing **sympathy** to people who don't want to talk about their loss?
6. If you own a pet, it's your **duty** caring for it.

CHAPTER 10

Spell Check

Circle the correctly spelled word in each group.

1. (charm)   chairm   sharm
2. forbidd   forbed   forbid
3. batle   baddle   battle
4. permitt   pirmet   permit
5. interfere   interefere   entirfere

6. protekt   proteckt   protect
7. puzle   puzzle   puzzel
8. du   due   doo
9. rush   rusch   raush
10. cheat   cheet   chete

CHAPTER 11

Spell Check

If a word is spelled incorrectly, rewrite it with the correct spelling in the space provided.

1. _____ **pause**
2. ____*succeed*____ **succede**
3. _____ **obey**
4. _____ **artifisial**
5. _____ **supply**

6. _____ **race**
7. _____ **wonder**
8. _____ **wership**
9. _____ **base**
10. _____ **trap**

CHAPTER 12

Spell Check

Circle the correctly spelled word in each group.

1. stirr   (stir)   stere
2. replac   replase   replace
3. slippe   slep   slip
4. poste   post   poast
5. chere   cheer   chear

6. modest   modast   modist
7. krowd   crowd   crowde
8. slaev   slaive   slave
9. rawh   raw   rawe
10. brave   braev   braive

CHAPTERS 10-12

Grammar Check

Correct the mistakes. In some items there may be more than one mistake.

1. You must **brave** in this world. Don't ~~slip a good chance~~ through your fingers.
   be — *let a good chance slip*

2. You should treat people **based** how they behave and not their **race**.

3. The photos made the hotel look a lot nicer. It not only **puzzled** us; we felt **cheating**.

4. We were thirsty and tired **due** the heat.

5. The church **supplied** people clothes and food after they lost everything in the flood.

6. Ken asked us not to **interfere** his plans.

CHAPTER 13

Spell Check

If a word is spelled incorrectly, rewrite it with the correct spelling in the space provided.

1. _____wise_____ wize

2. _____ freedom

3. _____ ideel

4. _____ eager

5. _____ rezerve

6. _____ steady

7. _____ fortun

8. _____ horison

9. _____ operate

10. _____ standard

CHAPTER 14

Spell Check

Circle the correctly spelled word in each group.

1. koncern   concerne   (concern)

2. actual   actuale   atchual

3. pease   peace   peece

4. acke   ache   aiche

5. courage   courige   couradge

6. expect   expekt   exspect

7. seperate   seprate   separate

8. mension   mention   menshion

9. pritend   pretind   pretend

10. blinde   blind   bligned

CHAPTER 15

Spell Check

If a word is spelled incorrectly, rewrite it with the correct spelling in the space provided.

1. _____ **inform**

2. ___*relieve*___ **releive**

3. _____ **dozen**

4. _____ **deaff**

5. _____ **blok**

6. _____ **pashence**

7. _____ **sharpe**

8. _____ **grateful**

9. _____ **defend**

10. _____ **respekt**

CHAPTERS 13-15

Grammar Check

Correct the mistakes. In some items there may be more than one mistake.

                            to   *went* [*Or: became* **blind**]

1. Hatice never **mentioned** us that her father **blinded** in his old age.

2. We're very **eager** for to go on our trip to California.

3. It was **wise** to **reserve** at the hotel. The city was crowded with tourists.

4. I was about ten **blocks** from home, so I was **grateful** with Mike for a ride home.

5. The doctor **informed** to me about the dangers of the operation.

6. The city **expects** us **separate** our garbage into plastic, glass, and paper goods.

CHAPTER 16

Spell Check

Circle the correctly spelled word in each group.

1. oficial   offisial   (official)

2. condision   condition   kondition

3. sheltre   chelter   shelter

4. postpone   postpoan   postpown

5. rough   ruff   raugh

6. praise   praize   prayse

7. waige   wadge   wage

8. sinsere   sinceer   sincere

9. bunch   bonch   buntch

10. loan   laon   loane

CHAPTER 17

Spell Check

If a word is spelled incorrectly, rewrite it with the correct spelling in the space provided.

1. _____deal_____ deale
2. _____ local
3. _____ posizion
4. _____ guide
5. _____ balance

6. _____ loyale
7. _____ honor
8. _____ hesetate
9. _____ suport
10. _____ matter

CHAPTER 18

Spell Check

Circle the correctly spelled word in each group.

1. (guard)   gaurd   gard
2. poizon   poison   poision
3. soare   sore   soire
4. envy   envie   envey
5. beatt   beat   beate

6. pointe   point   pointt
7. arrest   arest   arrezt
8. evil   evill   evile
9. beig   beg   begg
10. rott   roat   rot

CHAPTERS 16-18

Grammar Check

Correct the mistakes. In some items there may be more than one mistake.

to me [Or: Will you **loan** me $10?]

1. Will you **loan** ~~to me~~ $10? I'll pay you back tomorrow.
2. The clown stood on a big ball. Then he **lost balance** and fell.
3. The **guard arrested** the customer of stealing clothes from the store.
4. I wanted to eat the last piece of cake, but my brother **beat** me at it.
5. My parents are sick and **in no conditions** to host a party; they'll have at **postpone**.
6. Hank hasn't been performing well at work. Showing up late today **made matter worse**.

CHAPTER 19

Spell Check

If a word is spelled incorrectly, rewrite it with the correct spelling in the space provided.

1. _____fresh_____ fresch
2. _____ klass
3. _____ permanint
4. _____ licquid
5. _____ exchange

6. _____ oportunnity
7. _____ interupt
8. _____ quality
9. _____ mild
10. _____ trik

CHAPTER 20

Spell Check

Circle the correctly spelled word in each group.

1. (express)   exprass   expriss
2. apear   appeer   appear
3. accept   acsept   axcept
4. datermine   determin   determine
5. increase   encrease   increaze

6. limitt   limmit   limit
7. examin   exsamine   examine
8. freequent   frequent   frequint
9. formale   formall   formal
10. hook   hoock   houk

CHAPTER 21

Spell Check

If a word is spelled incorrectly, rewrite it with the correct spelling in the space provided.

1. _____ suit
2. _____immediate_____ imediate
3. _____ century
4. _____ border
5. _____ formere

6. _____ native
7. _____ split
8. _____ necesary
9. _____ spred
10. _____ hire

CHAPTERS 19-21

Grammar Check

Correct the mistakes. In some items there may be more than one mistake.

1. Because of my large shoe size, my choice of shoes at any store is often **limited** ~~with~~ _to_ a few pairs.
2. If you want **hired**, it's **necessary** to dress for success.
3. Don't **spread** yourself out too thin. Do you have time for all these activities?
4. Yi-Hsuan **expressed** an interest for learning more about the British school system.
5. Is there time to **freshen up** myself before we go out?
6. Ray helped Megan move to her new apartment in an **exchange** for a nice dinner.

CHAPTER 22

Spell Check

Circle the correctly spelled word in each group.

1. konfess   (confess)   confes
2. graduall   gradule   gradual
3. bargain   bargen   bargian
4. litareture   literiture   literature
5. apply   aply   appliy

6. regrett   regret   rigret
7. disappoint   disapoint   dizappoint
8. private   privite   praivate
9. shaim   shame   chame
10. host   hoast   hoste

CHAPTER 23

Spell Check

If a word is spelled incorrectly, rewrite it with the correct spelling in the space provided.

1. ____*prevent*____ **privent**
2. _____ **desire**
3. _____ **obzerve**
4. _____ **kompanion**
5. _____ **suffer**

6. _____ **mannere**
7. _____ **cureous**
8. _____ **heale**
9. _____ **remind**
10. _____ **pure**

CHAPTER 24

Spell Check

Circle the correctly spelled word in each group.

1. comittee   (committee)   commitee
2. possess   posess   posses
3. advantige   adventage   advantage
4. realise   realize   realiz
5. responsable   responsibel   responsible

6. proparty   praperty   property
7. depand   dipend   depend
8. adopt   addopt   adoapt
9. solfe   solive   solve
10. taxe   tax   taxx

CHAPTERS 22-24

Grammar Check

Correct the mistakes. In some items there may be more than one mistake.

1. Do you think everyone should pay the same amount of **taxes?** <u>*It/That*</u> **depends**.

2. Isabella is very **curious**. Her **desire** of knowledge never weakens.

3. Could I please speak to you in **privacy**?

4. I must **confess** that I **regret** about not going on the trip.

5. How can we **prevent** Ted not to spread lies about us?

6. Dale had no higher education; this put him in a **disadvantage** in his job search.

CHAPTER 25

Spell Check

If a word is spelled incorrectly, rewrite it with the correct spelling in the space provided.

1. ___*whisper*___ **wisper**
2. _____ **enemy**
3. _____ **owe**
4. _____ **comand**
5. _____ **defeet**

6. _____ **greed**
7. _____ **disgust**
8. _____ **feint**
9. _____ **surfase**
10. _____ **cruel**

CHAPTER 26

Spell Check

Circle the correctly spelled word in each group.

1. pravide	(provide)	provaide	6. store	stor	stoar
2. demand	dimand	damend	7. avoid	avoide	avoyd
3. kombine	combaine	combine	8. reech	reach	reatch
4. offer	ofer	offere	9. fitt	fite	fit
5. figure	figyure	figyere	10. press	pres	prass

CHAPTER 27

Spell Check

If a word is spelled incorrectly, rewrite it with the correct spelling in the space provided.

1. _____ crop

2. ____*tame*____ taim

3. _____ voyige

4. _____ admire

5. _____ steep

6. _____ remane

7. _____ society

8. _____ civilise

9. _____ attrakt

10. _____ soil

CHAPTERS 25-27

Grammar Check

Correct the mistakes. In some items there may be more than one mistake.

1. My roommate leaves dirty clothes all over the floor. It's ~~disgust~~. *disgusting [Or: It **disgusts** me.]*

2. I tried to become a part of that club, but I just couldn't **fit** myself **in**.

3. Gail says she was **attracted** by Tom from the first day she met him.

4. Our art teacher has a deep **admiration** with the works of Picasso and Dali.

5. Martin has two jobs and works hard to **provide** to his family.

6. Kenji **took** the **command** for the players, and they quickly **defeated** the other team.

CHAPTER 28

Spell Check

Circle the correctly spelled word in each group.

1. advence   advanse   (advance)
2. manufacture   manufachure   manufature
3. satisfie   satisfay   satisfy
4. spill   spille   spil
5. discover   dizcover   descover

6. stain   staine   stane
7. aford   afford   afforde
8. recent   rescent   recint
9. cace   caze   case
10. edge   edje   edige

CHAPTER 29

Spell Check

If a word is spelled incorrectly, rewrite it with the correct spelling in the space provided.

1. _____particular_____ **particuler**
2. _____ **detaile**
3. _____ **multapply**
4. _____ **object**
5. _____ **sorte**

6. _____ **rappid**
7. _____ **miss**
8. _____ **common**
9. _____ **forse**
10. _____ **value**

CHAPTER 30

Spell Check

Circle the correctly spelled word in each group.

1. (gentle)   gentel   gentil
2. steer   stere   stear
3. wrapp   wrappe   wrap
4. traid   traed   trade
5. hight   height   highte

6. solide   sollid   solid
7. harvest   hurvest   hervest
8. folde   fold   foald
9. pippe   paipe   pipe
10. dive   daive   dife

Grammar Check

Correct the mistakes. In some items there may be more than one mistake.

1. I saw Milena ~~recent~~ <u>recently</u>. She looked well and sounded **satisfied** ~~about~~ <u>with</u> her new job.

2. Don't waste paper. We can't **afford** buying more.

3. People can still have something **common** even if they don't share all the same **value**.

4. Are you throwing out that meat? **Wrap up** before you put it in the trash or it will smell.

5. Do you want to **trade** that book with this one? Then we can both read something new.

6. Phanuwat studied history in college. It gives him **edge** as a tour guide in Thailand.

KEY WORD INDEX

Here you can find the words that are taught in this book and the chapters in which they are introduced. Every word comes from the General Service List (GSL) of the 2,000 most common words in English.

A

accept   20

ache   14

actual   14

admire   27

admit   6

adopt   24

advance   28

advantage   24

afford   28

allow   2

ancient   8

appear   20

apply   22

arrest   18

artificial   11

attempt   2

attract   27

avoid   26

B

balance   17

bargain   22

base   11

battle   10

beam   6

beat   18

beg   18

blame   8

blind   14

block   15

blow   7

board   6

bold   4

border   21

brave   12

bunch   16

C

case   28

cause   2

century   21

certain   4

charm   10

cheat   10

cheer   12

civilize   27

class   19

coast   3

combine   26

command   25

committee   24

common   29

companion   23

compare   3

compete   9

compose   7

concern   14

condition   16

confess   22

consider   1

contain   3

courage   14

course   8

creature   4

crime   6

crop   27

crowd   12

cruel   25

cure   2

curious   23

D

damage   2

deaf   15

deal   17

defeat   25

defend   15

degree   4

demand   26

depend   24

desire   23

destroy   6

detail   29

determine   20

develop   3

disappoint   22

discover   28

disease   2

disgust   25

dismiss   9

disturb   6

dive   30

divide   9

doubt   5

dozen   15

due   10

duty   7

E

eager   13

edge   28

effect   3

enemy   25

entire   8

envy   18

evil   18

exact   7

examine   20

exchange   19

exist   4

expect   14

experiment   3

express   20

F

faint   25

faith   6

feast   1

field   9

figure   26

fit   26

fold   30

forbid   10

force   29

formal   20

former   21

fortune   13

freedom   13

frequent   20

fresh   19

G

gain   5

gather   8

generous   1

gentle   30

gradual   22

grateful   15

greed   25

guard   18

guide   17

guilt   1

H

habit   5

handle   5

harvest   30

heal   23

height   30

hesitate   17

hire   21

honor   17

hook   20

horizon   13

host   22

I

ideal   13

immediate   21

improve   5

include   9

increase   20

industry   9

inform   15

inquire   7

interfere   10

interrupt   19

L

lead   5

limit   20

liquid   19

literature   22

load   1

loan   16

local   17

loyal   17

M

manner   23

manufacture   28

matter   17

mean   1

mention   14

mild   19

miserable   7

miss   29

modest   12

motion   8

multiply   29

N

native   21

necessary   21

O

obey   11

object   29

observe   23

occasion   1

offer   26

official   16

operate   13

opinion   9

opportunity   19

origin   5

owe   25

P

particular   29

patience   15

pattern   4

pause   11

peace   14

permanent   19

permit   10

pipe   30

pity   7

point   18

poison   18

population   6

position   17

possess   24

post   12

postpone   16

practical 8

praise 16

press 26

pretend 14

prevent 23

private 22

probable 7

produce 9

proof 1

proper 7

property 24

protect 10

provide 26

public 3

pure 23

purpose 8

puzzle 10

Q

quality 19

R

race 11

raise 2

rapid 29

raw 12

reach 26

realize 24

recent 28

record 2

reduce 5

regret 22

relieve 15

remain 27

remind 23

replace 12

reserve 13

respect 15

responsible 24

result 5

reward 5

ripe 6

rise 4

risk 2

rot 18

rough 16

ruin 8

rush 10

S

satisfy 28

sense 3

separate 14

serve 4

settle 1

shallow 4

shame 22

sharp 15

shelter 16

shore 2

sincere 16

skill 3

slave 12

slip 12

society 27

soil 27

solid 30

solve 24

sore 18

sort 29

spill 28

spirit 1

split 21

spread 21

stain 28

standard 13

steady 13

steep 27

steer 30

stick 4

stir 12

store 26

succeed 11

suffer 23

suit 21

supply 11

support 17

surface 25

sympathetic 7

system 3

T

tame 27

tax 24

threat 8

trade 30

train 9

trap 11

treat 9

trick 19

V

value 29

voyage 27

W

wage 16

warn 6

whisper 25

wise 13

wonder 11

worship 11

wrap 30